T5-AWJ-591

MARTIN BUBER ON MYTH

THEORISTS OF MYTH
(VOL. 3)

GARLAND REFERENCE LIBRARY OF
THE HUMANITIES
(VOL. 918)

Theorists of Myth
Robert A. Segal, Series Editor

MARTIN BUBER ON MYTH
An Introduction

S. Daniel Breslauer

GARLAND PUBLISHING, INC. • NEW YORK & LONDON
1990

Library of Congress Cataloging-in-Publication Data

Breslauer, S. Daniel.
    Martin Buber on myth : an introduction / S. Daniel Breslauer.
        p.   cm. — (Theorists of myth ; vol. 3) (Garland reference
library of the humanities ; vol. 918)
    Includes bibliographical references and index.
    ISBN 0-8240-3721-9 (acid-free paper)
    1. Buber, Martin, 1878-1965—Contributions in concept of myth.
2. Myth—History—20th century. I. Title. II. Series.
III. Series: Garland reference library of the humanities ; vol. 918.
B3213.B84B74   1990
291.1'3'092—dc20   90-38866
                                                              CIP

Printed on acid-free, 250-year-life paper,
Manufactured in the United States of America

SERIES EDITOR'S FOREWORD

As a Jewish thinker and philosopher of religion, Martin Buber needs no introduction. Daniel Breslauer, an authority on Buber and author of *The Chrysalis of Religion: A Guide to the Jewishness of Buber's "I and Thou,"* provides a pioneering analysis of Buber as a theorist of myth. Breslauer not only points to Buber's interpretation of myths worldwide but, far more, reconstructs the theory of myth implicit in Buber's interpretation of Jewish myths in particular.

Myth for Buber originates in the mythmaker's encounter with God and, in recording that encounter, functions to evoke a similar encounter in the reader of the myth. Buber is hardly the sole theorist for whom myth serves to trigger experience, and Breslauer contrasts Buber's view to the views of, among others, Mircea Eliade and Carl Jung. Where for Eliade myth liberates one from the fallen, present world and returns one to the time of the primordial experience that inspired the myth, for Buber myth enables one to garner in the everyday, present world an experience akin to the original experience. Where for Jung both experiences are really of the unconscious, for Buber both are truly of God.

Breslauer most helpfully contrasts Buber's theory of myth to the theories of various others—among them Rudolf Bultmann, Adolf Jensen, Theodor Reik, and William Robertson Smith. Breslauer does so in the process of presenting in detail Buber's interpretations of the Biblical myths of creation, Adam and Eve, Enoch, Moses, Job, and Psalms. Where many, though not all, Biblicists have conventionally praised the Hebrew Bible as historical *rather than* mythic, Buber declares the Bible mythic and historical alike. Indeed, myth and history work hand in hand. History roots myth in actual, concrete events, and myth transforms history from merely a record of past events to an ever-beckoning opportunity for present ones. Myth keeps religion alive. Like most Biblicists, Buber still pits Judaism against paganism, but the opposition is no longer between history and myth. It is between one variety of myth and another.

Breslauer attends most fully not to Biblical myths but to Hasidic ones. Here, too, he contrasts Buber's view to the views of others—most notably, Gershom Scholem. Here, as elsewhere in the book, Breslauer continually places Buber's theory of myth within his overall philosophy. Buber, we are told, asks of myth what he asks of life as a whole: openness to other persons and things as well as to God.

Breslauer notes that Buber, for all his advocacy of myth, acknowledges its limitations—limitations that, it might be pointed out, are close to the ones that Jung, a fellow evangelist for myth, grants. For both Jung and Buber, myth can capture only a portion of the experience that engenders it. For Jung, the inexhaustibility of any of the archetypes that comprise the unconscious guarantees that myth will fall short of encompassing all of its subject. For Buber, the third-person, "I-It" nature of the medium skews the second-person, "I-Thou" message. Yet both laud myth for encompassing as much as it does. Both write to revive myth for moderns, who miss its meaning and power by literalizing it. Both berate those who spurn myth as merely primitive. Where Buber, who subsumes myth under religion, urges moderns to return to the myths of their traditional religions, Jung, who allows for secular myths, beseeches moderns to seek myths outside of religion as well as within it.

As admiring of Buber as Breslauer is, he is not uncritical. He concedes that Buber's imaginative readings at times fit Buber's theory better than the myths themselves. Breslauer faults Buber at once for defining myth too broadly and for taking the function of myth too narrowly. In passing, Breslauer gingerly broaches some of the criticisms of Buber's underlying philosophy itself—most conspicuously, the core distinction between "I-Thou" and "I-It." Overall, Breslauer's sympathetic and patient analysis makes his book a fine introduction to Martin Buber as theorist of myth.

CONTENTS

Chapter 3   Buber and the Bible

Chapter 4   The Meaning of Eden

Chapter 5   The Exodus

Chapter 9 Evaluating Buber

PREFACE

This book summarizes and evaluates the
contribution of Martin Buber as a theorist
of myth. Although best known as an exponent
of dialogical thinking and respected as an
interpreter of Jewish religion, the Bible,
and hasidism, a late flowering of Jewish
mysticism, Buber also provides explicit
guidelines for understanding and evaluating
myths. Buber describes reality as twofold:
people live either in a world of things, to
which they relate as a subject controlling
its objects, or in a world of self-conscious
others, with whom one relates as fellow
subjects. Human beings require both types
of reality, but also a means of moving from
one to the other. Buber understands myths
as one such means by which people pass from
I-It reality, the reality of one subject
manipulating objects, to I-You meeting, the
reality of dialogue among equal subjects.
In studying myths, he focuses on the myths
in the traditions he knows best, but offers
his advice and interpretation of mythology
and scholarship about mythology generally.

While some critical essays about Buber's
approach to myth have appeared, they usually
concentrate on his biblical scholarship, his
relationship to other scholars, and the
evolution of his thought. Despite these
efforts, however, Buber's unique approach to
myth suffers neglect. Too often critics
focus on his catch-phrase "I and Thou" (or
"I and You") without investigating his
special application of that idea to myth.
Because they look at the technical language
rather than its relationship to Buber's
ontology, these critics fail to grasp his
special view of myth. He does not relegate
myth to a primitive stage in human thought,
an animistic stage in which people view
reality anthropomorphically.

Buber's distinction between I-You and I-
It reality cannot be equated with the more
normal distinction between emotional and
rational modes of interacting with the
world. Buber's view of myth needs
particular study at the very least to
distinguish it from the views of others
using his same terminology for different
purposes. Buber's use of I-Thou thinking as
a characteristic of myth differs
considerably from that of others using the
same term. A contrast with other theories
helps illuminate Buber's uniqueness, but
Buber's peculiar theory of myth requires
study in its own right. His theory develops
on several levels, each of which requires its
own discussion in keeping with both the
subject matter and the method Buber uses.
This book, therefore, offers a coherent and

unified study focusing on Buber's approach to myth as part of his entire system of philosophy. That exposition sometimes contrasts Buber to others who share his language, such as Henri Frankfort and Ernst Cassirer, but also to those, such as Theodor Reik and Mircea Eliade, who do not.

Since Buber focuses on biblical and Jewish myth, the following chapters look at those examples of mythic expression. Since, however, Buber uses these examples to illustrate his general theory of myth, and in turn of existence, the chapters examine his work as an interpretation of human myth-making and of human experience generally. Buber's terminology and, more precisely, its translation into English often leads to confusion. Buber distinguishes between two ways a person interacts with the world. One way consists of manipulating things, of an individual subject using everything else as a mere object. He terms this relationship to reality "I-It." He describes the second way of interaction as "meeting" or "dialogue." By this he means that each participant in the meeting considers the other as an independent subject. He claims that such meetings do not manipulate others but enable them to express themselves, to "speak" (the terms "dialogue" or "speech" are misleading since Buber claims meeting occurs with both animate beings such as other people and inanimate objects such as a tree). The essential characteristic of this way of interacting with the world lies in its attitude: a willingness to consider the other participants as independent subjects

on their own. Buber called this
relationship "Ich-Du." Because the German
language distinguishes between the second
person singular (thou) and the second person
plural (you "all"), Buber's term was first
translated as "I and Thou." Walter Kaufmann
argues, correctly, against this translation
since English uses the distinction between
"thou" and "you" to designate archaic and
modern usage rather than singular and
plural. His new translation of Buber uses
"I and You" in place of I and Thou.
Throughout this book I fluctuate between the
two usages. Although I prefer Kaufmann's
term, most of the translations of Buber into
English and nearly all the secondary sources
use "I and Thou." When citing or
summarizing these sources, I use that latter
term. When describing Buber's views in my
own language, however, I follow Kaufmann's
lead. Although this inconsistency may be
confusing, readers should recognize that the
problem stems from Buber scholarship in
English and cannot really be avoided.

     I begin by summarizing the importance
and paradoxical nature of Buber's thought
generally. The first chapter introduces
Buber as person and thinker, suggesting the
relevance of Buber's general philosophy and
personal life as a Jew and scholar for
understanding his interpretation of myth.
The second chapter begins where the first
concludes and looks more closely at Buber's
investigation of myth. Myth has often been
understood as an "explanation" of reality;
Buber rejects that characterization, whether
meant as a positive or negative valuation.

The chapter concludes by contrasting Buber's
understanding of the myth of Enoch with that
of other scholars. The third chapter
introduces the first major focus of Buber's
study of mythology: myth in the Hebrew
Bible. Scholars debate the presence and
significance of myth in the Hebrew Bible.
This chapter charts Buber's place in that
debate. The following chapter focuses
specifically on Buber's interpretation of
the myths in Genesis and the myths from
Persia that Buber felt completed and
complemented those myths. Buber's view of
such myth as a memory of "I and Thou"
contrasts with the way other theorists of
myth interpret the biblical stories of
creation. The final chapter, centered on
the Bible, focuses primarily on Buber's
understanding of Moses and the legendary
myths associated with him. Buber's
rejection of sociological or psychological
reductionism places him at odds with such
theorists of myth as either W. Robertson
Smith or Theodor Reik.

The sixth chapter introduces Buber's
view of hasidic myth and the criticism he
received because of it. The chapter focuses
on Buber's Jewish critics, but highlights
how he sought to show the universal
relevance of hasidic tales. The seventh
chapter takes the controversy between Buber
and Gershom Scholem as its point of
departure but then focuses on Buber's
understanding of myth as an analogy to
language, an analogy clearly parallel to the
arguments of Ernst Cassirer. The eighth
chapter struggles with Buber's understanding

of hasidism as a response to modernity,
contrasting his thought with those who
identify hasidic religion with a strictly
orthodox Jewish tradition. Although the
first chapters in both the biblical section
and the hasidic section introduce critical
views of Buber, the ninth and final chapter
of this book evaluates Buber as a theorist
of myth. The chapter asks whether Buber's
use of myth, despite many shortcomings,
contributes to a modern appreciation of
myth.

The bibliography attached to this study
does not aim at completeness. It begins by
noting two general bibliographies, both of
which, however, are limited to works written
before 1978. Although they each provide
points of departure for the student of Buber
as theorist of myth, neither is fully
satisfactory. The work by Willard Moonan
provides an index entry on "Myth" that
should be used with caution since neither is
it exhaustive nor does the annotation always
justify the inclusion of a particular essay
under this rubric. The references included
in the select bibliography attached here
suggest the works to be consulted in further
study of Buber as a theorist of myth. The
various works cited, especially those by
Friedman, Glatzer, and Wood also contain
bibliographical information.

Support for the preparation and publication
of this book has been given by the Small
Grant Fund of the University of Kansas.
That support is gratefully acknowledged.

Martin Buber on Myth

Chapter 1 The Student of Myth

MARTIN BUBER: THE HONORARY STUDENT

European students often assemble to celebrate the birthday of a favorite teacher. They gather around the professor's house in the evening, serenade the chosen hero of the day, and raise a jubilant cry. While a frequent tribute to beloved educators in Europe, this celebration had never occurred among students at the Hebrew University in Israel. On the evening of February 8, 1963, however, the first such tribute took place. Over 500 students gathered to honor an eighty-five year old sage whom they had not even known as a teacher but whose writings had touched their lives and changed their views of reality. The evening festivities reached a heightened pitch.

The man they honored appeared before the students. Two representatives approached him. They acknowledged his influence on them and conferred on him a singular title.

Henceforth he would be an honorary student
of the Hebrew University. The man responded
joyfully to the honor, remarking that while
he had received many honorary degrees, now
for the first time he had become an honorary
student. Johan Huizinga, he commented, had
called humanity "Homo Ludens," "Humanity the
Player." In contrast, he considered study
the distinctive mark of human life. The
human being is a studying person: "who
aspires to know the truth in order to erect
upon it a structure worthy for people to
inhabit."1 That man was Martin Buber,
philosopher, translator, and interpreter of
Judaism who spent his life learning how to
construct a worthy structure for human
existence.2

BUBER AS STUDENT OF REALITY

     Buber's early life consisted of
desperate attempts to derive order out of
chaos.3 Born into an assimilated Jewish
family in Vienna in 1878, he experienced
emotional dislocation. His mother deserted
her husband and child to follow a lover when
the boy was only three years old. Sent to
live with his scholarly grandfather, Solomon
Buber, and his intellectual and forceful
grandmother, Martin became something of a
"child recluse." After his father's
remarriage, he resisted reintegration into
his primary family and later recorded
suicidal thoughts at the age of fourteen
that only Kantian philosophy resolved. His

early political and intellectual efforts
gave coherence to a life that fate had
seemed to tear apart.

Buber "the honorary student" pursued an
education framed by books. Later, however,
he discovered that learning extends beyond
such formal boundaries. A person learns not
by assimilating knowledge from outside
sources but by open meetings with others.
Knowledge only appears as a set of "facts" a
person can "master." "Humanity the
student" fulfills its aspirations for
knowledge by self-transformation; knowledge,
Buber finally decided, grows from within, as
a mark of the changes one undergoes because
of meetings with other people. Reflecting
on his development, Buber once commented
that he had originally preferred the company
of books to the company of other people.
Eventually, however, he discovered that
"the many bad experiences with men have
nourished the meadow of my life as the
noblest book could not do...."4 Buber's
adventure as a teacher grew from an impulse
leading him from reading books to meeting
others.

Buber turned from studying books as
self-contained entities to seeing them as
invitations to meetings with other people.
His previous study created what the
philosopher, translator, and student of
Buber, Walter Kaufmann, called an "imposing
and multidimensional achievement" that "won
for him countless admirers."5 The diverse
enterprises making up this achievement did
not immediately form a "way," a single path

or direction. Only gradually did Buber's
studies take shape as a coherent whole. The
turning point came in 1914. Buber felt
dissatisfied as the oracular mystic guiding
his disciples from afar, but did not know
the source of his dissatisfaction until an
event in 1914 that he describes as "a
conversion."6 He had enjoyed a morning of
"religious enthusiasm" and when, in the
early afternoon, a young man visited him, he
treated him cordially but distantly.

When Buber learned that the youth
shortly thereafter committed suicide, he
realized that he had avoided the "real"
questions the man had asked. Upon
reflection, Buber discovered that he had
lived in one sort of reality: a self-
absorbed existence in which he alone
appeared as a true "subject" and in which
everything else appeared as a mere "object"
of his subjectivity. In contrast, the youth
had approached him hoping for another sort
of reality: one in which independent
subjects respect one another's autonomy and
personal value. Buber resolved to give up
"mysticism," by which he meant the self-
absorbed reality that blocked him from
responding to the young man's real
questions.

As Buber developed his insight about the
two types of reality that people experience,
he learned the necessity of each in any
human life. This lesson gradually impressed
itself on him, not the least because in 1921
he began a personal relationship with Franz
Rosenzweig that revealed the ideal of

interpersonal meeting just as the earlier
"conversion experience" revealed the
inadequacy of self-absorption. While Franz
Rosenzweig, one of the central figures in
modern Jewish thought and, with Buber, a
leading exponent of Jewish existentialism,
had met Buber previously to 1921, that
reacquaintance proved a critical moment for
both thinkers.7 Rosenzweig, previously
distrustful of Buber, discovered him no
longer the "mystic" he had been before.
Buber found in Rosenzweig another
philosopher of dialogue who could help him
develop his earlier insight about reality.
Rosenzweig provided Buber with a forum, his
newly created Jewish school for adults, the
Freies Judisches Lehrhaus, in which to
expound his ideas. Buber did so in a set of
lectures on religion as presence, lectures
that eventually became his seminal offering,
I and Thou.8

DEVELOPING I-THOU PHILOSOPHY

Under the impact of Rosenzweig and the
stimulus of preparing public lectures, Buber
clarified his original insight into two ways
people experience reality. Human beings
relate to the world and to each other in one
of two ways. The human self (the "I") may
seek to manipulate what stands over and
against it (the "It"). The human self may
also encounter the other as an "I", as true
self on its own (as a "Thou"). At first,
these two alternatives appear as ways of

looking at the world. Buber, however,
insists that they are ways of <u>constructing</u>
the world. When people talk "at" the world,
they have constructed it as a set of things.
When people talk "with" the world, they have
constructed it as a universe of discourse.
This dialogical terminology may seem
metaphorical. When recognizing others as
independent subjects, it is <u>as if</u> we
addressed them and they addressed us; when
manipulating the world it is <u>as if</u> we were
speaking at an audience. Buber denies that
his terms are metaphorical. Actions are
also language. What people do either
addresses the world or assaults it. He
calls the two modes of being in the world
the "two basic words" that "establish a mode
of existence." As Ronald Gregor Smith puts
it, these are words that "being spoken...
bring about existence."9

Buber's insistence that his two basic
words constitute more than ways of
interpreting the world forms the foundation
of his entire corpus of work. Reality
itself, he claims, changes with the change
of human perspective. When human beings
meet the world as a cluster of others, both
they and their fellow subjects change one
another. When human beings manipulate the
world as a set of inferior objects, not only
do they "see" the world differently, but the
world itself and they themselves <u>are</u>
different. How people live in the world,
then, determines the very world within which
they act. Buber, accordingly, offers an
"ontology," a theory about reality. People
construct reality depending upon their

choice of either dialogue with other subjects or manipulation of objects.

Buber's view of the two realities does not, at least in theory, advocate one reality above another. Human beings need to inhabit both spheres. The realm of the word I-You provides the context for personal growth. People develop by meeting other subjects, by allowing the reality of other selves to challenge them, to call forth a response, to change them in one way or another. By saying "Thou" to others in the world, a person abandons the protective isolation that prevents an object from making demands upon a subject. The realm of I-It provides the material context in which people live. They cannot exist in an environment filled with independent selves, each of which requires acknowledgement of its unique reality. Alice, when she passes through the looking glass, it may be recalled, nearly starves because when she is served her meal each new dish introduces itself to her. The Red Queen refuses to let her "cut" anything with which she has such a personal relationship.10

Buber understands the necessity for impersonal relations and realizes that people require an I-It reality for their very existence. He notes that "The basic relation of man to the It-world includes...the preservation, alleviation, and equipment of human life."11 Without that type of reality, human life would wither and die. Human beings create a framework of institutions and

interconnections. They build homes, oversee
businesses, and organize activities. Each
of these has a utilitarian function. People
use other people and other things. They
think of themselves as "I" and everything
else as a tool, an instrument of their
desire, an "It." This person is not a self-
contained being but a "banker" or a "client"
or a "teacher." These "roles" replace the
living people who, while fulfilling these
roles, also think of themselves as "I."

Buber objects, however, when people
subsist only in I-It reality. By itself I-
It may seem oppressive but is no longer so
for one "who is not confined to the It-world
but free to step out of it again and again
into the world of relation."12 Moving into
I-You reality allows a person flexibility,
the potential for self-transformation, and a
recognition of the variety possible in life.
The manipulative "I" remains static; it
controls the world for its own sake and does
not, therefore, see a need for growth,
change, or development. I-You reality,
making use of the apparently identical
material context, enhances human existence
by demanding change. In such a reality, a
person no longer remains a constant and
unchanging entity. Rather, the person grows
and develops in accordance with an activity,
by participating in a meeting with others.
Buber describes this development of
personality as "an activity in which I
participate without being able to
appropriate it ... The person becomes
conscious of himself as participating in
being, as being-with, and thus as a

being."13 Because this participation involves action and reaction, the "I" addressing the "thou" cannot remain unmoved and unchanged.

I-You reality does not occur "outside" of normal human living, but within an everyday context. Saying "Thou" occurs as the material environment slips into the background, as a context for a meeting rather than as the purpose of the meeting, when the living others become more important for themselves than for what they represent. On such occasions, Buber suggests, people engage with one another without thought of gain or consequence; they respond to the humanity of the other person standing with them. Such a meeting must occur within the material context provided by I-It reality since Buber contends that I-You reality can "never act independently upon life" but must rather emerge "in the world--with its force which penetrates and transforms the It-world."14 Sometimes the formal purpose of a business meeting, of a social gathering, of a commercial exchange gives way to a more spontaneous response. When this occurs, the other whom the "I" encounters no longer assumes a "role." That other stands as an independent "I" that addresses another "I" as a living person. Both participants affirm the other as an "I" and affirm themselves as a living "Thou," as a responding person. Both subjects in such an exchange open themselves to vulnerability. They both allow the other to make demands upon them; they perceive the other as a full self with needs, desires, and legitimate

concerns. This meeting of equals usually
leaves each participant transformed.

BUBER AS STUDENT AND TEACHER

   Buber's view of reality suggests that
the I-It world offers a point of departure
for I-You meeting. Nevertheless, that I-It
reality often becomes impenetrable and
sometimes seeks to engulf humanity, claiming
for itself exclusive truth. Buber laments
the case of the man who, when faced by I-It
reality, "lets it have its way, the
relentlessly growing It-world grows over him
like weeds...."15   Responding to that
concern, Buber, the student, became Buber
the teacher, learning how to be a pedagogue
of I-You meeting, studying education itself
as a key to releasing modern people from
enslavement to I-It reality.16   Buber
understands that teachers, in order to
fulfill their educational task, must remain
aloof from their pupils. He concedes that
while teachers expect students to say "Thou"
to them, they cannot relinquish control by
saying "Thou" to their pupils: "the
educational relationship is incompatible
with complete mutuality."17   Buber, as
teacher, taught his pupils his own technique
of learning: that of heeding a message that
demands response. The educational setting
draws attention to, even if it cannot
exemplify, the reality shaped by I-You
meeting.

Such teaching about reality entailed a critique of a political arena often capable of recognizing I-It truths alone. Buber's teaching in Germany under the Nazis from 1933 to 1938 exemplified his thinking that political forms need not repress I-You meeting. He wrote of the "Kingship of God" as an antidote to the "Kingship of the Reich." He explored how Judaism generally and the Bible in particular offered a critique and alternative to Nazism. Delivering an address at the Frankfort Lehrhaus in 1934, Buber spoke of the spirit "in search of its own reality. That is why it takes possession of man for the sake of hallowing the world."18 Buber taught his students to look beyond the reality forged by political institutions to seek the alternative reality of the spirit, of I-You meeting. As Maurice Friedman suggests, the Nazis "dimly sensed that his spiritual resistance represented a danger for their 'new order.'" Buber's alternative order created by human beings opening themselves to one another contradicted the Nazi vision of a controlled society.19 He continued as a student of I-You reality even in Hitler's demonic bureaucracy of the I-It.

Even after emigrating from Germany to Israel in 1938, Buber continued pursuing the reality he had glimpsed in 1914 and sharing his discoveries with others. In the land of Israel disciples now expected practical advice and pragmatic political directives. The advice he provided often shocked his audience. He admonished his students to prepare themselves for I-You meeting rather

than remain fixated on I-It concerns. When
the British White Paper of 1939 appeared,
denying Jews the right to escape from Nazi
Germany to Israel, many Zionists bewailed
the act. Buber accused these leaders of
losing sight of the true problem. Zionists
should learn a lesson from this failure.
"We relegated the banner of Zion to a
political interest," he commented. Rather
than focus on the I-It sphere of political
reality, Buber advocated creating an
environment of dialogue in which Jew and
Arab could join equally in mutuality. "The
main thing," he declared, "is to set our
hearts today in that <u>direction</u>, in which we
must search, experiment, expand and win
souls."20 Once again, as in Germany, he
taught by drawing attention to a reality
other than, but as accessible as, that of I-
It political life.

BUBER AND JUDAISM

Buber's teaching, then, placed the
possibility of I-You meeting before his
students no matter what the content he
chose. Originally, however, in his lectures
for Franz Rosenzweig, he focused on the
content of religion. He used the difference
between I-It and I-You existence to posit
two types of religion: one type allows its
adherents the freedom to respond anew to
stimuli from the past; the second type,
however, stifles growth and learning by
demanding adherence to a fixed system of

dogmas and rituals.21 Buber dedicated his studies of religion to the former type, to learning the living dimensions of a responsive tradition. Buber's lectures, entitled "Religion as Presence," ranged beyond Jewish subjects to probe the meaning of religion in human life and explore the varied dimensions of human experience, concluding that human beings discover God through their interaction with one another, through their discovery of presence and being present, through the meeting of an "I" and a "Thou."22

Although early in his career Buber distinguished between "religiosity," of which he approved, and "religion," which he opposed, his later thought enabled him to explain himself more clearly. Buber, unlike other thinkers, did not reject institutional forms as such. Instead, he provided a test for determining their validity. He called institutional religion a "chrysalis" in which the religious spirit lay latent. Religious forms such as prayers, myths, and social activities enable people to recapture the original experience that religion reflects.23 A student of religion, according to Buber, works backward from the religious form to its originating spirit. Studying myth, for example, entails tracing the stages of development by which an event becomes a myth. Buber describes three such stages. In the first stage, people undergo an event shatters their normal expectations and resists expression in usual forms of communication. The second stage occurs when, reflecting on this event, people try to communicate the inexpressible by creating various forms of expression such as stories, rituals, and theologies. These forms necessarily alter the remembered event since that event surpassed human means of expression. In a third and final stage, the forms stimulate an event similar to that which originally inspired their creation.

Buber defines his tasks as a student of religion in relation to these three stages of development. He begins by describing as accurately as possible the religious forms of a particular tradition -- whether these are myths, actions, or beliefs. They represent the reported data with which a student must begin. Buber, next, uses critical analysis to probe behind the forms of religion to describe the event that catalyzed their creation. He refuses to take the form as the primary datum. Neither the developed theology nor the details of a religious myth represent the facts of a religious event. They evade the real experience; Buber seeks to decode that experience from the relics left behind in the later forms. Finally, Buber assesses a myth's adequacy in stimulating the reemergence of spiritual life from the chrysalis of institutional forms.

BUBER AND THE HEBREW BIBLE

Buber approaches the Hebrew Bible as a document of religion exemplifying the evolution from I-You to I-It to renewed I-You reality. Buber's biblical scholarship includes a close study of textual traditions, historical context, and linguistic meaning. Working with Franz Rosenzweig, Buber created a translation of the Hebrew Bible into German that combined critical analysis of meaning with an evocative style. The volumes of that translation appeared from 1926 until its completion in 1962 (when Rosenzweig died in 1929 Buber continued his friend's labors, working alone). While the renowned scholar of Jewish mysticism Gershom Scholem often criticized Buber's views, he acknowledged Buber's greatness as an interpreter and translator of the Bible. When the final and completed edition of the work appeared, Scholem commented that the thirty-five years of work and "the opportunity to rework it [the translation] in recent years" enabled Buber to make the final "definitive and complete" edition fully in harmony with Buber's thinking in his "mature years."

The text of the Bible translation, then, represents Buber even more than Rosenzweig. Scholem pays tribute to Buber's knowledge and exegetical skill, commenting that people now turn to the Buber translation as they turn to medieval Jewish commentators for explanation and elucidation of the text.24 During the time he spent on that translation, Buber explicated his work and his understanding of the Bible in a series of books, monographs and articles that sought to describe the biblical text, its meaning and background; to discover behind

it an event experienced by ancient Israel
that defied full expression; and to evoke a
similar event in the lives of Buber's
audience.

Buber accepts the necessity for close
study of the Bible as a document; historical
and linguistic studies are needed to "remove
layer after layer" from the received text
"in order to arrive at the earliest of all."
That earliest of all, however, is not a
reconstruction of "the course of events
themselves" but rather "the manner in which
the participating people experienced those
events." Thus Buber moves from the
inherited form of religion to its
experiential nucleus.25 Buber also analyzes
the Bible for its relevance to modern Jews.
He argues that close attention to the
inherited biblical text enables modern Jews
to recapture the immediacy of their
religion. Each person must "enter into the
dialogue of the ages" but must do so through
community without sacrificing
individuality.26

The biblical record, according to Buber,
shows how as individuals absorb and apply a
nation's literature and rituals, its
spiritual creations, they discover God. By
taking the cultural legacy of community
seriously, people learn the path to their
own personal meeting with the divine.27
Thus while biblical religion began as a
response to an overpowering experience that
exceeded human expression, institutional
forms eventually replaced that spontaneous
response, distorting ritual and cultic

forms. A modern Jewish life, however, can regain access to the original stimulus by removing late accretions from biblical religion. Thus Buber explores the meaning of Genesis 1:1-11:9, noting, as do most biblical scholars, the fluctuating vocabulary, changing perspectives, and stylistic peculiarities. He moves beyond these details, however, to suggest the social and personal context within which the author's experience of reality so strongly challenged preconceived views that only such stories as those in the biblical record could express them. Finally, Buber offers a modern audience his evaluation of the "truth" which they, too, can experience by heeding the story. Similarly, Buber studies the "key words" of certain biblical psalms to illustrate their structure more clearly. He then suggests the human experience that gave rise to those psalms and finally invites his readers to discover the same experience themselves.28

BUBER AND JEWISH RELIGION

In its original context, that of Buber's lectures to the Frankfurt Lehrhaus, the new philosophy that he and Rosenzweig eventually used to decode biblical meaning proposed a new approach to studying Judaism. Buber applied his insight into living as meeting, his intuition about "presence" as a form of being, to the received Jewish tradition. The "meeting with a given religious

tradition" became an opportunity to revive a
genuine encounter in which an "I" confirms a
"Thou."29 This new understanding of Judaism
changed Buber as a student of Jewish
religion. Whereas he had formerly
disparaged traditional forms of Jewish life,
he learned to affirm the validity of those
forms. His earlier approach had seemed to
"create an artificial platform outside of
the tradition." Now he studied Judaism as
one attached "to the great sequence" of the
past. He remained the great student of
Jewish religion, but his attitude as student
altered.30 As an exponent of how religion
moves from I-You to I-It reality and back
again, Buber approaches Judaism as a dynamic
organism.

While accepting the legacy of countless
generations from the Jewish past, Buber
finds a new way of unfolding the meaning
transmitted by those generations; he sees
each as an independent subject, as a "Thou"
directly addressing him. This way of
appropriating the past differs greatly from
the traditional Jewish approach. Many
traditional Jews express the distinctiveness
of Judaism in terms of its covenantal
commands. They define Judaism as a
compendium of laws set by God before the
Jewish people. To be a Jew entails, for
them, obedience to that collection of
imperatives. In contrast to these
traditionalists, liberal Jewish thinkers in
the nineteenth and twentieth centuries
define the "essence" of Judaism in
theological or philosophical ways as
"ethical monotheism" or the "attainment of

the absolute."31 Buber replaces both
characterizations with one drawn from his
own thinking. The Jew, he claims, "dares to
relate himself to God in the immediacy of
the I and Thou—as a Jew."32 That
presupposition underlies Buber's exegesis
of Judaism. He selects those forms of
Jewish expression that he thinks most
adequately express the daring event of
immediate relationship to the divine. While
he sometimes mentions rabbinic Judaism, he
finds the "truer" aspects of Jewish religion
in the mystical tradition of hasidism. Even
in his study of hasidism, however, Buber
begins with his principle of verification:
those expressions of the tradition most
likely to stimulate contemporary response
represent the most genuine reports of the
religious event.

Buber himself describes his approach to
Jewish religion in an open dialogue with
Franz Rosenzweig explaining his inability to
accept the entire tradition as a divine
mandate. He refuses to "accept the laws and
the statutes blindly" and asks again and
again whether a particular law addresses
him. Thus Buber admits that "at one time I
may include myself in this Israel which is
addressed, but at times, many times, I
cannot."33 Buber's view of reality as
divided into I-You and I-It realms teaches
him to evaluate the truth claims of a
tradition by its ability to open the way to
I-You. When Buber finds a tradition
allowing him to do so, he accepts it; when
he finds it blocking his way, he rejects it.
He admits that his construction of Judaism

represents neither an orthodoxy nor a heterodoxy but a "personal standpoint."34 That approach to Judaism enables Buber to take a more positive view of Jewish mythology than many of his contemporary scholars. He welcomes myth as another portal to I-You meeting no less valuable than ritual or theology.

BUBER AS A STUDENT OF MYTH

Buber finds in Jewish myth the best expression of Jewish religion; myth provides the most effective I-It medium into which a religion can convert I-You reality and the most flexible form out of which religion can allow I-You reality to emerge. Some scholars like Ignac Goldziher, one of the German-Jewish Semiticists of the nineteenth century, evolve evolutionary schemes to oppose "the confusion of the Mythical and the Religious." Goldziher attributes myth to an early and irrational stage of human thinking. As human thought progresses, religion develops using myth as its raw material. Finally, religion outgrows its mythic origins and becomes purely rational. Religion moves from a primitive world view to the stage at which it can "sever its connexion (sic) with Mythology and unite itself with the scientific consciousness."35 Most contemporary scholars of religion no longer accept such a negative view of mythology. Alan F. Segal, for example, denies that the term "myth" implies a false story. While "foolish myths" do exist, that is myths that fail to function adequately for their believers, other myths convey a truthful picture of reality for their adherents. Segal's positive exposition of the term exemplifies a general viewpoint now widely shared by students of Judaism and Christianity.36

Buber's theory of myth grows out of his view of reality. Zeev Levy, an Israeli scholar of modern Jewish Existentialist thinkers such as Franz Rosenzweig and Moshe Swarcz who uses their thought to illuminate general problems of contemporary theology and philosophy, shows how Buber's general approach to reality, teaching, and religion shaped his view of myth.37 Myth for Buber, Levy indicates, evolves from the natural response of the human spirit, expressing the memory of a meeting, and acting as a psychological stimulus for future human meetings. A myth represents an I-It version of an event people experienced in I-You reality.

This view of myth draws, as does all Buber's thinking, on his insight into the two ways of relating to reality: I-It and I-Thou.38 Buber had studied Jewish myth before coming to his I-You insight. His later presentations of biblical myth and hasidic myth reflect that insight. The insight itself suggests that human communication inevitably impoverishes the reality it seeks to transmit. Human beings address the world in the immediacy of I-You meeting and manipulate it through I-It distancing. Myth reflects this duality as a

necessary I-It recapitulation of an original
I-You meeting. Myth, in this way, resembles
all human forms of communication and
teaching. Such efforts at recording I-You
meeting in I-It language face the same
difficulties. Human beings seek to convey
the immediacy of event in reflective words.
Buber suggests that any teaching "stands
ready to become a You ... at any time,
opening up the You-world."39 For Buber,
then, myth serves the I-You relationship
even while using I-It language. As such, it
holds the positive potential of leading into
new I-You experiences but also the negative
potential of closing off such possibilities.

Buber's view of the relationship of myth
and religion makes him wary of
institutionalized myth. He feels that myth,
as part of religion, reflects a genuine I-
You reality. Religious institutions can
appropriate myth as a means of preventing
new personal encounters with I-You reality.
This possibility explains Buber's
ambivalence toward myth. He approves of
myth only when its relationship to I-You
meeting remains uncontaminated by later
structures. Buber regards myth favorably,
characterizing it as an early and immediate
response to an I-You meeting. When religion
accepts myth as part of its own tradition,
however, it alters its nature. Religion
fixes myth at a stage in its development; it
exalts the "I-It" form the response has
taken rather than the I-You meeting to which
the form points. Thus Buber considers myth
either   "the noblest freedom for a
generation that lives it meaningfully," or

"the most miserable slavery for the habitual inheritors who merely accept it."40

Buber uses a biological analogy to compare positive and negative religion. Religion either flows freely through a culture as its life's blood or becomes so thick and clogged that the culture cannot survive. All cultures need religion, just as bodies need blood to survive; hardening of religion, however, like hardening of the arteries, causes death. By using myth, religion infuses it with its own positive and negative attributes. Myth, then, can either carry the living nourishment of I-You reality or harden and thus prevent the easy transition from I-It to I-You experience.41

Buber, for example, agrees with many thinkers that the "myth of the hero" represents a central feature in many cultures.42 Buber locates the creation of that myth in the meeting between "the sublimest event, the life that he has lived" and "the profound emotion of the simple." He claims that "the greater the experienced event, so much the more compelling the myth-forming power." The event of the hero's life, however, does not itself create the myth. Only reflection on that life, only that life as "refracted in a prism," becomes myth. The story arises when the experience demands expression and transmission. The myth as such, then, holds the key to the central event in religious life even if it does not literally describe that event.

Buber admits, however, that the creation of myth may sometimes undermine its validity. He notes that "the myth of the saviour already contains in germ the insignificant miracle and the misuse of the truth of salvation and redemption."43 Religion, the institutional representative that shapes lived experience into I-It phenomenon, may keep myth at the I-It level of reality. Buber verifies myth according to its purpose and function. In this case, each person who hears the myth must stand once again before the master, turn to the central man who "brings to the teaching no new element, rather fulfills it; he raises it out of the unrecognized into the recognized...."44 Telling the myth of the savior makes that man present once again and enables others to stand before him. Sometimes the custodians of myth emphasize the literal details of its story rather than the experience to which it points. When that happens, myth loses both its veracity as a report of the past and its truth as a point of departure for the present. The story of the hero, then, becomes a set of doctrines in which one must believe, a tale of miracles in which one must have faith, a doctrine rather than a way of living.45 In that case, Buber comments, religion "holds religiousness in chains."46 He decries the degeneration of mythic religion in modern times.

Buber views myth as a special type of story: a mythic story begins in an I-You event that defies rational explanation; it takes shape in an effort to transmit that

irrational event; it functions pedagogically
to teach of the I-You reality and stimulates
a rénewal of that reality. Hasidic tales,
Buber thinks, follow this mythic paradigm,
although at times he calls them legends and
at other times merely tales. Thus he
introduces a collection of hasidic tales by
suggesting the purpose of storytelling
itself. A disciple of the Baal Shem Tov,
Buber relates, was once asked to tell a
story. He replied that a story must be told
so that "it constitutes help in itself." To
illustrate that point the disciple told how
his lame grandfather had once described the
Baal Shem Tov's dancing at prayer. While
describing the event, the grandfather could
not contain himself. Words alone did not
convey his meaning, so he began to dance.
"From that hour on he was cured of his
lameness. That's the way to tell a
story."47 The story sought to transmit the
I-You reality created by the Baal Shem;
telling the story should move beyond the
details of the tale to recapture its I-You
vitality; the grandfather's curative dance
represents the renewed I-You truth. Buber
concentrates on Jewish myths for the same
purpose the grandfather told of the Baal
Shem Tov, but he aims at curing a lameness
of the spirit rather than a lameness of the
limbs.

Buber studies Jewish myth to separate
the "false" I-It encrusted part from the
living myth that can point to a vital
Judaism for modern Jews. Buber advocates
Jewish myth because he laments that modern
people no longer recognize the possibility

of I-You meeting; they have lost their
sensitivity to interhuman relationship. He
notes that as human beings become incapable
of relating to mythic images they also lose
the ability to enter into relationship with
one another and with God. He offers his
analysis of myth to help the person he calls
a "spiritual pupil" who no longer knows how
to decode the stories about humanity and God
to "catch a glimpse of the appearance of the
Absolute."48 Buber explicates myth so that
such students might reclaim Jewish myth as
the center of Judaic religious life.

This theory of myth applies to non-
Jewish myth no less than Jewish. Buber
himself looked beyond Judaism to the myths
of world religions. He compiled and
translated Chinese ghost stories, retold
Finnish legends, collected Celtic tales, and
compiled the testimonies of religious
mystics from greatly diverse traditions.
Buber's work as translator and interpreter
of world mythology won him an admiring
audience. Buber as theorist of myth hopes
that Jews and non-Jews alike will learn to
glimpse the possibility of I-You reality by
reading back from a myth to its originating
event and leaping forward from it to an I-
You meeting of their own.

BUBER AND HIS CRITICS

Each of Buber's contentions about myth
met opposition. Scholars opposed his view

of reality as sentimental and dogmatic; they objected to his relegation of myth to a pedagogic purpose. Jews often found his reconstruction of Judaism untenable. Scholarly debate centers on several key concerns over the origin, meaning, and function of myth. As noted throughout this study, Buber often engaged other scholars in debate. He argued against Jewish thinkers who refused to allow myth a place in Jewish religion; he opposed "mythologists" who relegated myth to primitive thinking; he corrected biblical scholars who, in his view, misinterpreted mythic texts. Appropriate reference to these thinkers occurs throughout this study (as in the following summary of Buber's dispute with Jung). Because this introduction to Buber as a theorist of myth, however, seeks above all to illuminate the unique aspect of Buber's thought, it does not project a comparative picture of Buber. This study introduces comparisons of Buber's approach to alternative theories of myth only as a means of clarifying Buber's own position.49

Buber's commitment to I-You reality leads him to criticize theorists of myth who, he feels, relegate it to I-It existence. While Buber admits that myth subsists as an expression of the basic word I-It, he expects theorists of myth to push behind and beyond phenomenal reality to glimpse the possibility of saying I-You. Buber demands an openness not just to other people but to "works of the spirit." He therefore objects when theorists reduce myth to a function of the psyche, of social

needs, or of the human imagination. His
controversy with Carl Gustav Jung that
shocked many supporters of both thinkers
when it burst into openness in 1951
demonstrates how his view of reality
conditioned not only his interpretation of
myth but his acceptance or rejection of
other theorists of myth.50   Scholars
discussing the disagreement between Buber
and Jung often couch their analysis in
personal terms. Some criticize Buber's
"underhanded way of doing holy business" and
wonder why Buber cannot use his renowned
gift for open dialogue to appreciate Jung.
Others claim that "Buber was ready to enter
into dialogue with Jung but Jung did not
want a dialogue with Buber."51

     Actually, the two differed on the source
and therefore, for Buber, the truth of myth.
Buber claims that Jung locates myth within
the human psyche. He objects that Jung
thereby makes religion "a relation to
psychic events ... to events of one's own
soul...." If myth arises out of inner human
prompting, not in relationship to an
external event, then Buber has entirely
misunderstood its meaning. Buber cannot
admit that myth derives from inside a person
if he is to consider myth an accurate record
of an externally real event.52   A
psychological analysis of myth has even more
devastating consequences for Buber. Buber
recognizes that Jung defines truth in
relationship to the human subject. God
exists for that subject as a psychic
phenomenon, as an element in the soul.53
Were that the case, then myth testifies to

an object in I-It reality; myth can be known
as a "thing." The problem seems to be one
of knowledge. How can the truth of myth be
known? Jung seems to think that it is known
by looking inward at the human psyche; Buber
believes it can be known by looking outward
to I-You reality. Indeed, Jung criticizes
Buber for seeking a "knowledge" of God, and
Buber laments Jung's lack of imagination,
being unable even to conceive of a view of
knowledge different from his own.54 The
real crux, however, is ontological, not
epistemological--concerned with reality
itself, not with how to know reality. Jung
denies the realm of I-You as an independent
and verifiable sphere of being; he must
therefore reject Buber's claims that myth
originates in such a sphere and points
forward to it. Buber, however, builds his
entire theory of myth on his construction of
reality and cannot allow the validity of a
divergent view.

Students seeking to establish the
integrity of myth felt threatened by Buber's
emphasis on myth as a transitional and
pedagogical link between two I-You meetings.
Christians, for example, often recognize
that Buber's interpretation of New Testament
tales undermines canonical authority and the
Christian claim to uniqueness.55 Rudolf
Pannwitz, a Christian theologian and student
of myth and Gnosticism with whom Buber
corresponded on a range of shared concerns--
political, poetical, and theological,
criticized Buber's interpretation of
Christianity and his favorable
interpretation of hasidism. Both myths,

Pannwitz contended, sought to explain reality. Buber denied an explanatory purpose for hasidic myth.

Buber's view of myth's function impels him to evaluate myth. He tests each story he studies to see if it contains a vital message, if it really records an I-You meeting, if it really opens into a new I-You meeting. Only when he makes a positive judgment on both counts does he accept the story as genuine myth. Those, who like Pannwitz, ask myth to teach doctrinal truth must reject Buber's demand for responsive myth. Buber, by contrast, considers such doctrinal concerns unproductive. They work against myth by encrusting it in religious forms. Doctrine seeks to appropriate myth for itself and thereby neutralize its true purpose. Buber studies myth to discover the I-You reality it indicates and thus conflicts with those who look to myth for propositional truths, truths that Buber associates only with I-It reality.56 The content of Buber's study often scandalizes students of Jewish religion. Biblical scholars debate whether the Hebrew Bible contains "myth." Scholars such as Yehezkel Kaufmann, the renowned Israeli Biblical critic, think that while it retains remnants of myth, it neutralizes them. These biblical scholars criticize Buber for misunderstanding the advance made by the Bible over primitive religion.57 In a similar way, students of Jewish mysticism often claim that Buber has misunderstood the meaning of Jewish myth by ignoring their doctrinal foundations.58

Many Jews exposed to Buber's view of
Judaism would agree that he does not
represent the tradition. Important Jewish
thinkers add their weight to this view of
Buber as an outsider to the tradition. As
an exemplar of "humanity the student," Buber
probes the meaning of Judaism without
creating any single model of "Judaism,"
thereby alienating traditionalists,
liberals, and Zionists alike.59 Buber's
studies of reality, pedagogy, and Judaism
challenge preconceptions held by many other
scholars. Buber delights in raising such
challenges as he seeks to free myth from the
prison of the "mythologists" who analyze the
dead form without looking at its living
significance. He champions myth as a
challenge to recapture the reality of a
meeting between an I and a You.60

MARTIN BUBER'S LEGACY

Such, then, was the man whom the
students of the Hebrew University sought
out, even if he was not their teacher. He
had written extensively on Jewish religion,
but his lesson was a universal one: studying
reality, pedagogy, and religion offers a new
perspective on existence generally and on
myth specifically. Such study, he teaches
by exemplification, leads to a new way of
seeing, a new way of interacting in the
world.

Buber's writings on myth educate
students on reality, learning, and religion
generally. His teaching must be understood
in this wider perspective. Responding to a
challenge from Rudolf Pannwitz, whose
correspondence with Buber over Christianity
elicited the response noted above, Buber
claimed that "I hold the myth to be
indispensable; yet I do not hold it to be
central, but man and ever again man. Myth
must authenticate itself in man and not man
in myth."61 A study of Buber the theorist
of myth necessarily focuses on Buber's study
of Jewish myth, but it cannot lose sight of
Buber's more general concerns. When Buber
died on June 13, 1965, mourned by world
Jewry, his stature rested on his many
achievements and on his exemplification of a
life of learning. A life dedicated to
learning had become a life of dialogue with
other human beings, a Jewish life that
entered into conversation with humanity as a
whole.   This study of Buber as theorist of
myth enters into that same conversation.

NOTES

1. Aubrey Hodes reports this entire
    incident in his <u>Martin Buber: An
    Intimate Portrait</u> (New York: Viking,
    1971), pp. 209-12. The cited words are
    given on p. 211. For "Homo Ludens," see
    Johan Huizinga, <u>Homo Ludens: A Study of
    the Play Element in Culture</u> (Boston:
    Beacon, 1955).

2. Among the many fine studies of Buber,
    the following are useful for those
    wishing an introduction to his life and
    thought: Samuel Hugo Bergman offers a
    brief but insightful overview of Buber's
    thinking in "Martin Buber: Life as
    Dialogue," in his <u>Faith and Reason:
    Modern Jewish Thought</u>, trans. and ed.
    Alfred Jospe (New York: Schocken, 1963),
    pp. 81-97; Eliezer Berkovits expresses
    the criticisms often raised by
    traditional and observant Jews of
    Buber's interpretation of Judaism,
    "Martin Buber's Religion of the
    Dialogue," in his <u>Major Themes in Modern
    Philosophies of Judaism</u> (New York: KTAV,
    1974), pp. 68-137; Malcolm L. Diamond's
    <u>Martin Buber: Jewish Existentialist</u> (New
    York: Oxford University Press, 1960)
    presents an affectionate, clear, and
    generally positive evaluation of Buber;
    Maurice Friedman's early biography of
    Buber, <u>Martin Buber: The Life of
    Dialogue</u> (New York: Harper and Row,
    1960), remains a classic and more
    accessible to beginning readers than his
    definitive three volume work cited in

later notes; Nahum N. Glatzer provides excellent analysis and personal reflection on Buber's thinking in "Aspects of Martin Buber's Thought," Modern Judaism 1:1 (1981) 1-16; those beginning study of Buber would do well to look at Alexander S. Kohanski, An Analytical Interpretation of Martin Buber's I and Thou, with a Biographical Introduction and Glossary (Woodbury, NY: Barron's, 1975) and his Martin Buber's Philosophy of Interhuman Relation: A Response to the Human Problematic of Our Time (Rutherford, NJ: Fairleigh Dickenson University Press, and London: Associated University Presses, 1982); Paul Arthur Schilpp and Maurice Friedman, eds., The Philosophy of Martin Buber. The Library of Living Philosophers, Vol. XII (La Salle, IL: Open Court, 1967) collects several valuable studies on selected aspects of Buber's thought and includes both Buber's response to his critics and his early autobiographical fragments; a recent and useful work by Pamela Vermes, Buber on God and the Perfect Man, Brown Judaica Studies 13 (Chico, CA: Scholars Press, 1980) should also be consulted; see also S. Daniel Breslauer, The Chrysalis of Religion: A Guide to the Jewishness of Buber's "I and Thou" (Nashville: Abingdon, 1980). Laurence J. Silberstein's recent work Martin Buber's Social and Religious Thought: Alienation and the Quest For Meaning (New York: New York University Press, 1989) provides an insightful study of

Buber, his intellectual influences, and his thought on language, myth, and religious revisionism. Many of Silberstein's conclusions parallel those advanced here although the focus of his study is considerably different.

3. Haim Gordon provides an interpretation of Buber's life generally and his early life in particular that emphasizes this fact in his essay "The Sheltered Aesthete: A New Appraisal of Martin Buber's Life," in Haim Gordon and Jochanan Bloch, eds., <u>Martin Buber : A Centenary Volume</u> (New York: KTAV, 1984), pp. 25-39. Gordon notes that Buber himself increased the difficulties facing the biographer. When constructing his "autobiographical fragments," Gordon comments, Buber portrayed a linear development from triumph to triumph. Gordon suggests that "only a person who decided what role he played in history and has greatly enjoyed playing that role can write thus" (p. 30).   The definitive study of Buber's biography is the three-volume work by Maurice Friedman, <u>Martin Buber's Life and Work: The Early Years, 1878-1923</u>; <u>Martin Buber's Life and Work: The Middle Years, 1923-1945</u>, and <u>Martin Buber's Life and Work: The Later Years, 1945-1964</u> (New York: Dutton, 1981).

4. Martin Buber, <u>Pointing the Way</u>, trans. and ed. Maurice S. Friedman (New York: Harper and Row, 1957), p. 3.

5. Walter Kaufmann, "Buber's Failures and
    Triumph," in Haim Gordon and Jochanan
    Bloch, eds., <u>Martin Buber : A Centenary
    Volume</u> (New York: KTAV, 1984), p. 4; see
    the entire article, pp. 3–18.

6. See Martin Buber, <u>Between Man and Man</u>,
    eds. and trans. Ronald Gregor Smith and
    Maurice Friedman (New York: Macmillan,
    1965), pp. 13–14; Maurice Friedman
    discusses this encounter with care and
    sympathy in <u>The Early Years</u>, pp. 187–92.

7. See the discussion in Friedman, <u>The
    Early Years</u>, pp. 282–302 (contrast the
    view presented here with that of
    Horwitz) and in <u>The Middle Years</u>, pp.
    31–58, in Rivka Horwitz, <u>Buber's Way to
    "I and Thou": The Development of Martin
    Buber's Thought and His "Religion as
    Presence" Lectures</u> (Philadelphia: Jewish
    Publication Society of America, 1988),
    pp. 163–74. Buber's biography by
    itself makes a fascinating subject as
    several of the books mentioned in notes
    1 and 2 make clear. While touching upon
    biographical aspects of Buber's
    development, such as the meeting with
    Rosenzweig mentioned here, the present
    study refers to Buber's life only to
    clarify his position as a theorist of
    myth.

8. See Martin Buber, <u>I and Thou</u>, trans. and
    intro. Walter Kaufmann (New York:
    Scribner's, 1970). Unless noted
    otherwise, references to <u>I and Thou</u> are
    to this translation. Kaufmann's long

introduction, pp. 9-50, summarizes
Buber's world view, his application of
that view to the various studies he
pursued, and the plan he abandoned after
completing this first of a projected
series of volumes. Kaufmann also raises
a question which plagues any work citing
Buber in translation. Buber uses the
familiar term "Du" as an intimate form
of the second person. In older English
that usage could accurately be
represented by "thou." Most
translations of Buber, following this
usage, speak of I-Thou relationships.
Modern English, however, no longer uses
"thou" in such an analogous way with Du.
Kaufmann, then, translates Ich-Du as "I-
You." While I usually follow that
translation and write of an "I-You"
meeting (relationship seems a
formalistic phrase), I also prefer to
speak of "thou" rather than "you." I
apologize for the inconsistency but find
it necessary to convey the sense of
Buber's meaning. Rivka Horwitz' Buber's
Way to "I and Thou" traces the
relationship between the lectures at the
Lehrhaus and the book that grew out of
it. See also her German edition of
those lectures, Rivka Horwitz, Buber's
Way to "I and Thou": An Historical
Analysis and the First Publication of
Martin Buber's Lectures "Religion Als
Gegenwart" (Heidelberg: Lambert
Schneider, 1978).

9. Buber, <u>I and Thou</u>, p. 53. See also Martin Buber, <u>I and Thou</u>, trans. Ronald Gregor Smith, 2nd ed. (New York: Scribner's, 1958), p. 3.

10. See Lewis Carroll, <u>Alice in Wonderland and Through the Looking Glass</u> (New York: Grosset and Dunlap, 1946), pp. 283-85.

11. Buber, <u>I and Thou</u>, p. 88.

12. <u>Ibid.</u>, p. 100.

13. <u>Ibid.</u>, p. 113.

14. <u>Ibid.</u>, pp. 99-100.

15. <u>Ibid.</u>, p. 96.

16. See Ernst Simon, "Martin Buber, the Educator", in Paul Arthur Schilpp and Maurice Friedman, eds., <u>The Philosophy of Martin Buber</u>, the Library of Living Philosophers, vol. XII (La Salle, IL: Open Court, 1967), pp. 543-76.

17. Buber, <u>I and Thou</u>, p. 178.

18. Martin Buber, <u>Israel and the World: Essays in a Time of Crisis</u>, 2nd ed. (New York: Schocken, 1963), p. 180. Buber notes that the Nazis recognized the challenge implicit in his call for recognition of an alternative reality. They therefore, after this address, forbade him from further public activity. He comments, "thus again I became conscious of the fact that though

the power of the spirit is the hidden
kernel of history--its visible husk
remains the spirit's lack of power" (p.
6.)

19. The cited sentence comes from Friedman,
    The Middle Years, p. 160; the various
    incidents described here as well as
    general information on Buber's
    activities during the time of the Nazis
    can be found in that work, pp. 157-76.

20. Martin Buber, A Land of Two Peoples:
    Martin Buber on Jews and Arabs, ed. with
    commentary Paul R. Mendes-Flohr (New
    York: Oxford University Press, 1983),
    pp. 138-42.

21. Buber's distinction between two types of
    religion resembles that of other
    thinkers who distinguish between dynamic
    religious movements begun by
    "charismatic" leaders in opposition to
    institutional forms and "routinized"
    movements in which bureaucratic
    authority and training legitimate
    leadership; see, for example, Max
    Weber's distinction among prophetic,
    priestly, and rabbinic religion in
    Ancient Judaism, eds. and trans. Hans
    H. Gerth and Don Martindale (Glendale,
    IL: Free Press, 1952), pp. 17, 40,
    98ff., 157, 386-88. On the tension
    between institutionalized religion and
    spontaneous religion see Thomas F.
    O'Dea, "Five Dilemmas in the
    Institutionalization of Religion," in
    his Sociology and the Study of Religion

(New York: Basic Books, 1970), pp. 240–55. Buber differs from these thinkers because he refuses to use an evolutionary paradigm. Instead, he uses a cyclical model in which the primary religious event must necessarily be institutionalized in a form that reawakens the primal occurrence again and again. He also focuses on the effect of the religion on its believers rather than on the type of leadership involved.

22. Rivka Horwitz in Buber's Way to "I and Thou" discusses these lectures and their importance for all of Buber's subsequent writings as well as the debt Buber owed to former thinkers, especially Ferdinand Ebner.

23. See Buber, I and Thou, pp. 148–50, 166–68, and Breslauer, The Chrysalis of Religion.

24. See Gershom G. Scholem, "At the Completion of Buber's Translation of the Bible," in his The Messianic Idea in Judaism and Other Essays on Jewish Spirituality, trans. Michael A. Meyer (New York: Schocken, 1971), pp. 314–19.

25. Martin Buber, Moses: The Revelation and the Covenant (New York: Harper and Row, 1958), p. 16. Compare the technique and focus in idem., Kingship of God, 3rd ed., trans. Richard Scheimann (New York: Harper and Row, 1967); The Prophetic Faith, trans. Carlyle Witton-

Davies (New York: Harper and Row, 1960);
and several of the studies in On The
Bible: Eighteen Studies, ed. Nahum N.
Glatzer (New York: Schocken, 1968).

26. Buber, Between Man and Man, pp. 7, 80.

27. See Martin Buber, On Judaism, ed. Nahum
N. Glatzer (New York: Schocken, 1967),
pp. 77, 174, 193.

28. See Martin Buber, Good and Evil: Two
Interpretations (New York: Scribner's,
1953).

29. See Paul Mendes-Flohr, "Martin Buber's
Reception among Jews," Modern Judaism
6:2 (1986), p. 120. On the Jewishness
of Buber's thinking despite its apparent
deviation from traditional Judaism see
also Breslauer, The Chrysalis of
Religion; chapter 1, "I and Thou as a
Jewish Hermeneutic," pp. 25-67, suggests
how Buber evolved a new way of making
Judaism alive for contemporary Jews.

30. See the discussion of this change by
Samuel Hugo Bergman, "Martin Buber and
Mysticism", in Paul Arthur Schilpp and
Maurice Friedman, eds., The Philosophy
of Martin Buber, The Library of Living
Philosophers, vol. XII (La Salle, IL:
Open Court, 1967), p. 303.

31. For an example of this thinking see the
philosophy of Hermann Cohen. Wendell
S. Dietrich's study Cohen and
Troeltsch: Ethical Monotheistic

Religion and Theory of Culture, Brown
Judaic Series 120 (Atlanta, GA:
Scholar's Press, 1986) examines a Jewish
and Protestant expression of this
philosophy.   Dietrich   discusses
Cohen's argument against Jewish myth in
relationship to Ernst Cassirer's
theories on pp. 67-68.

32. Buber, On Judaism, p. 9.

33. Franz Rosenzweig, On Jewish Learning,
    ed. Nahum N. Glatzer (New York:
    Schocken, 1965), p. 114.

34. Buber, Israel and the World, p. 28.

35. Ignac Goldziher, Mythology Among the
    Hebrews and its Historical Development,
    trans. Russell Maretineau (New York:
    Cooper Square, 1967), pp. xxx, 2-15.

36. See Alan F. Segal, Rebecca's Children:
    Judaism and Christianity in the Roman
    World (Cambridge: Harvard University
    Press, 1986), pp. 3-4.

37. Zeev Levy, "Demythologization and
    Remythologization," in Bar Ilan Annual
    vol. 22-23 (Ramat Gan, Israel: Bar Ilan
    University Press, 1987), pp. 223-24; see
    the entire essay, pp. 205-7.

38. See Vermes, Buber on God, p. 31, who
    emphasizes how Buber's work led up to
    and drew upon his I-Thou thinking; see
    also Moshe Swarcz, Language, Myth, and

Art (Tel Aviv: Schocken, 1966), for a similar discussion.

39. Buber, I and Thou, p. 92.

40. Buber, On Judaism, p. 11.

41. See Buber, Between Man and Man, p. 18; The Legend of the Baal Shem, p. 13.

42. Buber, Pointing the Way, pp. 34-43; compare Otto Rank, The Myth of the Birth of the Hero and Other Writings, ed. Philip Freund (New York: Random House, 1959), pp. 3-96.

43. Buber, ibid., p. 36.

44. Ibid., p. 39.

45. Buber contrasts the "myth" of the Sermon on the Mount with the set of "but I say unto you..." proclamations that follow it. He thinks that the former represents Jesus as hero whose life "fulfills" the law, that is it gives witness by its very essence to the possibility of living the law; the latter, however, represents I-It doctrines that must be believed, a catechism to be followed as authoritative. Ibid., p. 39.

46. Ibid., p. 36.

47. Martin Buber, Tales of the Hasidim: The Early Masters, trans. Olga Marx (New York: Schocken, 1947), pp. v-vi.

48. Martin Buber, Eclipse of God: Studies in the Relation Between Religion and Philosophy (New York: Harper and Row, 1952), p. 120.

49. Robert A. Segal presents a useful and bibliographically suggestive overview of theories of myth and groups them by helpful categories in his "In Defense of Mythology: The History of Modern Theories of Myth," Annals of Scholarship I:1 (1980): 3-49. Isaiah Rabinovich presents a penetrating analysis of Jung's view of religion and its effect on modern literature in his Roots and Trends: Essays on Literature [Hebrew] (Jerusalem: Bialik Institute, 1967), pp. 40-54.

50. See Friedman, The Later Years, pp. 169-76; Buber, Eclipse of God, pp. 78-89, 133-37.

51. Friedman, The Later Years, p. 172.

52. Buber, Eclipse of God, p. 79.

53. Ibid., pp. 133-34.

54. Friedman, The Later Years, pp. 173-76.

55. Thus John M. Oesterreicher, a pioneer in Inter-faith dialogue, recognizes the "incomplete" nature of Buber's understanding of Christianity. Buber, he feels, misconstrues the myths, rituals and dogmas of the New Testament. Buber, of course, applies his critical

criteria of "authentic" myth to Judaism
and Christianity alike and in this way
cannot be charged with "discrimination."
Perhaps Michael Wyschogrod understands
this best when, in his introduction, he
characterizes Buber's method as socratic
stimulation rather than prophetic
proclamation. See John M.
Oesterreicher, The Unfinished Dialogue:
Martin Buber and the Christian, intro.
Edward A. Synan and Michael Wyschogrod
(New York: Philosophical Library, 1986).

56. Friedman, The Middle Years, pp. 98-99,
176, 182.

57. See Yehezkel Kaufmann, The Religion of
Israel: From Its Beginnings to the
Babylonian Exile, trans. and abridged
Moshe Greenberg (Chicago: University of
Chicago Press, 1960), pp. 20, 60-63 and
idem., Toldot Haemunah HaYisraelit, vol.
I (Tel Aviv: Dvir, 1937), pp. 9-11.
Compare the discussions, for example, in
Irving M. Zeitlin, Ancient Judaism:
Biblical Criticism From Max Weber to the
Present (Oxford: Oxford University
Press, 1984), especially pp. 2, 18-35;
note the argument against such a view
presented by Benjamin Uffenheimer, "Myth
and Reality in Ancient Israel," in The
Origins and Diversity of Axial
Civilization, ed. S. N. Eisenstadt
(Albany, NY: SUNY Press, 1986), pp.
136-67. Compare the discussion of
different views of biblical myth in J.
W. Rogerson, Myth in Old Testament

Interpretation, BZAW 134 (Berlin: Walter
de Gruyter, 1974).

58. See the discussion in Moshe Idel,
Kabbalah: New Perspectives (New Haven:
Yale University Press, 1988), pp. 1-16.
Hayam Maccoby discusses myth in Judaism
generally and as understood by both
Buber and Gershom Scholem, the scholar
who singlehandedly transformed the study
of Jewish mysticism into an academic
discipline, in his "The Greatness of
Gershom Scholem," in Harold Bloom, ed.,
Gershom Scholem (New York: Chelsea
House, 1987), pp. 137-54; compare the
remarks on Buber's view of myth in
Kohanski, Martin Buber's Philosophy of
Interhuman Relation, pp. 159-60.

59. See the various responses to Buber in
Berkovits, "Martin Buber,"; Mendes-
Flohr, "Martin Buber's Reception among
Jews," pp. 111-126, and Gershom G.
Scholem, "Martin Buber's Judaism," in his
On Jews and Judaism in Crisis, ed.
Werner J. Dannhauser (New York:
Schocken, 1978), pp. 126-71.

60. Buber, Between Man and Man, p. 214.

61. Martin Buber, The Origin and Meaning of
Hasidism, ed. and trans. Maurice
Friedman (New York: Horizon Press,
1960), pp. 248-49.

Chapter 2   Buber on Myth

PROBLEMS IN BUBER'S APPROACH

Buber claims that his studies of myth recapture "a corporeally real event" and show how the event was "impressed upon" human beings who "perceived and presented (it) as a divine, an absolute event." He contrasts true myths, reflecting real events occurring in I-You reality, to stories told as lessons about I-It reality, stories he calls "fables." He considers various kinds of stories (legends, tales about creation, tales about miracles, tales about good and evil) equally "mythic" if they report a real I-You event; they are not "mythic" if they merely reflect the author's imagination. Buber also judges among myths: he approves of those that accurately recall an I-You event and lead to its reenactment and deplores those that remain in I-It reality.1

Buber, however, never provides clear criteria for determining whether the I-You event he identifies with a myth <u>actually</u> occurred. By its very nature, I-You reality

defies such verification. Buber responds
subjectively, sometimes recognizing the
truth of I-You reality in a story and
sometimes judging such reality lacking.

Once while discussing the New Testament
with the Christian biblical scholar James
Muilenburg, who generally favored Buber's
insights into the Bible, Buber voiced doubt
about the authenticity of a certain passage
from the Gospel of Matthew. Muilenburg
pressed him for evidence, and Buber refused
to reply since he had no objective proof.
Finally, Buber declared "It is merely my own
subjective feeling.... I do not hear the
voice of Jesus in it." Muilenburg became
upset, although Buber reminded him that "he
had been warned."2 Academic honesty demands
more than an impressionistic judgment of a
myth's truth.

TESTING BUBER'S DEFINITION

This criticism of subjectivity affects
Buber's view of myth because he attempts to
establish the veracity of some myths and the
illegitimacy of others. Scholars have long
debated how to evaluate the truth claims of
mythic stories, contesting the historicity
of the narratives, the existential relevance
of mythic meaning, and metaphysical accuracy
of mythic world views.3 Insofar as Buber's
I-You philosophy claims to verify or falsify
the truth of any particular myth, the
subjectivity of this method undermines its

credibility. Buber, however, anticipates myth's use as a catalyst for entering I-You reality no less than he looks backward to its origins in I-You meeting. In this way he helps readers discover a personal meaning in the myths he discusses.

This consequence of Buber's studies is no less subjective than his search for the origins of a myth. It proves valuable, nonetheless, for both academics and non-academics interested in myth. Buber's aim in pointing to new possibilities of I-You meeting goes beyond merely academic exercises. He sought to involve readers in the material he presented. He claimed accuracy not only as an archeologist of the spirit, discovering the sources of myth, but also as a spiritual mentor, pointing the way for moderns seeking authentic living. Testing Buber's success in achieving this goal demands different standards from those normally used in academic studies. As Paul Mendes-Flohr contends, "It would thus be amiss to judge Buber's interpretive endeavor strictly by the standards of academic scholarship."4 Buber requires an academic reading that takes his own criterion of success as its point of departure. Nevertheless, any evaluation must itself guard against unwarranted subjectivity. Although Buber rejected evidence from I-It data to prove or disprove I-You reality, his own writing clearly takes place in I-It reality. Books represent secondary reflections on truth, not unmediated truth itself. As writings about myth, then, Buber's theory is susceptible to I-It

evaluation. Haim Gordon suggests that as
modern interpreters of Buber struggle to
find a way of "clarifying" his thought, they
should use Buber's own approach.5 That
approach provides a model by which to weigh
Buber's success or failure.

Buber invites his readers to respond to
the personal appeal of his words. He claims
that he would fail in his own eyes were
readers to stay at the analytic level.
Buber feels that a reader should do more
than assent to the power of a logical
argument. He relates that once he convinced
a man to abandon a preconceived belief and
"shattered the security of his
Weltanschauung." Buber realized, however,
that he had failed in his ultimate purpose.
He had won an argument but left a human
being confused. His debating skills meant
little if, after having persuaded a person
to give up his traditional beliefs, he could
not "live with him, win his trust through
real life-relationship, help him to walk
with me...."6 Buber sees his success
depending less on his scholarly expertise
than on his ability to move and inspire the
reader to share his experience.
This personal anecdote points to a
criterion by which to judge Buber as a
theorist of myth. Buber hopes to be taken
seriously as a scholar of myth, as an
academic who reveals the actual origins of
myths, whose system of verification guides
the study of myth. This present study must,
therefore, summarize Buber's reported
findings. The subjectivity of those
findings, however, render them less than

fully credible. Nevertheless, Buber remains
an impressive theorist of myth because of
his effect upon readers. The major focus of
this study will be on Buber's retelling of
myth, on his presentation of certain myths
to enhance their appeal for modern readers.
The final evaluation of Buber remains
subjective: has Buber succeeded better than
other scholars in conveying a modern meaning
for ancient myths? While that conclusion
must remain subjective, readers, by
following Buber's method and comparing his
interpretations with other scholars who
study the same stories but use a different
theory of myth, can reach their own decision
about his success.

MYTHS OF LEADERSHIP

     As noted earlier, Buber's concern for
spontaneous religion in contrast to
institutionalized religion parallels, even
though it cannot be identified with, the
distinction sociologist Max Weber makes
between charismatic and routinized
leadership. Weber sought to understand the
connection between religious diversity and
different types of leaders. When one
leadership group contends against another,
diversity takes on a political and readily
observable shape. Such conflicts often
arise between a routine or bureaucratic
leadership group based on training or
heredity and a more spontaneous type of
leader drawing only upon personal qualities

and relying only upon the acceptance of followers as self-justification. The former type favors continuity and stability; the latter initiates change and revolution.7

Weber recognized in myth, no less than in leadership, an indication of religious diversity. Folk religion may emphasize magic and heroism. A more middle class or bourgeois religion turns to "sentimental legend which has a tendency toward inwardness and edification." The Christian myth's "soteriological," or salvation-oriented, approach responds both the social needs of the new bourgeois class and by harnessing the "widely diffused soteriological myths" that "generated a tremendous growth in pneumatic manifestations of charisma."8   Weber saw that the changes occurring in myths of heroes may indicate religious change and development. Myths of leaders reflect the diversity within a particular tradition.

From the biblical period onward the myth of Enoch functioned in Judaism as such a view of leadership. Whether alluded to in a few biblical verses or associated with an extended mystical tradition, Enoch plays an important role in Jewish mythology. The myth itself developed in a complex evolution. The original story of Enoch seems lost in antiquity. Various texts from the Bible through eighteenth-century Jewish writings make use of Enoch as a religious hero. The references, however, are scattered and often seem haphazard. Enoch's role as charismatic hero, as an unconventional leader, remains constant in each of the variants although no single work presents the myth as a unified whole. When scholars consider an "Enoch tradition," they do so by piecing together fragments from different sources drawn from very distinctive times and places.

Nonetheless, Judaic scholar and student of the Kabbalah Moshe Idel confirms a relationship among the early, later, and intermediate traditions about Enoch as a mystical and pious ideal. He concludes with a valuable methodological reflection in which he justifies using texts from diverse places and historical periods to create a coherent Enoch tradition. He carefully compares disparate texts from different periods in the development of the tradition and shows how some texts from a late period reflect a tradition more ancient than that found in earlier material. He shows that each variant reflects on Enoch as a model of the charismatic individual who, whether accepted by normative leaders or not, acts as an inspiration to others.9

THE ENOCH TRADITIONS

Buber, among others, interprets the Enoch tradition, commenting on which variants he considers genuine and which spurious. His main intent, however, seems to be evocative: Buber hopes to actualize Enoch as an ideal for contemporary readers.

His attempt at presenting the Enoch
tradition should be evaluated in
relationship to the interpretations given by
other scholars. Some scholars understand the
Enoch story as one example of a general
motif--that of the ascension of the hero.
According to that myth, the hero ascends to
the gods, who invest him with rulership and
send him back to earth with special
authority. Many cultures tell similar
stories. A great man from the society
performs heroic feats; he engages in special
rituals; the gods seize him. Ascending to
heaven or descending to the netherworld, he
discovers a task, a social role. Returning
to earth, he takes up his new duties and
legitimates his authority by telling of the
events that occurred on his journey.

A sociological interpretation of such
myths notes their implication for
leadership. For example, Adolf E. Jensen,
an ethnologist drawing on anthropological
findings, exemplifies this interpretation.10
Jensen interprets the myth as a
legitimation of social leadership. Myth,
together with cult, expresses the social
realities of a community. When religious
leaders dominate a society, the myth tells
of exalted spiritual souls who ascend to a
deity and receive the authority to govern.
An alternative version of this myth
emphasizes that only the king can make such
a celestial journey; civil rather than
religious authority possesses the power to
face the divine forces. In either case, the
story records a test or ordeal through which
leaders must pass. A legitimate leader must

leaders must pass. A legitimate leader must prove worthy of leadership through divinely sanctioned trial. Jensen notes that the destination of the journey described depends upon the theological tradition of the culture involved. Those who assume a celestial deity tell of a visit to the heavens; those who picture the gods ruling in the underworld portray a descent to the netherworld. Every such myth, however, contains the theme of investiture with power after a divine examination.

This myth of the hero who ascends to receive authorization as a leader seems to legitimate the religion of the status quo. On a psychological level, however, the myth symbolizes human frustrations and restlessness. Thus historian of religion Mircea Eliade explains that the myth acts as a coded symbol of inner human drives.11 The deepest desires of the human psyche surface in the mythic stories of primitive peoples. Such myths, he suggests, arise as human beings struggle to transcend the routine of daily life. Not only primitive people but every person, he contends, requires a sense of transcendence, of surpassing normal experience. People today, he explains, live diminished lives because they no longer experience the meaning that myth provides. Without the message given by ascension myths, they feel trapped in mundane existence. They intuit the futility of their lives but lack the mythic symbols needed to transcend their everyday lives. This desire motivates all people and belongs to no particular class or social stratum.

Because of this view Eliade opposes the sociological interpretation often offered as an explanation of ascension myths. He claims instead that celestial flight "is not the monopoly of sovereigns" but rather portrays an ecstatic experience that should not be taken literally. The magical flight, in his view, has an existential referent. It expresses a "break with the universe of everyday" existence in which people transcend their limitations. Thus, unlike Jensen, Eliade interprets the myth of ascension not as a sociological tale legitimating leadership but as an expression of a universal longing for freedom and a universal need to surpass everyday life. When modern people read that myth, he claims, they can learn of their own yearning for the same experience of liberation and transcendence.

Jewish tradition includes an exemplary ascension myth: that of Enoch. Although the Hebrew Bible provides only fragmentary evidence of this myth, and although later Jewish tradition offers strikingly dissimilar variants of the tradition, most scholars agree that the Enoch story as such exemplifies the ascension motif. Enoch, an antediluvian hero whom God "takes" and who, therefore, does not die, figures in both biblical and postbiblical Jewish stories as the model of the pious Jew whose mastery of spiritual mysteries enables him to travel in celestial spheres. Buber's explanation of the Enoch story as an exemplification of the ascension motif not only shows an alternative to the interpretations of Eliade

and Jensen but also illustrates how his
approach makes myth accessible for
contemporary readers.

ENOCH IN THE HEBREW BIBLE

The story of Enoch exemplifies the basic
motif of a hero's ascension.   Enoch,
according to all the versions, links heaven
and earth in a cosmic journey. From the
Hebrew Bible through the early modern
version of the story told by Jewish mystics
of the eighteenth century, however, few
variants agree on much else. The Hebrew
Bible provides only two references to Enoch.
Genesis 4:17-18 relates that "Cain was
intimate with his wife who conceived and
gave birth to Enoch, so he built a city
calling it by the name of his son Enoch."
Genesis 5:18-24 tells of Enoch's birth, his
fathering a son, and then his disappearance:
Enoch walked with God after the birth of
Methuselah three hundred years and had other
sons and daughters. Thus Enoch lived three
hundred and sixty-five years. Enoch walked
with God and then was not, for God took him.

Both these notices are very brief and
give little information about Enoch.
Biblical scholars therefore look to
comparative Semitic stories to discover
their meaning. Following the works of
nineteenth century ethnologists like Max
Müller, some critics see the 365 years
mentioned in Genesis 5 as a veiled reference

to the sun. They posit, by comparing the
Bible with Babylonian stories, an original
story of a nearly god-like being deified as
the Sun God. Originally, the story told how
a great hero was placed in the heavens and
makes the circuit in 365 days, which
corresponds to his life on earth.12   While
attractive, this theory only accounts for
the reference to Enoch in Genesis 5 and
cannot really explain the differences
between that story and the Babylonian myths
to which it is compared.

    Other scholars such as Hermann Gunkel,
the noted German biblical critic associated
with form critical studies, explore the
social and historical background that can
explain the references to Enoch.   Gunkel
notes the parallels in Babylonian myth with
Enoch and the common themes of leadership,
walking with God, and the founding of cities
linking this story to other biblical tales.
In the course of development, Gunkel
suggests, an author inserted the story and
name of Enoch into the story of evolving
human culture. Finally, the story took on a
meaning of its own: Enoch symbolized
religious piety rather than any other form
of human culture.13 By its final stage the
story removed earlier influences and
transformed Enoch into a model of human
piety. The biblical narrative includes
brief hints of Enoch's history and
significance. This lack of detail deprives
the story of the specificity found in the
sources from which it was taken, leaving it
merely a suggestive indication of religious
living and the rewards accompanying it.14

The key phrase concerning Enoch in Genesis 5 claims that he "walked with God." Genesis 5:22 suggests that Enoch's walking with God occurred during his life. Genesis 5:24 is more ambiguous but can still be interpreted as a description of how Enoch lived on earth. In that case, the phrase refers to an ideal of religious living. The Bible applies that phrase to two early heroes, Enoch and Noah. When the biblical story turns from humanity's early generations to recount the history of the Israelites, the term for piety changes. God commands Abraham, the progenitor of the Hebrews, to "Walk before me and be perfect," (Genesis 17). From this time on, walking before God replaces "walking with God." The Bible has therefore reduced the Enoch myth to a legend about an early human hero, one whose greatness approaches but does not equal that of the founder of the Hebrew people. Enoch has been reduced to merely human size. The author reluctantly supplies only bare hints as to his significance. Reading the verses in Genesis, one learns little about the characteristics of the hero, what he experienced, or how he exemplified "walking with God."

Modern biblical scholarship considers Genesis 4 part of the Yahwistic document, the product of an author during the times of the Davidic kings of Judah about 1000 B.C.E. (David, Solomon, Rehoboam), and ascribes most of Genesis 5 to the priestly document, finally compiled and edited about 450 B.C.E.15 That historical background

illuminates the use of the Enoch story and
its function in both narratives. The one
characteristic that the mentions of Enoch in
Genesis 4 and 5 share is that they associate
him with an important social, cultural, or
religious innovation. Ancient Israel in the
time of the Yahwist experienced rapid
urbanization and social change. The
agricultural basis of the economy gave way
before commerce and international trade. A
tightly controlled central monarchy replaced
the diffuse and autonomous organization of
regional groups.

The story of Enoch suggests a double
truth in Genesis 4. Urbanization occurs as
a necessity of human progress and survival,
but it derives from the violent, painful
aspects of human nature. Enoch, whose birth
provides a catalyst for change in primal
times, symbolizes the new, and apparently
disturbing impetus to urban life experienced
by Israelite leaders during a time of
painful changes. The post-exilic leadership,
represented by the priestly authors of
Genesis 5, faced different problems from
those of the earlier leaders. They returned
to their former national home as clients of
an imperial power. Subservient to the
Persian government, these Judeans could not
afford to anger their overlords. They
needed to affirm a piety that transcended
political life. The heroes of the past,
represented by the post-deluvian patriarchs,
kings, prophets, priests, and judges, all
exercised social control. Their tasks had
focused on furthering national goals and
aims. These leaders no longer served as

realistic models in the post-exilic period.
Seeking for more realistic options, the
returning Judean leaders used the myth of
Enoch to indicate the possibility of a non-
political hero. Enoch's piety transcends
mundane affairs and thus suggests new
patterns of religious leadership. Since the
returning priests had not yet determined the
shape of their communal power, they could
afford to use the myth of Enoch as a hint of
possibilities derived from a more primal
model than Israel's political heroes.

Other appearances of the ascension motif
in the Hebrew Bible illuminate the Enoch
tradition. Prophetic stories about
ascension share with the Enoch tales an
emphasis on personal piety and alternative
leadership. The story of Elijah the
prophet, for example, recapitulates the
social dimension of the ascension motif.
Elijah, a solitary prophet at odds with his
society and characterized by an intensely
personal piety, eventually despairs of his
battle against idolatry and leaves his
disciple Elisha behind to continue his work
while he ascends to heaven (I Kings 17-19, II
Kings 1-2). His story intertwines social
and personal themes.

BUBER ON THE ASCENSION MOTIF

The theories of either Jensen or Eliade
adequately account for the complex tradition
represented by the biblical sources.

Jensen's view illuminates the myth's
function in legitimating a necessary change
in leadership. Eliade's perspective shows
how changing possibilities for self-
transcendence elicit different means for
attaining the same goal: that of advancing
beyond the routine of daily experience.
Buber's view integrates both perspectives.
He begins by dividing myths into two types:
the "myth of world preservation" and the
"myth of world redemption." The latter
emphasizes personal transcendence to the
exclusion of social interaction. The
former, which he associates with Enoch,
combines social legitimation with
sensitivity to personal concerns.

Both myths, Buber thinks, derive from
specific events that people experience, from
real relationships between leaders and their
followers. The concrete event at the heart
of the first type of myth occurred when
people associated with a leader whose life
did not differ significantly from their own.
The hero did not exhibit any apparently
supernatural behavior; he lived among them
and shared their lives. Nevertheless, he
exuded a sense of spirituality. Thus others
experienced his life as higher than that of
everyday existence. From such a leader
people learned that life, without being
changed and without alteration in personal
behavior, can take on new meaning and
purpose.

Thus the "myth of world preservation" tells
of a hero whose personality transcends the
limitations of a specific historical

setting. The hero shows, by example, that a
person can live within the world and still
experience transcendence. One need not
leave the world or even transform it to
enter a reality beyond it. The strange
combination of everyday ordinariness of
action with an extraordinary spirituality of
presence led to the construction of stories
such as those about Enoch, Noah, and Elijah.
An ascension myth asserts the importance of
both transcendence and return to daily
living; it refuses to allow its heroes to
escape reality by transcending it.

The second myth tells of heroes who
retreat from the world into themselves; they
live lives for which the outside world is
irrelevant. As "holy men," they "dominated
the inner world" but ignored external
reality. They show how to deny everyday
life and transcend it. This myth, unlike
the ascension myth, grew out of people's
experience with a leader obviously different
from themselves, whose perception of the
world and whose actions radically challenged
their own routines. These heroes impressed
on their followers the realization that life
could be different than they imagined it,
that the world itself, and not just they
themselves, could be transformed into
something different and other.16

Buber notes the danger present in the
myth of world redemption. The danger of
this myth lies in its temptation to avoid
political reality. When ancient Israel had
a vibrant national life it could afford to
risk myths of redemption, since national

existence maintained its force. Noah and
Enoch, the two biblical heroes who "walk
with God," represent a pre-nationalistic
model. Buber suggests that the value of the
story lies in that characteristic. The myth
evolved from meeting with a type of person
whose spirituality was liberated from
national identity, tied only to a person's
private piety and not to that person's
public religiousness. This myth, finally
recorded in the biblical stories, becomes a
new point of departure whenever public
religion decays, leaving people faced with
"nationless" religion. The myth of Enoch
and Noah, of the ascension to heavenly
consciousness while living a common and
ordinary life, invites those heeding it to a
similar piety in the midst of their own
lives. The biblical use of the ascension
motif both preserves a pre-national
religious option and legitimates that option
for future generations.[17]

DEVELOPMENT OF THE ENOCH STORIES

Later Jewish writers developed the
biblical references to Enoch and added
details to that material, making exlicit
connections to other ascension heroes.[18]
Many later authors, however, view both Enoch
and Elijah rather negatively, imagining them
as exponents of a nontraditional type of
religious life. Because Elijah failed in
his earthly task, he became an angel
eternally dedicated to that task. Rabbinic

angelology links Elijah and Enoch as leaders
who, failing their earthly duties, become
immortal as punishment for their failures.
Jewish mystics who focused attention on
private piety and personal devotion,
however, continued to consider Enoch a hero
worthy of emulation. Stories circulated in
these circles legitimate him as a fully
traditional Jew. In this tradition Enoch
acts as an observant Jew whose obedience to
divine commandments counteracts the
disobedience of the primal man.

Early texts describe the details of
Enoch's ascent and his relationship to
angelic beings, while later stories tell of
his atonement for the original sin of Adam.
In both types of tales Enoch functions
positively, as a religious model, as the
ideal zaddik, that is to say righteous man,
a redemptive hero whose supernal adventures
benefit humanity. One variation of this
post-biblical view of Enoch occurs in early
Christian writings. As the tradition
evolved, it attracted diverse and often
conflicting religious ideas and views. The
texts now extant appear as compendiums of
beliefs and hopes that evolved over three
centuries. Elements from that tradition
entered into and deeply influenced
Christianity. The New Testament reflects
this tradition in its own "savior myth" that
conditions its views of Jesus, its
ascription of titles to Jesus, and its
portrait of the supernal world of angels and
demons. Christians took the motif of the
pious leader who ascends to heaven and

reveals hidden secrets and applied it to
other worthies of the past.

The texts concerning Enoch specifically
appear late in the development of Christian
literature. The New Testament rarely refers
to him. The letter attributed to Jude
mentions Enoch as a prophetic messenger
announcing judgment against the godless
sinners. The ascension motif itself
receives even more attention when applied to
other figures from the Hebrew Bible such as
the prophet Isaiah. Although some writers
claim that parts of the late work The
Ascension of Isaiah represent Jewish
apocrypha, all agree that its final shape
comes from Christian writers. In this
version Isaiah, like Enoch, travels to the
heavenly spheres and returns with visions
and prophecies for future generations.19
Enoch provides human beings with information
essential for their salvation. He instructs
people on the actions necessary for
spiritual and physical survival in a time of
trouble.

The development of the Enoch tradition
enters Christianity as a model of religious
life, an alternative to normative Jewish
leaders. Several groups in the
intertestamental world competed for
dominance. Although eventually Christianity
and rabbinic Judaism would claim ultimate
victory, during the Greco-Roman period rival
sectarian leaders struggled for power. The
motif of Enoch supplied a justification for
leaders who opposed the established power
groups of priests and exegetes. In

opposition to the priests, the Enoch stories
provided new rituals, alternative calendars
of holidays, and prayers putatively culled
from heavenly archetypes. In opposition to
authoritative ideologues, the Enoch material
introduces new beliefs, interpretations of
traditional stories, and concepts derived
from Greek philosophy and religion.

The motif remains unchanged: a human
hero ascends on high to receive a divine
commission. This motif suggests the
psychological concerns animating writers of
the intertestamental period. People felt
restless with their religious situation.
They felt trapped in a materialistic and
socially stratified world. Flight to a
cosmic realm of spirit appealed to their
desire for transcendence and satisfied their
desire to escape the realities of political
contention. Those realities, however,
demanded that a group follow authorized
leaders and that it legitimate its right to
exist. The Enoch tradition provided an
ancient model that justified a group's
claims. The holiness ascribed to Enoch
could legitimate opposition to established
priestly forms. The specific nature of
Enoch's experiences on high, the esoteric
teachings ascribed to him, and the graphic
descriptions of heavenly behavior given in
the Enoch literature reflect the needs of
this later period.

While the biblical authors who pressed
Enoch into service for themselves needed the
freedom allowed by a broad, general allusion
to Enoch, the competitive nature of the

intertestamental period required more
particular attention to detail. A sectarian
group needed to define the rituals, beliefs,
and promises that made it more attractive
than its alternatives. The sociological
necessity of self-presentation altered the
telling of the Enoch myth so that it might
fit the context of its times. This shaping
of the tradition reflects the diversity of
religious life addressed no less than the
changed political context in which the myth
would be understood. When a group such as
the rabbis, gained power, they opposed the
Enoch tradition and associated charismatic
prophecy with punishment. Other groups
maintained that charismatic piety might
accompany and not contradict normative
piety. Still others explored variations of
religious living, whether Jewish or
Christian. The changing fortunes of Enoch
as hero and the diverse guises the legends
about him wore underscore the social and
political contentiousness of the times.
Despite differences in content, then, the
Enoch story in the intertestamental period
functioned as in the biblical canon. The
story legitimated a new type of leader
better able to confront new realities.

BUBER ON THE LATER ENOCH STORIES

The sociological and psychological
explanations of the ascension myth offered
by Jensen and Eliade can interpret the
expanded Enoch stories similarly to their

interpretation of the biblical tales.
Buber, however, introduces a new element
when he looks at these later views of Enoch.
Buber wonders why, if the purpose remains
constant, the myth should undergo change.
Although a different social group might
raise its claim to charismatic leadership,
that group could appropriate an earlier myth
without changing it. Buber, however, claims
that the later stories represent the natural
regression of I-It reality as it moves
farther and farther from its source of
origin. The myths of the intertestamental
period seek a more defined hero than the
vague intimations of the biblical tradition
allow. They "reveal" more about the hero
and, Buber thinks, therefore betray their
original intention.

Buber looks at the biblical material as
creatively impressionistic. Genesis merely
hints at Enoch's piety; the prophetic canon
gives very little information even about
Elijah's religious life and certainly seems
reticent about such figures as the
"suffering servant" in Isaiah, whom Buber
claims as an extension of the Enoch
tradition. The later versions of the story,
he felt, resolved the inherent ambiguity of
the biblical tales and thus fell into a
literalness that prevents religious growth.
The suggestive early myths allow individuals
to experiment themselves so that they can
duplicate the earlier experience. The later
tales fix the story in history: it happened
in a certain way to a certain person at a
certain time in the past. The unique,
unrepeatable act of the hero replaces the

open invitation to action that Buber finds
in the early stories.

Buber criticizes Christianity for what
he considers a stagnating reduction of the
original mythic tradition and a literalism
that prevents a transition from I-It to I-
You reality. He argues that stories about
Jesus, unlike the authentic Enoch story,
remove the hero from the "hidden quiver" of
God to ascend in an unambiguous personal
transfiguration. In this way the story of
Jesus replaces the model of transcendence
that Buber thinks lies at the heart of the
myth.20 Buber's critique of Christianity
lacks sympathy for that mythic tradition.
The New Testament makes creative use of the
Enoch motif, particularly in the Gospel of
John. Buber, however, fails to note the
presence of the Enoch myth in John 3.
Modern scholars remark on the heavenly
journey motif apparent when Jesus says to
the rabbi, Nicodemus, "Unless one is born
anew, he cannot see the kingdom of God ...
Only he who has descended from heaven, the
Son of man, can ascend into heaven" (John
3:3, 13). Jesus rejects the ideal of a
heavenly ascent for all people. By
following him and being born anew,
Christians no longer need to emulate an
Enoch-type hero. Most recently, the New
Testament scholar William C. Grese has
commented that whereas traditional ascension
stories offer manuals for a heavenly journey,
"John 3 does not describe how to enter
heaven for a revelation but how to obtain
the revelation to be found in Jesus," a
particularly significant variation on the

traditional theme.21   As in the earlier
Enoch stories, so too here, the theme
focuses on alternative forms of leadership.
Disciples discover in their relationship
with Jesus that they no longer require
heavenly charts to show them the way to
transcendence. Rebirth depends on
discipleship, not magic.

Despite Buber's critique of the New
Testament, his view of myth illuminates the
story in John 3. Jesus says to Nicodemus
that the road to the World to Come lies not
in a formula or manual of heavenly ascent.
Instead, the earthly task must include
finding a master whose life transmits the
heavenly secrets and whose charisma brings a
sense of rebirth. In a similar way, Buber
recounts the story of Moshe Teitelbaum, who
dreamed that he had been in the paradise of
the early rabbinic teachers (Tannaim).
There he saw the rabbis studying talmudic
tractates and cried, "This can't be
paradise." The angels corrected him, "You
seem to think that the Tannaim are in
paradise, but that's not so: paradise is in
the Tannaim."22   Buber himself considers
the relationship between teacher and
disciple the "quintessence" of hasidic
life. He considers the foundation of
hasidism to lie in "the life between those
who quicken and those who are quickened."
The truth of hasidism, as Buber saw it, lay
in discipleship rather than intellectual
prowess, human ties with a human leader
rather than a doctrine to be mastered,
revival through life with another rather
than revival as return to a philosophical

proposition.23 From this perspective, both
Jensen and Eliade catch only part of the
meaning of the myth. The myth does
legitimate a new type of leader and does
point to self-transcendence. It also,
however, as Buber recognizes, points to an
event occurring between disciples and
leaders. Buber shows that this dynamic
relationship remains open to any set of
leaders and disciples and need not be locked
in the past.   Whether the Christian story
violates this sense of presentness, as Buber
seems to think, may be argued (Buber's
prejudices probably enter into his inability
to read the Gospel of John sympathetically).
Yet, using Buber's own approach does show
how the pattern of the Enoch story appearing
in the Gospel of John exemplifies the themes
of that myth.

THE HASIDIC ENOCH

     Later Rabbinic and Medieval Jewish
mysticism expanded and altered the Enoch
tradition. According to this later and more
elaborate theory, Enoch became the angel
Metatron, who links the heavenly and earthly
spheres. Medieval Jewish mystics focused
their attention on Metatron and sought to
emulate him and, by uniting with his
potency, become a living bridge between the
cosmic and mundane spheres.24 Late in the
Middle Ages another story appeared about
another figure called "Enoch the cobbler."
Scholars debate the connection between this

Enoch story and the tradition about the patriarch in Genesis who became an angel. Later hasidism took the tale as exemplary for its followers. The entire teaching of the Baal Shem Tov, and thus of hasidism as a whole, sought to enable people to emulate the wondrous activities of the hero of this tale. Hasidic leaders claimed that they taught how every secular act or word could bind the lower and upper worlds, just as Enoch reportedly did.25 Modern scholars seek to decode this story and decide where it belongs in the long chain of tradition from the biblical Enoch.

Gershom Scholem, the foremost modern scholar of Jewish mysticism, in his survey of Jewish mysticism discusses this story in a comment on the Enoch tradition, calling it "scurrilous" and dating its first appearance in the fourteenth century. The tale tells of a poor cobbler whose devotion reaches such a height that as he pursues his trade he effects cosmic changes. Binding the top part of the shoe to the bottom, the cobbler binds the upper worlds to the lower ones. He unifies the spiritual levels of the cosmos with the material ones, overcoming the separation of the holy and the profane through an apparently ordinary act. Scholem never explains his adjective applied to Enoch the cobbler. Certainly Enoch is a "common man." The tale in itself, however, can hardly be called "vulgar" or "evil."26

The very ordinariness of Enoch actually suggests how the main themes of the myth reappear in the hasidic version. This

version of the story not only regards Enoch
as a common cobbler but also lacks any
mention of leaders. Enoch undergoes no
special training, attaches himself to no
specific master, and demonstrates no
proficiency in Jewish observances. The tale
rather claims that transcendence occurs when
people dedicate themselves wholeheartedly to
their ordinary pursuits. This new version of
tale legitimates the common person,
contending that the religious experience of
ordinary workers succeeds more effectively
than that of the elite leadership. Here the
myth serves to democratize charisma.
Enoch's very existence threatens the
official leadership since a mystic has no
need for institutional authority. Mystics,
the myth suggests, no longer need leaders
not because they oppose social and political
authority but because everyday life provides
the path to transcendence.

     This strategy worked well for Jewish
mystics. By the Middle Ages, Jewish
leadership had divided into three main
strands: the legalist, the philosophical,
and the mystical. Jewish historians
sometimes point to exemplary individuals
such as Moses Maimonides, Joseph Karo, and
Elijah Gaon of Vilna, who gained prestige
and power in more than one of these fields.
Even these luminaries, however, rarely
influenced more than a select audience:
those who respected Maimonides the legalist
often rejected his philosophy; Karo's legal
work, the <u>Schulchan Arukh</u>, overshadows his
mystical aspirations.27

More often, leaders would find success in a single area. As long as they remained content with that concern, they encountered little resistance. When mystics like the hasidim telling the Enoch story compromised with power, they survived. When they sought to replace it, as the messianic pretender Sabbetai Zevi attempted, they failed. Once again, the Enoch story adapts its theme of charismatic leadership to fit a new situation. The new democratization of the charismatic authority it legitimated suited a new social and political reality demanding compromise for the sake of diversity.

BUBER ON THE HASIDIC ENOCH

Buber claims that his method of interpreting myth reflects the event giving rise to the the myth of the savior hero more adequately than alternative approaches. For Buber, the myth originally reflected on the extraordinary experience of encountering the transcendent within the everyday. At first the myth expressed this experience through describing the life of a hero whose life illustrated the astounding possibility of I-You living. As the story developed, according to Buber's claims, the hero rather than the possibility he illustrated came to dominate. In hasidism, however, the original vision returned, that of the ability "ever again to invest the holy with effect and influence in the realm of the profane." The biblical myth suggests how

this transformation occurs outside of
nationalistic institutions. The hero's
sanctification of daily life transcends
institutional identity.28

Later variants of the story, by
contrast, emphasize institutional forms.
Hasidism recaptures the primary insight and
shows how "...man influences eternity, and
he does this not through special works, but
through the intention behind all of his
work." The hasidic story, then, more
clearly than even the biblical version,
preserves the memory of an experience of
transcendence occurring in an unmediated
relationship between people and their own
work. 29   Here, again, Buber points to a
broader understanding of the myth than
either Jensen or Eliade offers. While they
interpret the general pattern of the
ascension myth, they cannot explain the
development of its variants.

Buber's view of myth can explain this
development. As a people's experience
changes, so too the myths used to preserve
that experience change. When surprised by
transcendence that occurs in daily life
without the need for a leader and yet
clearly related to what earlier generations
also experienced, people revised the story
of Enoch. The transformed myth testifies to
a transformed experience of transcendence,
one that lacks both great leadership models
and extraordinary techniques. Buber does
not explicitly point to the social and
political environment in which the hasidic
myth arose. He seems to think that the myth

springs from an eternally valid human
potential.30 Nevertheless, his theory
points beyond his own recognition. A purely
sociological or psychological explanation of
the hasidic story misses its responsiveness
to changing personal possibilities. The
myth varies not just because new leadership
groups arise or because of a continuing need
for self-transcendence. The myth varies
because people live differently and see
different options for themselves in
different historical settings. Buber's
interpretive stance enables him to grasp
this point clearly.

THE LIMITATIONS OF BUBER'S VIEW

    This positive value of Buber's
interpretation, however, must be balanced
against Buber's misreading of certain
features of the hasidic myth. While Gershom
Scholem's criticism seems strange and
extreme, that of other scholars shows how
Buber's argument lacks cogency. Perhaps his
opposition comes from a conviction, shared
with another student of hasidism and Jewish
mysticism, Louis Jacobs, that the message of
the story advocates a mystical experience
"totally different from Buber's I-Thou
relationship." 31 This judgment may be
historically accurate in its relationship to
the original Enoch stories. Modern research
in the Enoch tradition, of which the cobbler
story may be the latest version, suggests
that he became the model of that unitive

mystical immersion in the divinity that
Buber opposed. Enoch was the ideal mystic
because by becoming one with the divine
potencies he took on their magical powers
and capabilities. Enoch the cobbler acts as
a secret mystic, a hidden righteous man, who
as he sews the upper leather of shoes to the
soles unites heaven and earth.

Perhaps Buber misunderstands this aspect
of the story because he envisions future
religious life as communal rather than
privatistic. He opposes "mystic" self-
absorption. The social and cultural setting
of Jewish mysticism, however, could have
cautioned him against importing a modern
meaning to earlier texts. As a theorist of
myth, he points to the modern meaning of the
tale as a development but not necessarily a
recapitulation of the hasidic version of the
Enoch story. That he did not merely shows
his own limitations as an exponent of his
theory, not the failure of the theory as a
whole. Buber's study of the Enoch myth
helps theorists of myth understand the
evolution of a mythic tradition.

NOTES

1. Martin Buber, <u>On Judaism</u>, ed. Nahum N. Glatzer (New York: Schocken, 1967), pp. 95, 99, 103.

2. See Maurice Friedman, <u>Martin Buber's Life and Work: The Later Years, 1945-1964</u> (New York: Dutton, 1981), p. 228.

3. This problem serves as the focal point for Robert A. Segal's article "In Defense of Mythology: The History of Modern Theories of Myth." <u>Annals of Scholarship</u> I:1 (1980): 3-49.

4. See Paul Mendes-Flohr, "Martin Buber's Reception among Jews," <u>Modern Judaism</u> 6:2 (1986), p. 120.

5. Haim Gordon, "Method of Clarifying Buber's I-Thou Relationship," <u>Journal of Jewish Studies</u> 23 (1976): 71-83; compare Walter Kaufmann's "Prologue," in Martin Buber, <u>I and Thou</u>, trans. and intro. Walter Kaufmann (New York: Scribner's, 1970), pp. 9-48, and Robert E. Wood, <u>Martin Buber's Ontology: An Analysis of I and Thou</u>, Northwestern University Studies in Phenomenology and Existential Philosophy (Evanston: Northwestern University Press, 1969).

6. Martin Buber, <u>Eclipse of God: Studies in the Relation Between Religion and Philosophy</u> (New York: Harper and Row, 1952), pp. 4-6.

7. Max Weber, <u>Ancient Judaism</u>, eds. and trans. Hans H. Gerth and Don Martindale (Glencoe, IL: The Free Press, 1952), pp. 17, 40, 98ff., 157, 386-88.

8. Max Weber, <u>The Sociology of Religion</u>, trans. Ephraim Fischoff (Boston: Beacon, 1963), pp. 103, 274.

9. See the presentation of the Enoch material given by Moshe Idel, "Enoch-- that is Metatron," in his <u>Ancient Jewish Mysticism</u>, (Jerusalem: Hebrew University Press, 1987), pp. 151-70, especially pp. 159-61.

10. See Adolf E. Jensen, <u>Myth and Cult Among Primitive Peoples</u>, trans. Marianna Tax Choldin and Wolfgang Weissleder (Chicago: University of Chicago Press, 1963), pp. 224-25.

11. See Mircea Eliade, <u>Myths, Dreams, and Mysteries: The Encounter Between Contemporary Faiths and Archaic Realities</u>, trans. Philip Mairet (New York: Harper and Row, 1960), pp. 99-122.

12. See Ignac Goldziher, <u>Mythology Among the Hebrews and its Historical Development</u>, trans. Russell Maretineau (New York: Cooper Square, 1967), pp. 127-29, and Umberto Cassutto, <u>A Commentary on the Book of Genesis: From Adam to Noah</u> (Jerusalem: Magnes Press, 1961), pp. 229 and 281-84. On the theory of a solar deity and its place in mythology see Richard M. Dorson, "The Eclipse of Solar

Mythology," in Thomas A. Sebeok, ed.,
Myth: A Symposium (Bloomington: Indiana
University Press, 1968), pp. 25-63.

13. See Hermann Gunkel, The Legends of
Genesis: The Biblical Saga and History,
trans. W.H.Carruth (New York: Schocken,
1964), pp. 95ff., and idem., Genesis,
seventh ed. (Gottingen: Vandenhoeck and
Ruprecht, 1966), pp. 135-37.

14. Compare Yehezkel Kaufmann, The Religion
of Israel: From Its Beginnings to the
Babylonian Exile, trans. and abridged
Moshe Greenberg (Chicago: University of
Chicago Press, 1960), pp. 77, 244, 316
and idem., Toldot Haemunah HaYisraelit
[Hebrew], vol. I (Tel Aviv: Dvir, 1937),
pp. 188, 211, 456. Kaufmann claims that
this transformation shows how biblical
authors neutralized the mythical aspects
of the sources they used.

15. See the discussion of the Yahwist and
Priestly writer and the bibliographies
given in Walter Brueggemann and Hans
Walter Wolff, The Vitality of Old
Testament Traditions (Atlanta: John Knox
Press, 1975). Common usage refers to
modern times as A.D. and to ancient
times as B.C. Those terms, however, are
theological ones. When Christians speak
of A.D., In the Year of Our Lord, or of
B.C., Before the Christ, they are
asserting that Jesus was the Christ, or
Messiah, and that with his advent the
world was changed. This book uses a
more neutral set of terms: "bce", before

the common era and "ce", the common era. These terms refer to a common mode of counting time, not to any putative events in the past.

16. Buber, On Judaism, pp. 106-7.

17. Martin Buber, On the Bible: Eighteen Studies, ed. Nahum N. Glatzer, (New York: Schocken, 1968), p. 32.

18. See Idel, "Enoch--that is Metatron," pp. 151-59; compare the sources he cites with intertestamental writings such as Wisdom of Solomon 4:10-11 and Ecclesiasticus 44:16; see the discussions in R.H. Charles, The Apocrypha and Pseudepigrapha of the Old Testament, vol. II (Oxford: Clarendon Press, 1913), pp. 163-87, 425-30. On the Enoch stories generally from their earliest forms through the later medieval Jewish and Christian materials see Jozef T. Milik, "Introduction," in J. T. Milik, ed. with the collaboration of Matthew Black, The Books of Enoch: Aramaic Fragments of Qumran Cave 4 (Oxford: Clarendon Press, 1976), pp. 3-135.

19. See H.H. Rowley, The Relevance of Apocalyptic (New York: Association Press, 1964), pp. 123-26; see also his treatment of the Enoch myth (which he calls "an ancient one"), pp. 57-64 and 93-99. Buber's treatment of the Christian elements in the story and his rejection of them are studied by Max

Brod in his "Judaism and Christianity in the Work of Martin Buber," in Paul Arthur Schilpp and Maurice Friedman, eds., The Philosophy of Martin Buber, The Library of Living Philosophers, vol. XII (La Salle, IL: Open Court, 1967), pp. 319-40; see especially p. 320.

20. See Martin Buber, Two Types of Faith, trans. Norman P. Goldhawk (New York: Harper and Row, 1951), p. 112, and his The Prophetic Faith, trans. Carlyle Witton-Davies (New York: Macmillan, 1949), p. 203.

21. William C. Grese, "Unless One is Born Again: The Use of a Heavenly Journey in John 3," Journal of Biblical Literature 107 (1988), pp. 677-93.

22. Martin Buber, Tales of the Hasidim: The Later Masters, trans. Olga Marx (New York: Schocken, 1947), pp. 189-90.

23. Martin Buber, Tales of the Hasidim: The Early Masters, trans. Olga Marx (New York: Schocken, 1947), p. 8.

24. See the discussion and references in Milik, pp. 125-35. Milik disputes the view of Gershom Scholem (see note 26) that emphasizes the identity of Metatron and Enoch; compare the entire study in Idel, "Enoch--that is Metatron."

25. Rivka Schatz Uffenheimer cites this comment in the introduction to her Quietistic Elements in 18th Century

Hasidic Thought [Hebrew] (Jerusalem: Magnes Press, 1968), p. 12.

26. Scholem discusses the Enoch story and its relationship to the Metatron legend in his Major Trends in Jewish Mysticism (New York: Schocken, 1961), pp. 40-43, 67-70; a footnote on pp. 365-66 calls the cobbler story "scurrilous." Perhaps he comes to this conclusion out of opposition to Buber. In another context, Scholem suggests the connection between the patriarch Enoch and the cobbler story and remarks that "Buber draws from this tale an inference diametrically opposed to that drawn by the sources in which it is quoted." On The Kabbalah and Its Symbolism, trans. Ralph Manheim (New York: Schocken, 1969), p. 132. Some of his other discussions of Enoch do not introduce the hasidic material; see his Kabbalah (Jerusalem: Keter, 1974), pp. 377-88.

27. The pioneering study of R.J.Zevi Werblowsky, Joseph Karo: Lawyer and Mystic (Philadelphia: Jewish Publication Society of America, 1962) offers a wide-ranging study of these issues, including an analysis not only of sixteenth-century legalism and mysticism but also of the "charisma" of Elijah Gaon of Vilna in the eighteenth-century.

28. Martin Buber, The Origin and Meaning of Hasidism, ed. and trans. Maurice Friedman (New York: Horizon Press, 1960), p. 87.

29. Martin Buber, <u>Hasidism and Modern Man</u>,
    ed. and trans. Maurice Friedman (New
    York: Horizon Press, 1958), pp. 181-85.

30. <u>Ibid</u>., pp. 151, 214-15.

31. Louis Jacobs, "Aspects of Scholem's
    Study of Hasidism," <u>Modern Judaism</u> 5:1,
    pp. 96-98.

Chapter 3 Buber and the Bible

MYTH AND BIBLICAL STUDIES

Nahum Glatzer, presenting several of Buber's studies on the Hebrew Bible, declares that "The central theme in Buber's biblical research concerns the concept of the kingdom of God, the origin of the institution of kingship in ancient Israel, and the inception of the idea of the Messianic kingdom."[1] Certainly Buber takes biblical politics seriously. Buber exalts the biblical criteria for true leadership, the Bible's contention that only YHVH should rule, and the messianic ideal of a perfected society as valuable teachings for modern times. Both biblical myth and biblical politics testify to a single message, a message he finds within the messianic vision that he calls a "mythicization" of "actual-historical" events.[2]

This view of biblical politics and messianism separates Buber's exegesis from that of other biblical critics.   Both Buber and Yehezkel Kaufmann, for example, recognize fantastic elements in the description of the End of Days found in Isaiah 2. Kaufmann emphasizes the theological meaning, the political significance, but not the mythical aspects of the description: the hero does not represent "a redeeming Messiah" but rather "the culmination of God's grace to Israel." The vision presents the "abstract ideal" of a universal humanity "expressed in the vision of the temple mount."3 Buber, like Kaufmann, reads the passage as a statement of ideal politics: it offers a "theopolitical realism" that establishes "the divine order of human community" through "human forces and human responsibility."

Nevertheless, Buber also remarks that the chapter provides a "mythical garb" for these ideas. The I-You realization of true community, for Buber, takes on I-It tangibility in myth. The Messianic king Isaiah describes "is the man in whom the likeness has unfolded" -- the likeness of God accessible to every person. Garbing that likeness in the mythical dress of a great king, Buber suggests, preserves the experiential insight that such political leadership may illustrate a generally human potential.4 Buber's approach to the Bible combines sensitivity to its political message with an awareness of its mythical content. Laurence Silberstein's study on Buber's social thought notes a "predilection for myth" that "departed from the norms of modern Jewish thought and scholarship," that

led many biblical scholars to question
Buber's thinking.5

Buber's interests often coincide with
those of contemporary biblical scholars.
James Muilenburg, however, correctly notes
the disparity. Buber may accept the agenda
of biblical criticism. He uses techniques
and methods very different from those
normally employed.6 Buber's distinctiveness
as a biblical scholar comes in no small
measure from his willingness to interpret a
biblical text as myth. The rationalist
outlook of modern biblical scholarship in
the nineteenth and early twentieth
centuries banished myth from true religion.
Julius Wellhausen, whose division of the
Pentateuch into various documentary sources
remains the point of departure even for
contemporary biblical scholarship,
contrasted the stories in Genesis to "myth."
Wellhausen argued that ancient Israel's
abolition of myth marked the advancement of
biblical culture beyond the lower stage of
religious evolution found in polytheism.

Nevertheless, as a sensitive interpreter
of literature, he lamented the inevitable
diminution of power resulting from the
change. He expressed his ambivalence by
remarking that "The pale colour which
generally marks the productions of the
earliest reflection about nature, when they
are not mythical theories, is characteristic
of Gen. 1 also."7 This judgment extends
biblical authors a compliment--they have
excised myth--while denying them creative
artistry--they offer only pale reflections

about nature. This double sensitivity
characterizes the discussion of biblical
myth throughout modern scholarship.
Wellhausen's double standard echoes through
modern studies of myth and the Hebrew Bible
that praise the Bible for its rationalism
and lament its loss of mythic lyricism.

Some authors emphasize the positive
aspects in the rejection of myth by claiming
that biblical Israel substituted history for
myth. This judgment reflects an
evolutionary view of human reflection on the
past. R. G. Collingwood, for example,
claims that "History as it exists today ...
has come into existence in the last four
thousand years" and seeks to elucidate its
stages and development.8 According to this
evolutionary paradigm, humanity advances
through several "quasi-historical" theories
to historiography as such and then to
philosophies of history. From a naive and
confused view of the past, people evolve a
universalist theory of events and their
meaning. Biblical Israel, according to
several modern theories, moved humanity
closer to a truly historical view of
reality.9 Rather than offer "pale"
substitutes for myth, these thinkers
contend, biblical writers elevated earlier
myths by historicizing them. Archeological
evidence apparently supports this claim
since biblical narratives differ from the
stories told in other ancient Near Eastern
documents. The Bible posits a single deity
who controls history and nature. That
supposition leads biblical writers to

construct a coherent theory of history and a scientific approach to cause and effect.

Texts from ancient Egypt, Mesopotamia, and Canaan reveal a contrasting cosmic vision emphasizing chaos. Conflicting and independent forces compete for control of the world. These forces, personified as divine beings, struggle among themselves. Human beings, at the mercy of these unpredictable deities, cannot construct a science that requires reliable laws and repeatable experiments. They cannot conceive a philosophy of history since events depend upon the whim of gods whose incessant competition precludes a constant balance of power or structure of meaning. G. Ernest Wright, respected as both a theologian and an archeologist, argued this case in 1950. Reviewing the comparative data, he insists upon the absence of "myth" from the Hebrew Bible. While admitting that "modern theologians revive the term 'myth'" in explaining the Bible, he contends that such usage is derivative and "not primary or original." Israel's literature "suddenly appears in history, breaking radically with the mythopoeic approach to reality."10 The Hebrew Bible alters the traditional mythology of ancient Near Eastern literature and introduces a theological innovation. By substituting history for myth, Wright suggests, Israelite thinkers advanced the cause of rationality. Since events followed predictable causes, not the whims of changeable gods, humanity could make long-range plans without fear. That rational predictability prepares the way for science:

the process of creating general principles of causation based on practical experimentation.

This theory seems to posit two ways of viewing the world: the mythic and the historical. In effect, however, it assumes three separate, if related, world views: science, myth, and history.11 Myth, according to this thesis, offers primitive explanations of reality, explanations disguised as stories. Myth portrays a world built out of imagination, based on an inaccurate science that provides a sense of environmental control to societies lacking technical skills. Science, by contrast, offers explicit explanations of the world, experimenting with the natural world to produce an accurate and rational assessment of cause and effect, enabling a more reliable means of controlling the world. Both myth and science, according to this view, offer explanations both of specific phenomena and of the general principles behind events. The explanations each provides are exhaustive and mutually exclusive.

One myth, for example, may explain how the worm gained power over the tooth, thereby causing toothaches. Primitive medicine might use that myth to cure people suffering from tooth decay. Science may explain tooth decay, however, by suggesting alternative causes, each requiring its own therapy. Some myths do more than explain the origins of one or another fact of human life; some, rather poetically, express a theory of life generally: events reflect the whims of supernatural beings who express their conflicts, inclinations, and responses to human actions through effects on the world. Scientists also sometimes articulate general theories that explain the operations of the world, whether a theory of gravity, light, or relativity. Myth narrates a story about origins, describing the initial occurrence of an event as if it brought a fact into being and established it forever. Science postulates certain reliable rules or "laws" that govern how things occur in the world. Myth and science, then, both seek to discover enduring and predictable causes active in the past, present, and future; in contrast a third approach, that of history, focuses on unique and nonrecurring events. What happened in the past need not foreshadow what will occur in the present or the future. According to this typology, a historical approach seeks to "understand" the past rather than to explain why it occurred, let alone to predict events. Those who hold this view argue that the Hebrew Bible represents a significant break with both earlier thought and modern science by introducing a sense of history.

THE TRANSITION TO HISTORY

With this distinction among science, myth, and history in mind, many scholars contend that biblical thought marks an advance in the history of human rationality.

Yehezkel Kaufmann, clearly agreeing with
Wright, argues for such a positive view of
the biblical innovation.12 Israel's folk
genius, he suggests, recognized only one
deity. This monotheistic insight provided
the foundation of modern science.

Kaufmann points to the biblical creation
stories as an example of how, despite
"vestiges" of ancient myths, the instinctive
folk response of ancient Israel removed all
traces of a "demonic realm" that might lead
to a chaotic view of the world. Events do
not occur because of the arbitrary and
unpredictable whims of conflicting deities.
Instead, history flows from the single will
of the one creating deity. This one God
stands behind joy and pain, good and bad
fortune. The stories picture singular
events occurring in the past that neither
explain the world nor offer people a means
of controlling it but rather emphasize
actions taken by human beings. Israel's
God, the sole, unique ruler of the universe,
banishes mythology.

Kaufmann admits that the Bible retains
vestiges of an earlier polytheistic
mythology. Images taken from pagan lore
reappear, transformed, in the biblical
tales. The authors of these stories
inherited mythic forms, Kaufmann suggests,
but filled them with a new content. The
older tales told of conflict among the gods,
of demonic forces throughout the world, of a
nonhistorical pattern of causation. The
Bible radically changes this approach by its
monotheistic revolution. Based on this

monotheistic content, biblical narratives
create a historical and non-mythic
tradition. While in <u>form</u> Israel's folk
religion might borrow from earlier
prototypes, in <u>content</u> its monotheistic
bias demanded the rejection of mythology.
The "isolated traces of pagan mythology"
have lost their force in the biblical
stories. The stories in fact emphasize a
single theme far closer to science than to
myth: God alone has fixed the laws of heaven
and earth, the world and all that is
therein.13

    Kaufmann's views influence many scholars
today. These scholars interpret the
biblical tales as a historicizing of myth.
Whereas myth tells of polytheistic deities
who continue the original acts of creation
and conflict again and again in eternal
struggle, the Bible tells of a single
divinity whose unique creative act initiates
a progressive history that continues to
unfold in accordance with an original plan.
Since the stories trace a historical
development rather than a static
"explanation," they represent a transition
from mythology to the scientific mode of
interacting with the world. The concept of
a "divine plan" explains the order and
predictability of the world. On the basis
of that theory human beings can analyze the
world, experiment with data, and draw
reliable conclusions from their work.
Jewish scholars who accept Kaufmann's lead
in emphasizing the absence of biblical myth
sometimes give grudging acknowledgment to
the critical apparatus associated with

Wellhausen, usually, however, only after
modifying it.14

While Kaufmann's approach emphasizes the
rejection of myth for history as the
foundation for scientific thought, other
scholars disagree. The influential scholar
of ancient Near Eastern culture Henri
Frankfort, for example, suggests that
biblical thinking moves directly from
ancient myth to historical myth without
developing a scientific view of the world, a
view which he claims comes much later with
Greek thought. The biblical perspective,
denying myth but not yet inculcating
science, leads, in his view, to a tragic
condition. Myth, he contends, inspired
ancient Near Eastern religions to discover
magical ways of manipulating the divine
forces shaping reality; Israel submitted to
the indecipherable whims of its deity.
    That one God takes full responsibility
for the diverse and changing elements of the
world, leaving no room for chance or
accident. Natural and human events alike
manifest a patterned history, a determined
program that needs decoding. Biblical
thinkers, heir to this historical
perspective, set about interpreting the
meaning of their deeds as isolated facts in
a grandiose scheme. Narrowing their focus
to such an investigation of history,
Israelites lost the tie with nature that
mythology had provided. Monotheism, with
its shift of emphasis from the interaction
of humanity with nature to an ethical and
historical introspection alienated humanity
as a singular creation.

Frankfort laments this replacement of ancient mythology by the exaltation of history. Ancient Near Eastern religion had taught its adherents to flow with the natural tides of the world. Rather than imposing a single pattern on life's diversity, polytheism explained and justified that plurality. Israel's God of the covenant, Yahweh, removed this justification of diversity and thereby undermined what Frankfort called "the greatest good ancient Near Eastern religion could bestow--the harmonious integration of man's life with the life of nature." By focusing on history, on a series of nonrepeatable events, Israel's covenantal thought left its believers unable to cope with the cycle of nature on which they depended for life. The resulting alienation from agriculture created an enduring sense of human unhappiness and tragedy.15

In opposition to Kaufmann, Frankfort claims that this monotheism prevented the development of science.

Frankfort describes the transition from paganism to biblical thought as a transformation in world view, a conversion of consciousness. In his view, the mythic consciousness arises from an animistic view of reality. The primitive human being fills the world with personality. Unable to conceive of an impersonal, scientific, or philosophical reality, pre-scientific thought imputes anthropomorphic qualities to all existence. Myth arises when people experience reality as composed of others who address them as a "Thou." He suggests that primitive peoples live expectantly, waiting for reality to reveal itself in a "playful fantasy" of a "Thou" that also contains an authoritative power. Frankfort notes that "Out of the repeated experience of the 'I-Thou' relationship a fairly consistent personalistic view may develop." These personalistic views characterize myth in the ancient Near East. The transition from myth to science shatters this I-Thou understanding of reality. Israel's transformation of myth into history, however, avoided that consequence. The Bible retains a personalistic view of the world--a mythic mentality, as it were-- without the mythic philosophy that usually accompanied it. Israel created an alternative myth, that of "the Will of God." While retaining the "I-Thou" experience, the Bible reduced all Thou's to a single personality.16 This transformation undermined ancient myth without permitting the rise of science and inspired a pessimistic view of human life.17

DEMYTHOLOGIZING THE BIBLE

Between the strong negation of myth advanced by the rationalists and the strong affirmation of myth made by their opponents lies a middle ground. The Bible contains myth, but the potency of its myths lies in the ideas they convey, not in their mythic form. Myth, according to this view, expresses philosophical ideas in a primitive and elementary way. The authors of the Bible used that primitive language because they addressed a primitive audience. More sophisticated readers of the Bible, however, need a more sophisticated language. The biblical message must be decoded from its mythic form and reexpressed philosophically. Scholars following this approach seek techniques by which to translate biblical mythic images into a more modern medium of communication.

One technique, championed by Rudolf Bultmann, explains the existential meaning in biblical myths. Myth, understood as a genre for transmitting ideas and claims about human existence, tells stories not to transmit literal descriptions but to evoke a particular world view. Modern readers can read apparently impossible stories and discover contemporary meaning in them. Tales about miracles, about supernatural events, about divine beings, actually point to a view of reality, an existential interpretation of life. Mythical references need not be taken as literal descriptions of natural phenomena. Instead, they convey signs and hints, indications of abstract ideas. Decoded in this way, biblical myths that correspond with myths in nonbiblical cultures point to a shared world view; the changes introduced by biblical writers into traditional myths point to a changed view of reality. This approach to myth, called demythologization, advocates a modern stance to the Bible. It does not pretend that the biblical authors themselves demythologized the material they inherited from the past. It merely suggests that they used mythic expression as a natural part of their world view. Biblical writers did not consciously translate ideas into stories. The stories, however, do contain ideas within them. Therefore, modern readers can demythologize the stories and learn thereby how the Bible differs from the other mythic works.

The Roman Catholic biblical scholar John L. McKenzie, for example, argues that the Bible is neither science and philosophy nor theology. It must be looked at as a type of "poetic embellishment" that neither substitutes for religion nor is identical to it. Myth serves neither as history nor as science but as a means of enunciating a response to the world. The modern biblical critic should translate the mythic language into discursive language about that response.18 This approach to the Bible accepts the presence of myth but refuses to emphasize myth as an end in itself. Myth has value only when it points beyond itself to general philosophical truths about existence. The dialogue between those who affirm the value of myth and those who deny it even a presence in the Bible often turns into polemic. A few of the older scholars anticipated this new affirmation of myth, among them Buber. Studying Buber's biblical investigations requires taking the intense polarization of Jewish approaches to the Bible as their backdrop.

BUBER AS BIBLICAL EXEGETE

Buber participated as an active partner in the debates and discussions that divided the critics and the advocates of myth as an element in biblical thinking. Like other scholars, Buber acknowledged the change monotheism created in Israelite thinking. Unlike them, he did not claim that monotheism necessitates a relinquishing of myth. Buber's early lectures on Judaism suggest two types of monotheism: one which abolishes myth and one which affirms it. The tension between these two types, he contends, tells the story of Judaism: "The history of the development of Jewish religion is really the history of the struggles between the natural structure of a mythical-monotheistic folk-religion and the intellectual structure of a rational-monotheistic rabbinic religion."19

Buber refuses to banish myth from the Bible. While at times, Buber admits, the Bible does historicize myth, on other occasions it presents "a mythisation of history." Buber strenuously opposes those who wish to strip biblical religion of myth because such denuding would reduce religion irreparably. Monotheism creates its own myths, different but no less powerful than the myths of polytheism because "only an abstract theological monotheism can do without myth." A living religion, one that looks to life, not merely to abstract theology, needs specific forms by which it realizes its abstract ideas. It needs myth as a sturdy and solid vessel for a religion of memory "in which its central events can be kept safe and lastingly remembered and incorporated."20

Myth affirms monotheism insofar as it serves memory honestly rather than seeking to replace the event to which it points. When myth acts as a servant to memory, it prepares the way for present dialogue. It opens a path through the past into the present and future so that what once became an opportunity for meeting can become so again. Myth acts in the present because it offers a valuable and irreplaceable testimony to an event in the past. Buber embraces the Bible's historicization of story even as he affirms myth. He contrasts "history" to "apocalypticism" rather than to "myth." The prophetic faith, Buber feels, emphasized history because within it human beings learned their responsibility. Not monotheism but ethics lies at the heart of the Bible's revolutionary view. History takes on importance because human deeds change the world; people supply an element of surprise, of spontaneity to creation. Buber lauds the prophetic insight that legitimates history. He considers it an expression of the "highest strength and fruitfulness." Prophecy, in this spirit, emphasizes moral freedom as characteristic of "God's partner in the dialogue of history."

The apocalyptic spirit, unlike prophecy, considers God independent of all creation, requiring no creature with whom to enter

into dialogue. What replaces history during
the "decadence" of Eastern culture and
religion is an unchangeable determinism.
Buber sees the struggle between Israel and
its neighbors not as one between a culture
at odds with nature and those at home with
it but as one between a culture that accepts
the responsibility of ethical living and
cultures that fatalistically deny the value of
moral decision making. Finally, Buber
considers this distinction crucial for
modern as well as ancient cultures. Every
human society must choose between history
and apocalypticism, and Buber considers
those societies which choose history "in
league with the prophets."21

Buber's approach combines an affirmation
of myth with an affirmation of history.
While many biblical scholars think such a
double affirmation impossible, Buber
considers it inevitable. Myth does not mean
the absence of history but rather a vivid
memory of it; history does not imply a
transcendence of myth but rather a
recognition of the choice every person must
make in the present. Buber characterizes
the theme of the Bible as a historical one:
"the encounter between a group of people and
the Lord of the world in the course of
history." The narrative evoking that
history, however, takes the form of myth.
Biblical myth, in all its variations,
reinforces history rather than
apocalypticism or a retreat to fatalism.22
Buber opposes interpreters who call for a
"demythologization of the Bible" and thereby
reduce the historical and prophetic stories

of the Bible to existential propositions.
He stands against demythologization, which
he calls "the postulate of the hour" because
"myth is not the subsequent clothing of a
truth of faith; it is the unarbitrary
testimony of the image-making vision and the
image-making memory, and the conceptual
cannot be refined out of it."23 Myth when
joined with history transcends mere
existentialist propositions. While some
critics claim that Buber accepts Bultmann's
conclusions too uncritically, in fact Buber
opposes reductionism, even that which
decodes myth as existential truth.24

   Benjamin Uffenheimer, an Israeli
biblical scholar who employs many of Buber's
techniques to subjects that Buber himself
did not analyze, offers an insight into
Buber's relationship to Bultmann. He
suggests that Buber opposes Bultmann for
transposing myth into something other than
itself. Buber refuses to refashion myth
into an abstract claim or even into a
historical claim. Myth remains a document--
a monument to an event. The religious
legitimacy of the myth lies in the honesty
of its representation, in its truthful
documentation of the original meeting.
Biblical myth does not need translation into
another language. The commentator need only
point to the function mythic language plays
so that readers may respond to the myth's
address.

   According to Buber, the Bible tells
stories neither to give a historical
explanation of events nor to provide a

mythic vision of life. Neither history nor myth truly describes the biblical intent. Rather, the Bible serves a single purpose: it publishes a "Gospel," a "good news." Whether using historical narrative, mythic poetry, or wisdom sayings, the Bible transmits a single message. That message consists neither of a mythic or scientific explanation of cause and effect nor of a series of historical events. Instead, it proclaims a continuing human opportunity: human beings stand in equality before the single God, are called upon to respond to that God as a commanding "Thou," and shape their lives as they answer the summons placed upon them.25 This language resembles Henri Frankfort's description of myth as an expression of a primitive, animistic world view. Actually, it differs from Frankfort by refusing to reduce myth to a function of primitive thinking. Buber's "I-Thou" expresses a generally human possibility rather than pre-modern or pre-scientific thinking. The biblical narrative has contemporary relevance because of its testimony to "I-Thou" relationships. As a witness to that possibility, it advances beyond either science or myth.

For Buber, the choice between a "historical" form and a "mythic" one makes little sense. Myth grows out of history. Historical events once retold become myth. Buber rejects a dichotomy between the mythic approach and the historical. Instead, he maintains that biblical myth arises from I-Thou meetings that occurred in actual history. The mythic form preserves a memory of those meetings with an immediacy that can stimulate a readiness to repeat them in the present. The stories reported in the Bible reflect upon events in human lives retold so as to convey an intangible meeting rather than the literal details of external happenings. Buber uses an admittedly subjective method by which to trace back the evidence of that meeting through historical reports, through prophetic utterances, through legends, and through myth.   Because of his subjective approach, Buber often wins respect but not acceptance for his theories.26

PAGANISM AND MONOTHEISM

Buber's distinctive interpretation of Jewish mythology appears in his contrast between Hebraic and pagan views of the divine. Like other thinkers, Buber distinguishes between Hebraic and pagan mythology. Pagan myths are wrong not because they are myths but because they misconstrue reality about the meeting with God and about the creatures encountered. Where pagan myths assume that God, humanity, and creation are all part of one continuous reality, biblical myth maintains the distinctions among the individual participants in the world. A meeting can occur only when God, humanity, and the natural creatures interact as integral and self-authenticated individuals. By dissolving the differences between the

spheres of existence, paganism prevents true
meeting. Biblical myth, because it is
monotheistic, not because it is myth,
captures the true nature of reality. Pagan
myth, because it is pagan, not because it is
myth, offers false testimony about reality.
The nature of Israel's God precludes the
type of myth found in pagan religion. Pagan
religion, Buber, like Frankfort, suggests,
seeks to master nature through appeal to the
gods. Rather than address the divine as a
"You," pagan religion asserts magical
control over it. Since "the scriptural God
is essentially different from the gods of
other national myths," the biblical myth
points to a different and more humanistic
reality.27 Buber recognizes the truth of
myth as a reflection of the duality of I-
Thou and I-It ways of living in the world.

Buber evaluates myth by determining its
accuracy as a reflection of the two ways of
being in the world. Biblical myth, on this
reading, retains a sense of the two
personalities involved in I-You meeting.
Where pagan myth dissolves this duality into
a false unity, biblical myth emphasizes the
integrity of every participant. Buber often
characterizes this aspect of Jewish myth by
using an expression common among nineteenth-
and early twentieth-century apologists for
Judaism: ethical monotheism. While other
Jewish theologians as well as Buber consider
this concept the key to Jewish religion,
Buber understands it in a special way. He
thinks of ethical monotheism as the entire
pattern of Israelite living, not merely as
an intellectual or moral idea. Biblical

myth reflects ethical monotheism when it
transmits a sense of the obligation to
discover life as an organic whole through
human meeting. When people discover their
responsibility toward the world as a field
of other selves, they respond, Buber claims,
by creating the myths of ethical
monotheism.28

Those who seek to evade that reality,
however, create myths to reinforce their own
illusions. The Bible, while sharing a set
of mythological themes with ancient Egyptian
and ancient Mesopotamian literature, employs
those themes differently. In Egypt, for
example, myth transmitted secret knowledge.
Those initiated into the myths of Ptah at
Memphis, of Amon in Thebes, or Aton at
Heliopolois received a special teaching that
guaranteed them salvation. They achieved a
gnosis of hidden truth. In contrast,
Babylonian myth was oriented toward cultic
practices rather than salvation. Its
diviner priests instructed people in daily
affairs and used magic to cure toothaches,
to plan military campaigns, and to predict
the future. Myths, in Babylonia, provided a
means of attaining magic, rather than
salvation.

Buber contrasts both the gnosis of Egypt
and the magic of Babylonia to Israel's "good
news." That news, he claims, focuses on the
reality of the meeting between the divine
and the human, on the equality and immediacy
of that relationship, and of the genuine
encounter between an "I" and a "Thou."
Buber takes his task to be that of

reaffirming the biblical message in contrast
to that of either the gnostic secrets of
Egypt or the magical practices of
Babylonia.29 Buber, then, clearly thought
of his analysis of myth as a discussion of
accurate or inaccurate mythic sources. He
interpreted the Bible as a compendium of
true myth. The modern scholar may well
wonder at Buber's confidence. He himself
faced an objection to his subjectivism.
Nevertheless, his approach offers an
insightful way of reading the Bible, even if
his truth claims about biblical myth seem
unsubstantiated by clear evidence. Even his
exaltation of the Bible in relationship to
other cultures can be read less as an
evaluative type of exegesis than as a way of
reading the text more carefully. Buber
illuminates the Book of Job, for example, by
examining its relationship to other ancient
Near Eastern mythical tradition.

MYTH IN THE BOOK OF JOB

Buber's approach differs from those who
interpret biblical religion as an advance
from a primitive, mythic world view to a
modern, scientific stance. This view
enables him to interpret strange tales that
seem to contradict the rationalistic
perspective. The Book of Job, for example,
teems with mythical allusions and images.
Biblical scholars struggle to understand
this work. Some affirm the mythical roots
of the tale, yet deny their crucial

importance. Others consider the book a
vestige of pagan traditions. Buber's
analysis avoids both extremes by
interpreting the story as a response by
post-exilic Jews to their new encounter with
the deity.30

The Book of Job develops in four stages.
The first stage tells of God's discussion
with his angelic court, numbering among them
the Satan, or the "adversary." In the
course of conversation with this angel, God
wagers that "his" servant Job cannot be
dissuaded from his piety no matter what may
occur to him. God and Satan agree to test
whether any fortuitous accident can unsettle
Job's conviction of divine justice. Several
disasters occur to Job, some of them the
work of natural forces without apparent
rationale (lightning descends to slaughter
his children) and some apparently the
decision of human beings following their own
inclinations (bandits raid his herds). The
author thereby implies that "unthinking"
nature and "free" human beings both act
according to a power that compels them. Job
never complains about this treatment.

The second stage of the story introduces
conflict and a different philosophical
stance. Job engages three friends in
dialogue. Job claims that God should act
justly and that the actions taken against
him are unjust. The friends defend God's
justice and suggest that Job must have
merited the suffering he has endured. In
the third stage, God confronts Job from out
of a whirlwind. God overwhelms Job with a

display of creative force and power so that Job admits his mortality and insignificance. The book ends with an epilogue. God justifies Job and condemns his friends. Job has "spoken truly" about the divine while the friends have not. Only through Job's prophetic intercession for the friends can they win God's forgiveness. Job fulfills his duty and prays successfully for his friends. Satan never reappears, and God restores Job to his former prosperity.

Most biblical scholars admit that the author of Job drew on ancient myths or legends.31 They suggest that the book's archaic language and dense images reflect the influence of pagan religion on Hebrew thinking. The theme, symbols, and content of the book have much in common with ancient Near Eastern literature. Some scholars, however, minimize the importance of these correspondences. Robert Gordis, for example, recognizes that the author of the book uses mythical allusions but claims that "he is not interested in imaginary creatures from the dim mythological past--he is concerned with the actual present, with the vast universe as it is governed by its maker." Gordis opposes those scholars who interpret the story as a mythic one. He suggests that they fail "to distinguish between mythological allusions and religious beliefs."32 For him, the book, then, far from representing myth, replaces it with a historical perspective.

Buber's concern for the book as "myth," however, moves beyond recognition of

mythical allusions or an original ancient
Near Eastern source that the author
borrowed. When seeking the lived experience
reflected in the story, Buber notes four
theological strands. The prologue and
epilogue of the book seem expressions of
determinism. A human being, confronting the
inevitability of fate, affirms fate as an
Other, as a You. The dialogue between Job
and his friends reflects two kinds of
"mismeetings" in the world: that among human
beings and that between humanity and the
deity. The portrayal of God in the
whirlwind points to a fourth alternative: an
I-You relationship that overwhelms but does
not destroy the human partner and thereby
confirms people in their significance.
Buber considers the portrayal of these four
kinds of meeting as accurate assessments of
human experience. Thus he considers the
story to "bear the stamp of an intractable
directness--the stamp of a first
expression."33 Job as myth arose to
characterize an event that shook its teller
by its unexpectedness and newness; the
author expressed this experience by placing
the new meeting within the context of older,
more traditional ones. The author of the
story could convey the significance of an
encounter with the You of God only by
relating a strange and perplexing tale that
encompassed all alternative theories.

Buber discerns four experiences of human
meeting with the deity. According to him,
the prologue (and one should also assume the
epilogue) portrays a capricious divine
tyrant: "a small mythological idol." This

God acts without regard for any other being and plays games with creation. The dialogue offers two views of deity. On the one hand the friends dogmatically affirm cause and effect: the deity must follow the rigid laws of scientific causation applied to the sphere of morality. God must submit to the inexorable logic of the human consciousness. On the other hand Job argues that while God acts for a purpose, the divine actions testify to injustice. God apparently "contradicts His own revelation" by promising rational purpose but acting irrationally, and this contradiction leaves Job irreconcilably confused. Neither the world nor God seems to make sense.

The author has suggested three ways people interact with the divine: they may see divine actions as irrational forces intersecting their lives without purpose or meaning; they may impose a human morality on divine actions without regard for the actual facts in any specific case; or they may try to affirm both experiences--defending the divine as purposeful and moral, but recognizing that divine actions are often irrational and immoral. The third alternative, Job's predicament, requires some resolution. The God who confronts Job from the whirlwind provides that resolution in a fourth alternative. Although appearing in the same story, "this God, Who answers from the tempest, is different from the God of the Prologue."34 As Buber understands this story, it reflects a person's surprised and shocked response to an amazing meeting. This person experiences God as creator and recognizes all the terror and horror of natural life. This person also experiences God in revelation, as the moral teacher who demands righteousness. Caught in the Joban conflict, the person then experiences a third reality: God affirms the confused and intellectually crippled human being as a worthy person. While the conflict between God as creator and God as moral teacher remains, the person also experiences God as one who reassures, who confirms even the confused person as important and significant. Job learns that God takes note of him, even if he cannot understand why God does so or how to reconcile his experiences of God.

According to Buber, the myth of Job rejects both pagan gnosticism, which thinks human beings can know the secrets of the divine and pagan magic, which thinks human beings can compel the divine. The experience of the prologue represents the former, that of the dialogue reflects the latter. Job's experience in the whirlwind reflects the truer myths of Hebrew thought: God is known neither intellectually nor magically, but only though I-You meeting.35 The meeting with God confirms human ignorance of the divine and human inability to predict or control divine acts, but it also affirms the value of being human.

Buber's method impels him to make a truth claim: Job's view represents the biblical vision of the prophets in contrast to pagan mythology. Buber suggests that where priests often turn to magic, much as

Job's friends turn to morality, as a means of compelling God to act in humanly comprehensible ways, prophets faithfully recall the ambiguity of their call to a religious vocation. While gnostics convey only hints and myths about their truth, seeking to reserve their knowledge to themselves (just as the opening sections of Job sketches the workings of the heavenly court with laconic suggestiveness), prophets seek to share the knowledge of God with all (thus Job, in the epilogue, intercedes on behalf of his friends so that they too may recognize the dialogical nature of divinity). Thus for Buber the Book of Job is made up of "reminiscences of prophetic life and language."36

Buber's explanation of the prophetic message in the Book of Job deepens an appreciation of its value for people today, even if his claim to have uncovered its distinctive difference from paganism may be challenged. Yehezkel Kaufmann may be right in seeing the biblical tale as a polemic against the wisdom tradition of the ancient Near East. He suggests that the story pits the "sage" who acknowledges the existence of God but who claims that divinity lacks any connection with morality against the "righteous man" who refuses to separate morality and justice from the deity.37 Nevertheless, while Kaufmann shows how the text might fit a cultural context in which pagan and Israelite competed against one another, Buber opens the book to modern reflection. The alternative perspectives he shows claim allegiance even today. While

Buber's own exegesis of Job never fully explains its presuppositions, and thus Buber may be using his own method too broadly, the careful reader can go beyond Buber himself. Such a reader may agree with Kaufmann that the Book of Job differs significantly from ancient Near Eastern mythic precedent. That reader might also admit that Buber may not have uncovered the intentions of the original author of Job; scholars may dispute Buber's evidence for locating the book in a particular time and place. An unprejudiced view, however, should also allow that Buber has pointed out themes and possibilities in the Book of Job that speak directly and significantly to modern people trying to make sense out of life.

MAGIC AND THE BIBLE

The Book of Job opens with what Buber identifies as a typical "Oriental myth": that of the divine council. God appears surrounded by divine beings who serve him as royal ministers. The book makes little use of this motif but still displays what Buber considers distinctive in the biblical use of such a myth: the supernal ministers appear anonymously. They have "neither individual names, nor individual forms, nor individual myths"; even "the Satan" applies only to a specific function, not a specific personality. Personality, Buber comments, befits God alone.38 The relatively minor role of this myth in the Book of Job

reflects its sphere of concern. Where the
author of Job focuses on what people may
know, the divine council myth centers its
concern on human power. Ancient magicians
often appealed to divine forces to aid their
work. Magic seeks to control earthly life
through the manipulation of heavenly powers.
Magic extends the causality of nature into
the spiritual realm. As human beings strive
to bend nature to fulfill their will, so
they use incantations and rituals to
influence supernal potencies for their own
gain. The biblical appropriation of this
myth challenges magic with its alternative
perspective. Buber's theory of biblical
mythology suggests that biblical authors
recognized the power implicit in ancient
magical myths of the divine council. While
inheriting that myth, they nevertheless
intuited how later transmission had
distorted its primal meaning. As magic, the
story obliterates the initiating impulse for
the myth. The author of Job therefore
restores the myth to its original meaning.
Buber conceives of this author as taking
"dogmas in process of formation" and setting
"over against them the force of the new
question, the question brought into being
out of experience."39 Biblical myth-making,
from this perspective, took traditional
dogmas, ideas, and images crystallized in
religion and revived them by connecting them
with experience.

Buber argues that this continuing
process leads from the story of Job to the
full-bodied rejection of polytheistic
paganism by Second Isaiah. Buber recognized

and affirmed this prophet's ridicule of idolatry and considered it a peculiar historical expression. The prophet who clearly "knows about the drama between God and man" no longer uses mythic images but creates a historical image: the servant of Yahweh hidden in the divine quiver awaiting God's use.40 Emphasizing this aspect of the development of biblical thought, Buber avoids using the terminology of "myth." His portrayal of the hidden messiah, however, linked with his interpretation of Job fits his own definition of myth. The line of evolution from Job, who seeks a personal I-You answer from the Creator, to Isaiah's servant, who anticipates the Creator's call to emerge from mystery, suggests a mythic continuity.

Henri Frankfort mentions both Job and Second Isaiah in his analysis of the "abysmal difference" between Hebrew and earlier ancient Near Eastern thought. Unlike Buber, he suggests that the emphasis on a relationship between the individual Israelite and the one deity who rules the world yields only despair. The Israelite who confronts this deity finds that everything else in the world has "shrivelled to nothingness before the absolute value which was God." Israelite thought removed the magical control that primitive people held over the world and replaced it with no suitable alternative. The biblical material retains traces of primitive myth but distorts those traces so completely that the Israelites have no power over their own destiny.41

An alternative approach interprets biblical myth as equally primitive and magical, but related to social rather than intellectual structures. In contrast to Buber's view, this approach traces the influence of ancient Near Eastern magical religion on the Hebrew Bible and suggests that the latter diluted rather than improved on the former. Frank Cross analyzes biblical myth from a comparative perspective and reaches a similar conclusion.42 He devotes attention to Israel's Psalms and their mythical allusions. Psalm 82, for example, uses the image of Yahweh in the council of the gods. The Psalm draws on the Canaanite notion of El as the prototypical king and may have originally sought to influence judicial decisions by an appeal to a higher court.

In its final shape, however, the Psalm takes on special significance in Israelite politics. Cross explains the sociological function that this Psalm played, claiming that "With the institution of kingship in Israel and the temple cultus, both institutions of Canaanite origin, the old myths became resurgent."43 The Psalm as myth could symbolize a social and institutional change. When Yahweh ousts El from the pantheon, the older deities lose their permanence and power. The Psalm need not reflect on the human condition but rather explains the transformed institutional cult, now centralized in one shrine--probably Jerusalem--in which one official--probably the king--performs the

ritual action.44 In their primitive form,
then, the Psalms offered the people of
Israel a magical means for protecting their
national prosperity. Only after losing
faith in that nation did they take on the
personal and individualistic cast they now
possess. From this perspective Frankfort is
right; the Bible reflects ancient Israel's
failure of nerve.

Buber's reflections on the Psalms reach
a very different conclusion.45 His German
(and English) presentation of Psalms 1, 12,
14, 73, and 82 place them in an order that
he claims reflects their answer to the
question of human existence, and he
describes his essay as an "existential
exegesis." The Psalms lead from the
problems of Psalm 12 to the solution in
Psalm 1 and then open the modern question:
how can an evil will exist if God exists?46
This structure seems to reveal the Psalms as
mythic responses to an I-You meeting. A
creative reading of the Psalms places a
person face to face with the divine other.
In such a case "they complete one another
like the stages of a personal way" and evoke
a contemporary response.47

The Hebrew presentation of the same
material, however, proceeds from Psalm 1
through Psalm 82. That study affirms that
what Franz Kafka could not discover in his
reality (a word of comfort) "is to be found
in this Psalm." Here the most clearly
mythical Psalm in which God appears in the
midst of the angels (literally "gods" or
"divine beings") serves to offer human

beings a glimpse of hope. Without claiming
that the entire structure represents one
mythic response, Buber's analysis pays
closer attention to detail than Cross' and
shows how an imagistic evocation of the
deity may recall and awaken the possibility
of an I-You meeting.48

The Psalm begins by announcing God's
presence in the angelic court and continues
with God's accusation that these gods are
unjust. The Psalmist then recognizes that
the pagan deities are of no importance and
will eventually be deposed from their high
positions. Most scholars point to Isaiah
14:12-15 and Ezekiel 28:1-10 as examples of
what may happen to such beings. The Psalm
ends with an invocation: the Psalmist urges
God to do in reality what the Psalm projects
him having done in the supernal realm. He,
the just deity, should take the reins of
government from the hands of the unjust
gods. The mythical image remains in place:
the heavenly council abides and controls
sublunar life. Nevertheless, the author
hopes that God's own action will end the
injustice of such a condition. Buber's
commentary characterizes the Psalm as a
polemic against understanding "the history
of the human race as a continuation of the
history of nature" and against "the delusion
that the way of man can be determined from
the general customs of the animals."49 The
members of God's council err because they
engage in power politics. They assume that
might determines who deserves the governance
of human life. The Psalm, on this reading,
addresses the historical human condition,

not some "cosmic circle of a heavenly host."
The author agrees that God does delegate
authority and that heavenly princes may well
adjudicate the fate of nations.
Nevertheless, the heavenly principle of
government, like the earthly one, remains
the basis for justice.50 The Psalm teaches
earthly rulers who, like supernal ones, act
as intermediaries between the divine being
and the human community that only justice
legitimates their power. Buber, here as
with Job, moves from this study of a text to
its originating event.

He traces the Psalm back to a human
experience, claiming that it only begins
with the testimony of the human author.
Later, Buber suggests, the author translated
his testimony about his life, into a
literary work. That poem sought to convey a
vision that confirmed God as ruler over the
world. Out of a private I-You meeting, the
poet crafted a moral lesson: "those who
were entrusted with the office of judge
succumbed to injustice" but were themselves
punished. The author moved from direct
experience to a general lesson: the chaos
of history does not represent the final
truth. Ultimately, righteousness, justice,
and human concern for the afflicted prevail.
This "true" experience of history
counteracts the "false" myths that evoke the
pessimistic determinism that Frankfort seems
to accept.51

Once again, Buber, if judged by his own
criterion, succeeds better than his more
scholarly opponents. While Cross may be

right about the history and politics behind
the creation of the Psalm, Buber evokes a
sense of its generally human importance.
While Frankfort may characterize paganism
accurately, the Psalm does not now reflect a
"failure of nerve" when people read it and
probably had ceased to do so even when
canonized by later generations of Jewish
leaders. In this way, Buber's
reconstruction, while historically perhaps
less exact than that of Cross or that of
Frankfort, nevertheless enables modern
readers to enter into the spirit of the
Psalm. Buber shows how biblical myth may
transcend science and magic, and, despite
Frankfort's opinion, retain meaning in the
face of changing social conditions.

MYTH AND THE NEW TESTAMENT

Buber's description of his
interpretation of the Psalms as "an
existential exegesis" seems to fall under
the general rubric of "demythologization."
Buber translates mythic language into a
theory about human existence, a technique
often associated with the German theologian
and New Testament scholar Rudolf Bultmann.
Introducing his study of Christian religion,
Buber acknowledges his debt to Bultmann.
Not only as an author and philosopher but
also as a colleague Bultmann helped Buber
learn the meaning of the New Testament.[52]
Despite this acknowledgment, however, Buber
disagrees with Bultmann's approach to myth

generally and to the myth of the New
Testament in particular. Bultmann claims
that myth does not "present an objective
picture of the world as it is" but rather
expresses human self-understanding. Myth
<u>appears</u> to describe externally real events
but in fact conveys an <u>attitude</u> toward
reality. On this reading "the importance of
the New Testament mythology lies not in its
imagery but in the understanding of
existence which it enshrines."53 Applying
this view of mythology to the New Testament,
Bultmann recognizes in Jesus both a
historical person and a mythical figure. He
suggests that if the mythological language
describing Jesus merely attempts to "express
the meaning of the historical figure of
Jesus and the events of his life," then the
important message lies in this meaning, not
"the objective form in which they are cast."
The facts of the New Testament stories,
then, are less important than "the meaning
of the Person of Jesus for faith."54
Bultmann therefore reads the stories of the
New Testament as mythical expressions of an
existential meaning, seeing the concrete
language as a vehicle for an intellectual
content that modern scholars can decipher.

Buber's approach differs radically. He
agrees that much of the New Testament
reflects a "crystallization" of the mythical
element, an element he traces back to Greek
rather than Jewish sources. He identifies
the core of the New Testament, however, with
Judaic, and more specifically prophetic,
religion. The message of the New Testament,
he claims, "has its origin not in the

mythical imagination but in the (prophetic)
view of historical reality."55 Buber's
studies of the New Testament seek out the
historical kernel around which the myth
formed. Since religion often distorts the
myths it uses, Buber pushes behind the late
forms of the myths to what he considers
their historical origins. At the heart of
the tales, he argues, stands the living
teacher Jesus. That teacher reached out to
other people, touched them with an I-You
relationship, and transformed their lives.

As Christianity developed, however, that
I-You immediacy became muted and eventually
lost. Buber remarks on the difference
between Jesus' dialogue with a rabbi in Mark
10, in which Jesus approves of the rabbinic
way to God, and the interchanges in the
Gospel of John. When John's Jesus
proclaims, "No one comes to the father
except by me," Buber no longer hears the
same voice speaking as in Mark. He admits,
"I hold to the former speaker (i.e., Mark's
Jesus) and not to the latter (i.e., John's
Jesus)."56 In his search for the
"authentic" experiences of Jesus found in
the New Testament, Buber rejects the Gospel
of John as a reliable witness. He considers
the myths its preserves no longer the
pristine Jewish myths that he associates
with the biblical tradition. The Gospel of
John seems to Buber a paradigm for
Christianity's distortion of "I-You"
meeting. He points to the conversation
between Jesus and Nicodemus in John 3 as a
primary example.57 The story seems to take
as its point of departure a historical

reality: Jesus used the symbols of Jewish
tradition, particularly those taken from the
Genesis creation story, to advocate personal
self-renewal. He called upon his audience
to "follow me," and led them through his own
example to a personal rebirth. The myth
preserves this call since "By what he says
Jesus does not intend to bar the way to
heaven to his nocturnal visitor, but to open
it." As the story evolved, however, it came
to mean the opposite of its original
intention and eventually taught an
exclusivist view of salvation. While Jesus
invited people to imitate his way, John's
Gospel identifies an elect group of those
who are meant to hear.58

   Already in 1949 Buber had corresponded
with Bultmann about this particular passage
in John. Bultmann had claimed that the
story could only be generalized: it teaches
a lesson about human salvation, not about a
real historical meeting in a particular
case. In his later commentary on John,
Bultmann says explicitly that the story "has
been dictated by the particular theological
interests of the Evangelist," who
"nevertheless gives the Gospel the
appearance of an historical narrative."
Bultmann concludes that the "scene" created
by the author draws on traditional forms and
motifs and is, in that sense, a literary
work; nevertheless, he calls this process
one of "historicizing" a mythic idea. He
looks first to the idea being expressed, not
to a historical event that then gave rise to
the idea.59

Bultmann discovers an existential message in the story: "In the encounter with the Revealer man is put in question in such a way that his whole past, which determines his present being, is also put in question. Only so can he be called to rebirth...."60 Bultmann emphasizes that this existential message, rather than the mythic forms and gnostic influences that he admits also abound in the passage, represents the contribution of Christian revelation. He contends that the text addresses an existential, not a gnostic, question. The point is no longer "a speculative account of man's descent, but a characterization of his nature," and thus, even in its mythic form, the Gospel represents a stage of "demythologization" within the New Testament itself.

The focus on gnosticism clarifies the implications of Buber's approach to myth. Buber insists that later Christianity, especially Paul, but also the Gospel of John, fell into gnosticism. Whereas myth "brings the inexpressible to speech," gnostic thinking, according to Buber, "tears it out of the historical-biographical ground within which it took root."61 By equating gnosticism with a move away from history, Buber, unlike Bultmann, identified the latest form of the Christian myth as gnostic. Demythologization, then, from his perspective, blurs distinctions between two opposed types of religiousness. His definition of myth as a historically real event, as an event that cannot be reduced to primitivism, magic, or existentialism, leads him to reject demythologization even as he rejected other reductionist explanations.

The modern reader may learn a more open approach to the Bible from Buber than from Bultmann. Bultmann's identification of a New Testament passage with a particular existential idea limits, rather than expands, its possibilities of significance. Buber's approach, however, invites readers to discover more and more nuances and meanings in a text and to use the text as a point of departure for their own living. A contemporary student of biblical narratives, Joel Rosenberg, reads those stories as interconnected systems of symbols and cross-references. He points to the irony and sophistication found in the Bible as signs of its complex creativity. He argues that "the Hebrew Bible presents itself as a text to be <u>reread</u>."62 Buber's understanding of biblical myth encourages such rereading. While the specific conclusions Buber himself draws concerning any single biblical passage may need revision, his method does succeed in awakening a desire for reading and rereading the text. In this sense, Buber achieves his purpose in analyzing biblical myth.

NOTES

1. Nahum Glatzer, "Editor's Postscript" to Buber, On Judaism, ed. Nahum N. Glatzer (New York: Schocken, 1967), p. 237.

2. Martin Buber, Kingship of God, 3rd ed., trans. Richard Scheimann (New York: Harper, 1967), p. 15.

3. Yehezkel Kaufmann, The Religion of Israel: From Its Beginnings to the Babylonian Exile, trans. and abrdg. Moshe Greenberg (Chicago: University of Chicago Press, 1960), pp. 390-1.

4. Martin Buber, The Prophetic Faith, trans. Carlyle Witton-Davies (New York: Macmillan, 1949), pp. 152-54.

5. See Laurence J. Silberstein, Martin Buber's Social and Religious Thought: Alienation and the Quest For Meaning (New York: New York University Press, 1989), pp. 52, 58.

6. James Muilenburg, "Buber As An Interpreter of the Bible", in Paul Arthur Schilpp and Maurice Friedman, eds., The Philosophy of Martin Buber, The Library of Living Philosophers, vol. XII (La Salle, IL: Open Court, 1967), p. 381.

7. Julius Wellhausen, Prolegomena to the History of Ancient Israel, preface W. Robertson Smith (Gloucester, MA: Peter Smith, 1973), p. 298.

8. R. G. Collingwood, <u>The Idea of History</u>, ed. T. M. Knox (London: Oxford University Press, 1946), p. 13.

9. Ironically, Collingwood credits Christianity with the "leaven" that leads to this great advance and contends that biblical Israel remained enthralled to a mythic "quasi-history." See <u>ibid.</u>, pp. 17, 46-56.

10. G. Ernest Wright, <u>The Old Testament Against Its Environment</u>, Studies in Biblical Theology, no. 2 (Naperville: Allenson, 1950), pp. 19-21; compare his continuing argument on pp. 21-45.

11. Compare the analogous triple distinction among "magic, science, and religion" in Bronislaw Malinowski, <u>Magic, Science and Religion and other Essays</u>, intro. Robert Redfield (Garden City, NY: Doubleday, 1948). In "Myth in Primitive Psychology," pp. 93-148, he emphasizes that "myth is a cultural force" and denies the consensus of "modern science at its best" that myth "explains" phenomenon. Nevertheless, by insisting that myth "supplies man with the motive" for action and by discussing the "myths of magic" at great length, his approach actually advances the "explanative" view of myth described in this chapter. I suggest alternative views of myth primarily to illuminate Buber's distinctive approach. For a more

comprehensive treatment of theorists of
myth see Robert A. Segal's essay, "In
Defense of Mythology: The History of
Modern Theories of Myth." Annals of
Scholarship I:1 (1980): 3-49.

12. Ernest S. Frerichs has drawn attention
to the parallel between Kaufmann's
thought and G. Ernest Wright's view of
biblical religion's historicizing in
contrast to paganism's myth. See his
"Ancient Israel's Scripture and Its
Religion: The Achievement of Helmer
Ringgren," in Jacob Neusner, Peder
Borgen, Ernest Frerichs, and Richard
Horsley, eds., New Perspectives on
Ancient Judaism, vol. 2: Religion,
Literature and Society in Ancient
Israel, Formative Christianity and
Judaism: Ancient Israel and Christianity
(Lanham, MD: University Press of
America, 1987), p. 29.

13. Kaufmann, The Religion of Israel, pp.
66-73.

14. See, for example, Nahum M. Sarna,
Understanding Genesis (New York:
Schocken, 1970). Sarna warns readers
against a "fundamentalism" and false
piety and recognizes the value of source
criticism and documentary analysis. At
the same time he claims that "the
disentanglement of literary strands does
not constitute the apotheosis of
scholarship" and argues for a reading of
the Bible as a whole, integrated work.
Thus Sarna accepts the findings of

documentary scholarship but moves beyond them. In that move he emphasizes Kaufmann's insights about mythology (see Sarna, pp. 6-12, 53-59, 193-94). Compare as well Irving M. Zeitlin, <u>Ancient Judaism: Biblical Criticism From Max Weber to the Present</u> (Oxford: Oxford University Press, 1984), esp. pp. 2, 18-35.

15. Henri Frankfort, <u>Kingship and the Gods: A Study of Ancient Near Eastern Religion as the Integration of Society and Nature</u> (Chicago: University of Chicago Press, 1948), p. 342; see the entire discussion, pp. 338-43.

16. Henri Frankfort, H.A. Frankfort, John A. Wilson, and Thorkild Jacobsen, <u>Before Philosophy: The Intellectual Adventure of Ancient Man</u> (Baltimore: Penguin Books, 1949), see esp. pp. 12, 15, 142, 244-48.

17. See the discussion by J. W. Rogerson, "The Old Testament Versus Mythopoeic Thought," in his <u>Myth in Old Testament Interpretation</u>, BZAW 134 (Berlin: Walter de Gruyter, 1974), pp. 85-100; see esp. pp. 93-96 on the "puzzling business of experiencing the phenomenal world as a Thou."

18. See the discussion throughout John L. McKenzie, <u>Myth and Realities Studies in Biblical Theology</u> (London: Geoffrey Chapman, 1963).

19. Buber, On Judaism, p. 99.

20. See ibid., pp. 99-100; and Buber, Israel and the World: Essays in a Time of Crisis (New York: Schocken, 1948), p. 22.

21. Martin Buber, "Prophecy, Apocalyptic, and the Historical Hour," in Pointing the Way, trans., ed., and intro. Maurice S. Friedman (New York: Harper, 1957), pp. 192-207.

22. Buber, Israel and the World, p. 89; compare the discussion on p. 98.

23. Martin Buber, Hasidism and Modern Man, trans. and ed. Maurice Friedman (New York: Horizon Press, 1958), p. 41.

24. See the discussions in Maurice Friedman, Martin Buber's Life and Work: The Later Years, 1945-1964 (New York: Dutton, 1981), pp. 85-99, and in Benjamin Uffenheimer, "Buber and Modern Biblical Scholarship," in Haim Gordon and Jochanan Bloch, eds., Martin Buber : A Centenary Volume (New York: KTAV, 1984), pp. 163-211.

25. Martin Buber, "The Language of Good Tidings," in his Darkho Shel Miqra [Hebrew] (Jerusalem: Bialik Institute, 1964), 272-83.

26. See Nahum N. Glatzer, "Buber as an Interpreter of the Bible," in Paul Arthur Schilpp and Maurice Friedman,

eds., The Philosophy of Martin Buber,
The Library of Living Philosophers, vol.
XII (La Salle, IL: Open Court, 1967),
pp. 261-380; James Muilenburg, "Buber as
an Interpreter of the Bible," in ibid.,
pp. 381-402; the quotation cited is on
p. 381; compare Glatzer's "Editor's
Postscript," in Buber, On the Bible, pp.
233-40 (the cited quotation is on p.
238) and Shemaryahu Talmon, "Martin
Buber's Way of Interpreting the Bible,"
Journal of Jewish Studies 27 (1976):
195-209; compare the discussion of Buber
in Eliezer Schweid, "Buber's
Interpretation of the Bible," in
Joseph Dan, ed., Binah: Volume 2, Studies
in Thought (Westport, CT: Praeger, 1989),
pp. 191-217. Schweid makes no mention
of Buber's stress on biblical myth but
does note the uniqueness of Buber's
approach and its difference from
traditional biblical scholarship.
Buber, Schweid suggests on p. 216,
"does not demand a return to the Bible
but a return to the unifying message of
life." Moshe Swarcz, "The Concept of
Myth and the Question of
'Demythologization' In Martin Buber's
System," in his Language, Myth, and Art
[Hebrew] (Tel Aviv: Schocken, 1966), pp.
216-49, discusses Buber's response to
Rudolf Bultmann; compare Malcolm
Diamond, Martin Buber: Jewish
Existentialist (New York: Oxford
University Press, 1960), pp. 79-80, and
Harold Schulweis, "Myth and
Existentialism," Judaism 6 (Fall 1957),
pp. 302-10.

27. Zeev Levy, "Demythologization and Remythologization," in <u>Bar Ilan Annual</u>, vols. 22-23 (Ramat Gan, Israel: Bar Ilan University Press, 1987), p. 222.

28. Buber, "The Language of Good Tidings."

29. Buber, <u>Israel and the World</u>, pp. 20-27.

30. See Buber's discussion in <u>The Prophetic Faith</u>, pp. 183-91, and in <u>Darkho Shel Miqra</u>, pp. 340-42.

31. See the discussion on this subject in Marvin Pope, <u>Job: Introduction, Translation, and Notes</u>, Anchor Bible (Garden City, NY: Doubleday, 1965), pp. xxi-xxv; l-lxvi.

32. Robert Gordis, <u>The Book of God and Man: A Study of Job</u> (Chicago: Chicago University Press, 1965), pp. 119, 318.

33. Buber, <u>The Prophetic Faith</u>, p. 188.

34. <u>Ibid.</u>, p. 196.

35. <u>Ibid</u>.

36. <u>Ibid.</u>, p. 197.

37. See Kaufmann, <u>History of Religion in Israel</u>, pp. 334-38, and the more extended discussion in his <u>Toldot</u>, vol. II, pp. 604-23.

38. Buber, <u>Kingship of God</u>, pp. 51-53.

39. Buber, <u>The Prophetic Faith</u>, p. 188.

40. Ibid., pp. 208-35.

41. Frankfort, Before Philosophy, pp. 242-45.

42. See Frank Moore Cross, Canaanite Myth and Hebrew Epic: Essays in the History of the Religion of Israel (Cambridge: Harvard University Press, 1973).

43. Ibid., pp. 71-72, 186-90.

44. Ibid.

45. Martin Buber, Good and Evil: Two Interpretations--Right and Wrong, Images of Good and Evil, trans. Ronald Gregor Smith and Michael Bullock (New York: Scribner's, 1953), pp. 3-60; Darkho Shel Miqra, pp. 139-62.

46. Ibid., pp. 3-6, 60.

47. Ibid., p. 3.

48. Ibid., p. 30; Darkho Shel Miqra, p. 162. For a recent scholarly treatment of the psalm see Mitchell Dahood, Psalms II, 51-100: Introduction, Translation, and Notes, Anchor Bible (Garden City, NY: Doubleday, 1968), pp. 268-71.

49. Ibid., p. 28.

50. Ibid., pp. 25-27.

51. Ibid., pp. 29-30.

52. See Martin Buber, <u>Two Types of Faith: A Study of the Interpenetration of Judaism and Christianity</u>, trans. Norman P. Goldhawk (New York: Macmillan, 1951), pp. 13, 117; compare Maurice Friedman, <u>The Later Years</u>, pp. 84-85.

53. Rudolf Bultmann, "New Testament and Mythology," in Rudolf Bultmann et al., <u>Kerygma and Myth: A Theological Debate</u>, ed. Hans Werner Bartsch (New York: Harper and Row, 1961), pp. 10-11.

54. <u>Ibid.</u>, p. 35.

55. Buber, <u>Two Types of Faith</u>, p. 109.

56. See Friedman, <u>The Later Years</u>, p. 85.

57. Buber, <u>Two Types of Faith</u>, pp. 117-26.

58. <u>Ibid.</u>, pp. 124-25.

59. Rudolf Bultmann, <u>The Gospel of John: A Commentary</u>, trans. R. Beasley-Murray, R.W.N. Hoare, and J.K. Riches (Oxford: Basil Blackwell, 1971), pp. 130-33.

60. <u>Ibid.</u>, p. 159.

61. Martin Buber, <u>The Origin and Meaning of Hasidism</u>, trans. and ed. Maurice Friedman (New York: Horizon Press, 1960), p. 249.

62. Joel Rosenberg, "Biblical Tradition: Literature and Spirit in Ancient Israel," in Arthur Green, ed., <u>Jewish Spirituality: From the Bible Through the</u>

Middle Ages (New York: Crossroads, 1986),
p. 87.

Chapter 4   Buber in Eden

BIBLICAL CREATION MYTHS

Buber's approach to myth focuses on historical memory. That orientation may prove a liability when investigating the meaning of general mythic themes. Mircea Eliade, for example, studies myths in detail and denies that the historical paradigm fits mythical narrative. He acknowledges that "Myth narrates a sacred history ... an event that took place in primordial Time." He also suggests that the meaning any myth conveys transcends this temporal event. Myth manifests certain realities that surpass changes of time and place.1 Eliade entitles one chapter on myth "Time can be overcome." He claims that the "tragic history" that myths tell "must not only be known, it must continually recollected." Such recollection entails telling the myth to bring back the original event.2 While history accepts the dictates of time and allows events to remain in the past, myth struggles against a sequential chronology of events. It struggles against time itself.3 Buber's view of myth emphasizes its remembrance of a unique event and its evocation of another unique event. He maintains that the biblical story of creation confirms this view of myth. Buber takes the story as a myth arising from a remembered event that points not to an inevitable human condition but to the possibility of future events:

> The Jew knows from his knowledge of creation and of creatureliness that there may be burdens inherited from prehistoric and historic times, but there is no overpowering original sin which could prevent the late-comer from deciding as freely as did Adam.4

Buber clearly notes that the story of creation influences Jewish religious life. He denies, however, that this influence takes the form of recreating the original event again and again. Instead, the story provides an object lesson from which individuals learn. This approach to a creation story contradicts that of Eliade, who emphasizes the need for continual "recollection" and re-reenactment of that creation event. Eliade, to be sure, notes that several traditions engage in a "demythicization" of creation stories but he denies that this apparent replacement of the need for continual renewal of primal acts actually abolishes myth.5 Analyzing biblical creation myths tests the grounds for Buber's historical view of myth against

the views of those claiming that myth
testifies to enduring and ever-recurring
realities.

   Two elements that the biblical creation
tales share with other mythic traditions
seem especially relevant to the question of
whether the stories record unique events of
history or seek to evoke a recreation of
perennial eternal actions: on the one hand
they explain the origin of time and change,
and on the other they portray the
deterioration of the human situation and the
appearance of evil (often associated with a
demonic figure). Genesis 1:1-2:4 describes
the beginning of the world as a series of
changes. With the distinction between dark
and light change and movement become
possible. Each additional creation supplies
new possibilities for development,
evolution, and genuine history. Genesis
2:5-3:24 describes how death and evil enter
human life, through a snake whom many
identify with the devil.

   Eliade comments on each of these two
themes. He suggests that retelling the
story of history's beginning overcomes its
tragedy. By telling how the world began, a
culture defends itself against the fear that
since time devours all things, it too will
perish. Creation stories mythically suggest
that "Deliverance from this world, and the
attainment of salvation, are equivalent to
deliverance from cosmic Time."6 From this
perspective Genesis 1 recaptures primal Time
and liberates people from cosmic Time.

The text does indeed seem to indicate such an intention. Genesis 2:1-4 portrays the divine rest that "sanctifies" the Sabbath day. The seventh day in every week becomes, as it were, a liberated day, a day in which time stands still and people can transcend history. Abraham Joshua Heschel views the Sabbath as such an "island" in time, providing refuge from the historical time in which people struggle. The Sabbath provides a "likeness of God" that is "eternity in disguise." He goes on to explain that through the Sabbath people become "aware that every instant is an act of creation, a Beginning, opening up new roads for ultimate realizations."7 The Sabbath provides transcendence by a weekly reenactment of the Genesis myth. It liberates those who follow it by a ritual performance that recreates the mythic event.

The second part of the creation story, Genesis 2:5-3:28, traces the development of evil in human life, a development traditionally associated with the devil. Eliade comments on such stories with the Genesis tale clearly in mind. Eliade notes the creative power of the devil in these narratives.8 More is at stake than merely "making a place for the Devil" in the world. These stories do more than explain the presence of evil. They show its necessity, its association with the divine, and its affirmation of evil as both unfortunate and creative.

The Genesis myths confirm this view. Even at the beginning of the story all is not well: God's creation lacks vegetation in the absence of both rain and human agriculture. When God creates a male human being, that creature lacks companionship. Thereafter God supplies animals and finally a woman to ameliorate the situation. One of God's own creatures, the snake, leads the human creatures into disobedience of a divine command. The three who participate in this act--the snake, the woman, and the man--receive separate punishments allotting each a specific function and task in the world.

Only when this drama concludes does human history as such begin. The story leaves readers with a sense of the recalcitrance of the world and the evil that seems necessarily inherent in creation. The biblical story seems to echo this mythical view. Paul Ricoeur, examining the Adamic myth, finds in it a model of human evil and human repentance. The myth goes beyond telling about an original event that once occurred in history. It also functions "to generalize the experience of Israel, applying it to all mankind at all times and in all places...."9 As Eliade suggests, then, myth does not record a unique historical event in Genesis 2:5-3:28 but rather evokes a continuing repetition of primal actions. This brief sketch shows that Buber's general approach to myth may not adequately explain the biblical stories of creation. He explicitly confronts these questions and uses his view of myth as a reflection on the meeting between an I and a You to answer them.

BUBER AND CREATION MYTHOLOGY

Despite his emphasis on the specific historical event at the heart of a myth, Buber recognizes the universal force of creation myths. He concedes that such myths point to a generally human truth. His discussion of these myths articulates his theory of why human beings require mythology at all. Myths not only convey a memory of an I-You meeting and stimulate a new one but also express a view of reality. Buber declares that myths help moderns to bridge the distance between what they know intellectually about the world and what they experience existentially about themselves. Myths of creation, he thinks, tell people about the chaos outside of themselves, about the potential for order and the destructive evils of the world in which they live. Myths, however, act on more than one level. They not only describe reality, they make those who listen to them, or tell them, internalize their message. Because the Bible tells about creation, people experience themselves as created; because the Bible tells about evil decisions, people recognize in their own lives the temptation to make wrong decisions. Myth, in Buber's words, provides a "bridge" from the knowledge people glean about the world outside of themselves to their own self-understanding.10 Genesis 1:1-2:4 describes a world of perfection, order, and meaning. The story confirms people in their beliefs about the rational world. The story also includes a command given to human beings

(Genesis 1:28-30). The combination of description and command makes the external description personally relevant, important for private decision-making. Genesis 2:5-3:28 describes the chaos and evil human beings encounter. As such, the myth affirms the experience people have of life's sufferings. The myth ends with a set of injunctions, of tasks. Accordingly, the myth moves beyond description of the world to the implications of that description for human acting.

By understanding Genesis myth this way, Buber makes the "historical event" from which the story originated relevant to all human beings. The new events the myth encourages are those of decision-making required of any and all human beings. Some biblical myths focus on social or political forms; some, like that of Enoch, wrestle with the meaning of religious leadership. While of general interest, the events celebrated in these myths may be of greatest use for others who share in the community of symbols, traditions, and history of those who tell the myth. Biblical creation stories, however, describe the more basic human search for meaningful ways of interacting with the created world. Buber, therefore, no less than Eliade, points to the universal truths embodied in myth. Buber prefaces his study of creation stories with a confession. He had pondered the difference between Jewish and Iranian myths of creation for some time. He first studied the problem in 1935 but waited over a decade before explicating his interpretation. The ideas "took so long to mature" because his understanding of myth had changed. At first he thought, much like Eliade, that myths of creation taught general truths about human life. Every human myth, in this view, would testify to a single verity of human existence.

If this paradigm were true, then the Jewish and Iranian myths contradict each other. A person must choose between the two and decide which is true. Buber's sense of myth as recollection of historical events, however, rebels against such a forced choice. Once he recognized that different historical meetings could produce different myths, he could reconcile apparent contradictions. While the Iranian and Jewish myths differ, they do not conflict. One need not choose between them since they represent different stages in any person's growing understanding of evil in the world. This final view suggests that myths differ from one another, insofar as each is true, because they spring from different events. When human beings interact with their world, they inevitably confront "evil." The nature of that meeting with evil, however, differs in different cultures. Sometimes a person discovers "evil" as an aimlessness, as a lack of direction. Sometimes a person grapples with a determined and focused opposition, an evil as self-consciously chosen. The biblical and Iranian myths differ because they preserve the memory of two "different kinds and stages of evil."11

This insight shapes Buber's method of describing the myth so that it differs considerably from Eliade's. He analyzes a creation myth to discover the historical meeting it recalls. He sets as his task that of recalling "an occurrence as reliably, concretely and completely remembered as possible." That event occurred to an individual person. Buber seeks to reconstruct that person's experience. He looks at a myth as "an image of the biographically decisive beginnings of good and evil."12 While Buber applies this to both the biblical and the Iranian myths, this chapter will investigate his view of the biblical creation stories as a contrast to Eliade's perspective. Since Buber does not expect the myth to solve the problem of "time" or to offer a positive interpretation of "evil," he begins by asking what in a person's life could account for the mythic narrative. If myth represents a response to an event in one's life, how does the response point back to its stimulus? Buber does not search for a meaning "obtained" in the myth or a solution that "has been gained," but rather an originating event.13

He locates that event in every person's encounter with the other creatures of the world. Human beings, for Buber, live in two ways: as partners with creation and as manipulators of it. When a person learns that authentic human existence depends upon dialogic partnership, not manipulation, creation myths arise. The context in which a person learns that lesson differs from individual to individual. Any aspect of the

world may reveal itself to a human person as
in need of dialogue. Creation myths begin
with such an experience, an experience
teaching that "the human lot is decided by
the dialogue between God and man, the
reality of which fills the whole life and
the whole world...."14 The mythic retelling
of creation stories reawakens awareness of
that event. Once before in human history,
and thus ever again in that history, human
beings heard a call to decision making,
faced the need in turn to accept the
responsibility of that call or deny its
force. Unlike Eliade, Buber does not insist
that the myth recreates the original event.
Instead, he argues that one person's
experience of the need for dialogue, for the
decision either to enter into partnership
with others or to manipulate them, becomes,
in myth, an invitation to all others to make
the same decision.

   Buber traces creation myths to human
experiences with failure as well as with
success. The tales of Adam, Eve, Cain
(which Buber spells Kain), Abel and their
descendents reflect events in a single life.
The author of these stories, he thinks,
creates the narrative out of the complexity
of one person's encounter with the world.
This author, Buber insists, "must have
experienced Adam as well as Kain in the
abyss of his own heart."15 He discovers in
the stories about creation an evocation of
that experience in which the possibility of
evil overwhelms human consciousness. From
this perspective the biblical myths do not
explain evil but rather acknowledge its

presence. Buber contends that the biblical myths by making this acknowledgement arouse a modern response to the evil still present as an inevitable temptation.16

MYTH, GENESIS, AND GOOD AND EVIL

Buber's exposition of the myths of Genesis recapitulates his general theory of good and evil. That theory provides the necessary background for understanding the biblical exegesis he offers in his commentaries on the Genesis narratives. According to that theory, the mythic evocations of good and evil reveal how "the factual life of the human person" consists of "two qualities of totally different structure." Recognizing the "factual life" helps describe those structures, although without demanding a response to them, as does myth.17 The biblical account uses myth to recreate God's demand that each person "turn" toward God and seek direction rather than drift aimlessly, "seduced" by lack of direction. Human beings encounter a divine call but often refuse to acknowledge it.

The story of creation for Buber reminds people of their role in creation, their ability to act as "helpers and companions" to the creator.18 The structure of good consists of readiness to act, of a willingness to choose in each new context. The structure of "evil," however, consists in detachment, in severing the connection

between one's primal drives and life itself.
Doing good means making decisions; evil
grows from a lack of choice, from allowing
impulses and urges rather than decision to
determine action.19 The central act that
Buber exalts occurs when a person turns
toward the divine purpose of creation. The
Hebrew phrase <u>teshuva</u> and its German
equivalent, <u>Umkehr</u>, describe what he
considers the key mythic event.

Philosophically, the terms suggest that
when humanity returns to its original
purpose, it fulfills its true nature. In
that way a Platonic view of a return to the
ideal combines with the Jewish emphasis on
turning toward the God of creation.20 On
this account, historically, and in the
present, people have felt bewildered by the
chaos of imaginative possibilities. They
drift in accordance with impulses of the
moment. Repeatedly, however, they recognize
a call reminding them of the need to choose
a direction, to decide on a course of
action.
The creation narratives recall an event
of decision making, an occurrence in one
person's life commemorated as a story about
primal time. Buber concludes from the myths
that "the humanly right is ever the service
of the single person who realises [sic] the
right uniqueness purposed for him in his
creation." He also contends that this ethos
"has its origin in a revelation ... of
human service to the goal of creation," so
that only mythic tales can convey the nature
of the good as a responsive event to a
divine call.21 The event of the turning

that Buber finds in the biblical myths
recurs throughout Jewish literature. Buber
alludes to an ancient Rabbinic teaching: a
person should learn to serve God with both
the good inclination and the evil one. He
wonders what such an injunction might mean
and concludes that the "evil" inclination
has been misnamed. In itself, the
inclination is not intrinsically bad or
wicked. Human decision determines whether
it serves or good or evil ends. Buber
claims that it becomes evil

> because man separates it from its
> compassion and in this condition of
> independence makes an idol of precisely
> that which was intended to serve him.
> Man's task, therefore,is not to
> extirpate the evil urge, but to reunite
> it with the good.22

Buber makes three points in this short
statement. So-called evil has no intrinsic
wickedness to it. When linked with
"compassion," when part of the entire field
of human thought, action, and choosing, this
impulse acts productively and positively.
Second, the impulse becomes evil only when
it is separated and made into an "idol."
Somehow, Buber suggests, by separating this
impulse from the whole of the human
situation, a person begins to worship it, to
allow the separated impulse to substitute
for the totality from which it has been
severed. By isolating this one impulse
that in essence acts for human good, people
become slaves to their own inner forces.
Evil refers to that aspect of the human

personality that when projected outward as a
force on its own masters the very humanity
that produces it. Third, Buber points to a
resolution, a means of redeeming evil and
returning it to its positive function by
reuniting it with the total human
personality. This view of evil sees it as
an alienated part of human nature that can
be reclaimed for human productivity.

This focus on "good and evil" provides
the universal aspect of Buber's
interpretation of the Genesis myths. That
interpretation argues that these myths
preserve a common human memory: that of how
evil begins. They point to the
possibilities of human action for either
self-realization or self-destruction. These
myths of good and evil bring together the
varied intuitions arising from human life.
They unite the intellectual intuition people
have about the world around them with the
experiential knowledge they gain about
themselves. As statements about the world
of the past, myths confirm a public
knowledge accessible to everyone. As
stimulants to personal involvement, they
awaken a uniquely individual way of knowing.

This judgment shows how myths of good
and evil illustrate Buber's general
understanding of myth as the memory of an
event. The myth recalls an event that once
occurred in the human past. It appeals to
those living in the present to learn from
and emulate the experience encapsulated in
the myth. Insofar as myth makes present
once again a crucial event in human history,

it confirms ideas about the world. Insofar
as it addresses each person's unique
situation and demands action in the present,
it speaks to personal knowledge about one's
own self. Buber traces this idea about the
world to an individual's encounter with
evil. The myths of Genesis differ from
other creation myths because the personal
event they recall differs from those
enshrined in the other myths. The
distinctiveness of the biblical view springs
from its distinctive core: a remembered
human event in which a person encountered
evil. Confronting Jewish myth with opposing
myths means discerning the specific event it
recollects. Myths may be equally true but
point to different primal occurrences; thus
different myths complement one another.
Nevertheless, Buber considers biblical myth
primary since "the process need not
necessarily go further than the first
stage." While Iranian myth portrays a real
and unfortunate human possibility, biblical
myth shows the challenge awaiting each
person and the way to avoid going beyond the
earliest forms of temptation to evil.23

GOOD AND EVIL AND "I AND THOU"

Buber enunciates his view of good and
evil in his introduction to I-Thou thinking,
I and Thou. According to that work, evil
stems from indecision. When human beings
evade their responsibility, they fall into
evil. When human beings make a decisive
choice, they avoid the trap of evil.

Indecision leads to detachment, isolation, and self-absorption. Evil occurs when people move through their lives without conscious choosing, without weighing the consequences of their own deeds. Evil springs up when the selfish drive, inherently unobjectionable, separates from the human awareness of community, from "the plasma of communal life," and allows it to grow untempered by relationship with others.24 Since the impulse is not by nature evil, it can be used for beneficent purposes. The evil impulse is not intrinsically wicked. It represents the claims of a choice not yet taken, an option not yet realized. When people choose consciously, they acknowledge the good even in that which they reject. To act truly, Buber suggests, entails funneling "all the force of the other," of the path not chosen, into the action that in fact has been chosen. Evil lies in seeing only one side of the picture, in affirming only one part of the entire whole.25

Nahum Glatzer, whose close personal association with Buber makes him a sensitive anthologist and interpreter of his work, contends that Buber's evaluation of biblical myth springs from his I-Thou philosophy.26 Glatzer demonstrates the affinity between Buber's reflection on the quest of "realization of the I-Thou relation" and the biblical language of events and concrete situations. Buber seems to find biblical ways of speaking generally, and prophetic language particularly, congenial to his own philosophy. In the case of the theme of the

creation myths, however, Glatzer suggests,
both Buber and the Bible as read by Buber
share a singular blindness. Buber, whether
as creative philosopher or as exegete,
"seemingly ignores, or at least
underestimates, the power of evil in the
world .... To Buber, the biblical attitude
to creation precludes the independent
existence of any evil power."27 Thus Buber
finds his own aversion to evil as a positive
force in the biblical writings. Buber
claims the reverse as true: his view of good
and evil derives from the Bible. His
explanation of good and evil in Genesis 1-3
sketches three stages: in the first stage
human beings confront the vast possibilities
presented by free choice; in the second
stage, overwhelmed by those possibilities,
they allow imagination and impulse to
determine their actions; at last, they turn
from impulse to decision.

GENESIS 1:1-3:24

The biblical creation stories represent
the culmination of a long and complex
tradition. While the evidence of influence
from nonbiblical sources cannot be denied,
those sources appear in altered guise. Most
scholars consider Genesis 1:1-2:4 a separate
narrative from the Eden story. The two
stories, however, intertwine so that now
"despite the difference in approach,
emphasis, and hence also in authorship, the
fact remains that the subject matter is

ultimately the same in both versions."28
Genesis begins with divine creativity.
Genesis 1:1-2:4, usually thought to come
from a late priestly source, suggests that
humanity receives a commission to cultivate
its image and become godlike. In that
version, everything occurs according to a
clear divine plan. God begins the creation
by distinguishing between light and
darkness. Each successive day brings a more
complex division among created beings or a
more complex set of creations. The creation
of human beings plays a distinctive role in
this plan. Only humanity shares a common
"likeness" with the creator and receives a
peculiar directive: not merely to propagate
itself but also to serve as the rule or
measure of everything else. God takes the
initiative and creates humanity, male and
female at the same time. Humanity is to the
world what God is to all of creation: the
symbol of its true purpose, the standard of
natural life.

The story has moved from a simple
division among existing things to a
consideration of the major yardstick in all
creation: humanity. The tale culminates
with a divine blessing. On the seventh day,
everything works as it should, and God
enjoys a cessation of work. God stops, but
the world goes on. This, relates the story,
is why the seventh day is special in God's
sight. Throughout the story, punctuating it
at distinctive points, the narrative cites
divine approbation of the world, "And God
saw that it was good," finally concluding,

"And the divine saw all creation, and, behold, it was very good."

Beginning in Genesis 2:4b, however, another story seems to unfold. In this story, God begins creating with an unproductive garden, since agriculture apparently depends on human work. God, experimentally, creates a human being from the soil. (Buber notes that the term "human" comes from the Latin humus, meaning earth just as the Hebrew name given the human created is adam, from the term for earth, adama.) Because that human being seems lonely, God decides it needs a partner. One after another, God creates the animals and brings them to the human, who names each one of them but does not consider any a fit partner.29 Finally, God puts the human to sleep and, from its rib, makes a female. At this point new names enter the story "ish" (or man) and "isha" (woman); henceforward even the generic "adam" seems to refer only to the male. The text comments that, since woman was taken from man, a man must leave his parents to follow his woman and cleave to her.

The story does not end happily here. Instead, tragedy occurs. The human was permitted to eat from all the trees in the garden except two: the tree of the knowledge of good and evil and the tree of life, warned that on the day of eating from it, death would follow. While never explaining the relationship among the man, woman, and the animals, the story quickly moves to a confrontation between one creature, the

naked/clever (the word used can have both
meanings) snake. This description is apt
since the snake entices the woman to reach
out for cleverness, and she thereby sees
that she is naked. The story tells that the
serpent suggests to the female human being
that God has forbidden her to eat from any
tree in the garden. She, of course,
contradicts the snake and notes that the
prohibition extends only to the fruit of one
tree. She, however, adds a touch of her own
that complicates the choice further by
claiming that God forbade not only eating
the fruit but handling it as well. The
snake tempts her by suggesting that she will
not die from the fruit but will rather
"become like divinity, knowing good and
evil." The woman looks longingly at the
tree and "sees" that its fruit is good to
eat. She eats from it and shares the fruit
with the man. After eating, the two become
aware that they are naked (notice the
artistic pun: they become aware that they
resemble the snake). Other, less immediate,
consequences follow. God adds special
privations to the natural results following
the attainment of the knowledge of good and
evil.

These consequences, usually understood
as punishments, focus on the role played by
each participant in the tale: the snake need
never labor for food but must eat the dust
of the earth and bear an eternal enmity with
humanity; the woman must "labor" in pain,
giving birth to children; and men must
"labor" in sweat, plowing the fields.
Although God pronounces these facts of life,

they flow logically from the deed itself.
The snake's cleverness leads to its own
degradation and alienation from humanity.
The woman's imagination leads her to accept
the pain of childbirth willingly. The man's
subservience to the woman provides the
foundation for that necessity and eros Freud
called the basis of civilization and its
discontents.

This division of labor in the aftermath
of human disobedience deserves detailed
analysis.30 God's decrees do not seem
arbitrary punishments but rather statements
of the human condition articulated in clear
relationship to the story as told. Here the
consequences of refusing decision take place
in the realm between partners in dialogue.
When dialogue becomes monologue, when deceit
rather than truth forms the subject of
speech, relationships suffer. Humanity and
the animals no longer enjoy companionship
but maintain an uneasy enmity. Women no
longer live as helpmates to men but waver in
a tense polarity of power: they are needed
as child bearers but have sexual passions
which make them dependent on men. Men
themselves, once at one with the soil that
gave them birth, must now live out an
ambivalent relationship with it. They
"work" the soil that reluctantly yields
briars for the laborer.

An epilogue adds a distinctive, and
probably once separate, note. Here the
consequences of the act are historical
rather than relational. Remarking that
human beings disobeyed one commandment, God

ponders their fate, eventually concluding that they must be exiled from their garden "lest they eat of the tree of life and become immortal." This prohibition combines with a very different kind of act as God clothes the man and the woman with animal skins. The story has the trappings of a ritual. God formally approaches the human couple, presents them with a gift, and assigns them their duties. This act may be called "a significant symbolic act that firmly distinguishes humans from the divine."31 Human beings, far from receiving punishment, emerge from the Garden of Eden with new dignity, status, and purpose. The woman, however, gets the best of the deal. At the end of the story she has received a real name, Eve, and declares, "I have got me a son from the Lord!" (Notice that the man is left out of this!)

The entire epilogue depends on an interaction of opposites, combining compassion with hostility, power with vulnerability. In effect, the narrative serves a single purpose: that of showing how human beings prepare for their mortal task. Were human beings to be unclothed, they would face the challenges of life with too great a vulnerability to hope for success. Were they to live forever, they could not reconcile themselves to the continuing disparity between their continued failure and their visions of success. Were women not given over to the sexual power of men, the race would disappear. Were women not given the power to name their children, they might not accede to their tasks. Taken as a whole, the final section of the story suggests that although the first humans erred and failed to make a decisive choice, new choices await them in the future; they have been better prepared for these choices than they were for the first decision that they evaded.

BUBER'S VIEW OF GENESIS

Buber's exegesis of the creation story illustrates his method of biblical exegesis. He traces the story of Adam in the Garden back to a core human meeting with the divine. The tale grows out of an individual's discovery of the choices of life. The experience of life's order followed by the chaos of social reality provides a biographical foundation for the biblical story.32 Buber thinks of the narrative as one that arises when a person sought to provide a "stammering account" of a personal discovery. He claims that a person necessarily stammers when describing the universe as "a chronological series of commands and 'works' from the divine workshop." Nevertheless, only such a chronology "does justice" to the reality that the person encounters: a reality that makes a demand, that moves from an "eternity" in which all remains static to a "history" in which actions play decisive roles. From this perspective the story of creation in Genesis 1:1-2:5 records how a person learned that the world is not eternal, that history is <u>not</u> eternal return, and that every individual act makes a difference in life. As Buber puts it, the myth fulfills "the task of stating the mystery of how time springs from eternity, and the world comes from that which is not world."33

Buber refuses to distinguish this part of the creation story from the narrative of Eden. (Biblical scholars usually separate Genesis 1:1-2:4 from the narrative in 2:5-3:28 as the work of two different authors.) The first story sets the stage for the second by establishing the reality and therefore the requirement for decision making. The second story describes evil as the evasion of that responsibility. That evasion, Buber suggests, arises from an abortive attempt to fulfill the ideal inherent in the first story: the ideal of imitation of the divine. The first story implies that humanity becomes like God through making decisions in the world. The second story, however, describes an alternative approach to the same goal. The experience in that story reflects an attempt to achieve the image by "seizing" it and leaping out of the human predicament to usurp divinity. The second approach seeks to perfect the "image" of God within humanity by arrogating divine power rather than by exercising divine discretion.

Both stories reflect on a single experience: they give "witness to the spirit's will to perfection and to the command to serve the spirit." Creation

itself, then, justifies two urges. The
impulse to become like God expresses itself
sometimes as an obedient fulfillment of
human potential and sometimes as a demonic
usurpation of divine reality. The
description of creation, then, provides
humanity with a goal and a warning: the goal
of becoming like God and the warning against
attempting to do so in ways other than
through perfection the image within the
human self.34 Since for Buber myth arises
from an event, he must uncover the core
experience to which this story responds.
Certainly he recognizes that the story
contains remnants of an ancient "myth of the
envy and vengeance of gods." Nevertheless,
he rejects that ancient myth as the basis
for the story. He looks instead at a
historical experience. One person, at one
specific time, encountered the boundaries of
freedom and recognized personal mortality.
This person stood both as the member of a
social group, that of ancient Israel, and as
an individual facing the general truths of
human existence.

The myth, Buber explains, shapes its
message in accordance with both aspects of
life; therefore the text uses the names
"YHVH Elohim" for God, combining a reference
to the deity who leads Israel in its history
with the universal divine force pervading
reality. As Buber puts it, "This God is the
sole possessor of the power both of creation
and of destiny." The individual experienced
the meaning of life as a combination of
social destiny and natural obligation, of
the limitations imposed by society and those

inherent in nature. The view of God in
these two stories seems "alien to the style
of the rest of the Bible" precisely because
it combines an experience of the individual
as a member of society with that same
individual's experience as a human being who
shares a common humanity with all other
people.35

The first story establishes the
generally human aspects of the formative
event: people face a cosmic obligation to
imitate the divine. The second story begins
with a more specific context: that of the
farmer tied to the soil. The connection
between the name for humanity given in this
text, adam, and that of the earth, the
adama, implies the nature of the ties
binding human beings to the soil. People
must treat the soil with respect and honor;
the soil also has responsibilities and "has
to answer for the offenses of man who
springs from and is dependent on it." The
historical memory at the core of the story
derives from a farmer's experience. Not
only have human beings come from the earth,
but they can also pollute and destroy it.
Not only does the soil nourish human life,
it can also thwart human intentions.

Buber emphasizes that the myth evokes a
person's duties to the land and of the
limits on a person's ability to transform
the land. Buber suggests that a person once
experienced the force of this mutual
obligation and created the myth out of
reflections on that experience. Not only
biblical myth but biblical ritual as well

preserves this experience. Buber illustrates this claim by pointing to the laws of tithing in Deuteronomy 26. The farmer must tithe his harvest, offer first fruits to the divinity, and remove corruption from the land. Although apparently only ritualistic, these actions reinforce the bonds of dependency linking humanity and the soil.36 What myth conveys through narrative, ritual communicates through actions. For Buber, the first two chapters of Genesis record a person's experience with the process of decision making. That person recognized an obligation toward the world through its order and perfection. The myth preserves as well a sense of obligation deriving not from the pattern of creation but from relations among the creatures. Human beings and the earth make claims on each another. Two sources of constraint shape a person's experience: the ideal, as established in the perfect blueprint of creation, and the actual, as encountered in the dialogue between that person and the natural environment. At this stage in the story "good and evil" do not yet take shape. Only their presupposition does: the human ability to choose, an ability brought to actuality through real decisions, through tests of humanity's use of it.

Buber understands the "command" placed on humanity, the caution against eating of the tree of the knowledge of good and evil, as arising from the memory of such a test. The historical event at the heart of the myth grew out of a discovery made in the midst of a crisis. The story conveys the intensity of that crisis as well as its presuppositions. The crisis begins because people face an ambiguous reality. The story, Buber suggests, shows that God does not "impose his will" on his creatures. The author of the myth makes it clear that a human being must make real choices; the demands of God implanted in creation itself and the demands of creatures out of their own needs often present people with conflicting possibilities among which they must choose. People may "accede to their creator or refuse themselves to him." This freedom provides the basic requirement for any choosing, any decision making, since without such a prohibition no decision would be either required or possible.37

DECIDING FOR DIRECTION

     After the moral dilemma has been set, the author evokes the decisive experience: that of temptation and its consequences. While couched in mythic terms, the story for Buber records a real event in the past in which a person, overwhelmed by the temptations flowing from reality, experienced a powerful ambivalence. One impulse led toward decisive choice; the other led to lassitude and a refusal to choose. Out of the conflict of these emotions an author translated the event from historical to mythical language. The freedom and obligation to decide depend upon an honest recognition of the choice presented. As the story of the test proceeds, Buber suggests that the protagonists move farther and farther away from true choice. Both the snake and the woman use exaggeration to misrepresent God's word. They merely "play" with the word of God. They abandon reality for fantasy and carry out the rest of the incident which occurs in what Buber calls "a strange, dreamlike kind of contemplation." The woman "sees that the fruit tastes good." Buber remarks that this quality could hardly be "seen." The actuality of existence has been transformed by imagination. Fantasy rather than reality motivates the action from this point forwards.

The historical experience at the heart of the story lies in this intoxication by imagination. The author reflects on the effects of such a drunken perception of the world. Buber claims that the story makes this imaginative intoxication the basis of a "dream-longing" that motivates the woman to eat the forbidden fruit. When the man eats as well, Buber also attributes this act to imagination. The man has lost touch with reality and acts "truly in dream lassitude." Throughout this "act" of disobedience none of the characters has taken the true prohibition seriously or acted out of conscious rebelliousness. "The whole incident," Buber concludes, "is built out of play and dream." The story reflects how an imaginative reconstruction of reality can overwhelm an honest appraisal of life.38 The story, however, does not end with this

moment at which a human being discovered the
terrifying power of imagination. The story
continues as the man and woman are
confronted by God and receive new
directives. The significance of those new
directives lie in their relationship to the
problems raised by imagination; they point
to a means for moving from dream into
reality.

Buber looks carefully at the biblical
narrative in Genesis 3 to discover whether
positive action indeed occurs. Instead, he
claims that the text records ever-increasing
complications and prevarications that
prevent true decision making. The key to
understanding the passage lies in the "tree"
from which humanity eats. If by eating
humanity gained the ability to make true
choices, to decide for the good and against
evil, then that ability must lie outside of
natural human ability. People must decide
to reach beyond themselves into the sphere
of good and evil. Such a reading
contradicts Buber's interpretation of the
myth. It cannot record an experience of
<u>falling</u> into evil but rather of <u>choosing</u> it.
Buber anticipates the problems raised by
such a reading of the text and responds by
insisting that evil remains indecision even
after humanity has attained godlike
knowledge. He suggests that the declaration
must be understood ironically. While
humanity may "know" good and evil, it cannot
create it. God knows good and evil as a
part of his essential being: "He encompasses
them, untouched by them." Human beings,
however, can "know" only at a distance;

humanity "capable only of begetting and
giving birth, not of creating," can feel
only the conflict of the opposites, only
their tension and not their resolution.39
The very meaning of the term "knowing good
and evil" supports the view that humanity
only increased its pain and anxiety by
achieving it.

Buber reviews the varied explanations
commentators give to this term and rejects
such common interpretations as those of
sexual knowledge and general cognition.
Instead, he cites evidence from other
biblical texts to show that the term implies
the knowledge of alternative options.
Humanity can now evaluate imaginative
possibilities as well as actual choices.
Humanity now lies helpless before the
onslaught of imagination. Human beings know
not only what they are but also what they
might become.40 Choice becomes even more
difficult in this situation. Buber explains
the new dilemma as the source of shame:
recognizing "this so-being" in relationship
to "an intended shall-be." Human beings,
then, have fallen into a chaos of
imagination. God must contend with a
humanity constantly shaken by fantasies that
have no basis in factual life. The so-
called "punishments" with which Genesis 3
concludes provide an antidote for the human
imagination.

Buber thinks that the conclusion of the
Eden story reflects the experience of a
person who, having fallen into imagination
and suffered its consequences, discovered a

continuing support for decision making and a
guidance for genuine choosing. The story
affirms that even if people must suffer
painful consequences from their dream-like
lassitude, they can still find direction and
can be rescued from their helplessness.
While the consequences of a person's lack of
direction may be painful, Buber thinks that
Genesis 3 refuses to call them punishment.
God responds to human failure by providing
new opportunities for development. Although
human beings fail one task, they can
confront new ones. Buber therefore stresses
that the biblical story does not imply
"original sin." God allows each person,
including the main actors in the myth, new
opportunities to make true decisions.

   Buber uses the second set of
consequences that Genesis 3 attributes to
the eating of the forbidden fruit to
reinforce his argument. God provides humans
with clothes while expelling them from
Paradise. These two actions seem
inconsistent. God shows compassion by the
first and, apparently, hostility by the
second. Buber, however, considers both
equally beneficial since both point to the
dynamic and creative aspects of human life.
Buber claims that the expulsion from Eden
reveals divine compassion. God, Buber
imagines, seeks to prevent "the thoughtless
human creature" from becoming immortal and
thereby being destined for interminable
suffering. Lest that occur, God grants
humanity the gift of mortality. Death
becomes "a haven, the knowledge of which
brings comfort."   Both men and women

advance beyond their fixed limitations and grow towards decision making.41 The Eden story recounts a human experience: faced with ambiguous duties, overpowered by imagination, a human person discovered that lack of direction combined with imagination leads to disaster but that even disaster does not leave a person totally bereft of guidance and support. The myth exposes the true choice lying before each person: that between defective intention and true intention, between indecisive and decisive choosing.42

GENESIS AND BUBER'S VIEW OF MYTH

Buber's explanation of the Genesis myths chronicles what he discovers as the formative event from which it evolved. Although narrated as a tale about primeval times, the myth really conveys how one person experienced life's temptations and the call to avoid them. Buber's emphasis on the historicity of the stories goes beyond this general description. He suggests a specific historical setting for the formative event, even if some of the narrative materials the author uses may derive from an earlier period. Buber claims that the myth took on its final form toward the end of biblical history after Israel had experienced first the success and then the destruction of its national life. The historical event undergone by the original author of the myth took on significance

because it addressed the reality of the
Jewish community. The older elements in the
story combined with the new perception to
awaken a distinctive way of interacting with
the world. Thus the creation narrative,
while "in its original content an ancient
composition," came to play a late
theological role.43

Israel began its career as a kingdom
during days of crisis under Saul and David.
Later, under David's son Solomon the nation
evolved strong and complex institutional
structures. That institutional religion,
according to Buber, led to a decline in
religious sensitivity. Prophetic leaders
suggested new ways of understanding divine
demands but went unheeded until the
Babylonians decisively defeated the Judean
nation and exiled its leaders to Babylonia.
The exile of Judeans to Babylonia created a
crisis that forced the people to reevaluate
their tradition. The Jews in exile turned
to their ancient resources and read them
with new meaning. Buber locates the
formation of the Genesis myths in this late
period in which earlier material takes on a
renewed importance. While the cosmic myth
may well have roots in early Israelite
religion, it remains unmentioned until the
later prophets. It takes shape in the
Genesis narrative as a rather awkward
synthesis of traditional sources. This
synthesis, however, reflects a genuine, and
creative, human event.

Jews in exile discovered that "every
creation, foundations, blessing,

commandment, judgement, punishment,
election, assistance and covenant-making in
early history is a kind of revelation."44
The stories begin as an expression of that
new discovery. Taking form as myth, the
stories evoke the possibility of discerning
direction and purpose in a period of
questioning and confusion. Written for and
by Jews who confronted crucial decisions in
their personal and national lives, the myth
invites a rereading of ancient texts and
provides reassurance that others before
them, when facing such decisions, met the
single divinity of all creation and found
support through that meeting. The myth
tells the story of one person's discovery.
As a myth, however, it initiates a process
by which others can imitate that person's
experience and discover anew the same
reassurance that the first author found.
The Genesis myths then, evoke a call, a
demand, a sense of response for all its
readers, even modern ones. At every stage a
person hears the invitation to "turn," to
abandon indecision and to move into the
structure of good. This message clearly
parallels that of Buber's own understanding
of evil in relationship to I-You meeting.
He decodes the Genesis myth as an example of
evil's potential for good that is central to
this own philosophy.

The myth portrays a vivid experience of
the event of a "fall," by which Buber means
a refusal to exercise one's inherent ability
make a decision. It offers a case study of
human evasion of choice and its
consequences. Buber claims that the

Genesis myth evokes the moment at which "the evolving human person" faces "the plenitude of possibility" as an overwhelming and distracting force. Each of these possibilities demands human attention. The indecisive person feels the attraction of each alternative and therefore sways "in the dizzy whirl" of temptation which leads to an uneasy compromise of a false suppression of alternatives—false because "wholeness can never be achieved ... where downtrodden appetites lurk in the corners."45 The myth presents modern readers, just as it presented its earlier readers, with an alternative possibility. Despite their weakness and vulnerability, they can risk decision making because of a divine presence supporting and guiding them.

When interpreting the Genesis myths, Buber repeats his earlier contentions about evil. These myths confront people today with the truth about evil: it "cannot be done with the whole soul" because it represents "a lack of direction." They testify that only using the "evil impulse" for God's purpose solves the problem of human indecision. The myths of Genesis provide an object lesson in the anthropology of good and evil to which Buber had already pointed in I and Thou.46 By heeding the myths, people evoke the call to decision addressed at each level of their existence and stand again ready to answer that call. Buber considers the story a paradigm for modern actions, not merely a memory of an unrepeatable historical event. Modern audiences discover their own potential by heeding the myth of the earlier writer. The story reveals to them their own biographical evolution as it traces the events experienced by the hero of the myth.

Buber's claim that the myths of Genesis portray the "prehistorical origin of that which we call evil" seems similar to Eliade's view of myth. In both cases a myth tells how the problematic condition of human life began, how people lost their original perfection, and how they might acquire it once again.47 Like Eliade, Buber insists on the modern relevance of ancient myth. The historical emphasis that Buber adds, however, changes the perspective taken to myth. Myth does not require the modern person to return to an earlier condition; myth does not demand a re-enactment of an earlier event. Instead, for Buber, myth requires a new act, a deed born in this moment, not one that simply recreates an earlier one. That difference seems crucial. While Buber perceives a similarity between the remembered event of the myth and the present possibility for a renewal of it, he also accentuates differences. The modern who reads an ancient myth must take responsibility for initiating a new action. Such moderns cannot merely accept the script of the myth as their own. They must utilize the peculiarities of their present moment as the point of departure for their imitation of the ancient myth.

Buber's analysis of the power of myth moves beyond Eliade's universalism. Eliade's inclusive studies merge Australian,

African, Christian, and humanistic sources
without analyzing the differences dividing
them. Buber, however, looks at the events
recorded by single traditions. While Buber
has a universal theory of myth as the
response to a formative event, he places it
in a specific cultural setting. In the
Genesis myths he succeeds precisely because
he points to a narrative coherence that
integrates its psychological, structural,
and historical elements without abandoning a
general and universal understanding of the
function of myth. Moreover, the particular
myth in question functions to illuminate a
general human dilemma: that of human choice.
Buber's insistence on the particular
historical origin of the myth adds to,
rather than detracts from, its universal
significance. Buber's interpretation of
myth as reflection upon an individual's
experience opens more possibilities for
modern readers than Eliade's because he
allows a greater flexibility of response.
Eliade's approach reduces diverse myths to a
single meaning, implying that moderns must
accept that single message. Buber, however,
takes the myth as a stimulus for new actions
that, because their cultural setting differs
from the original event, are different from
it.

NOTES

1. Mircea Eliade, <u>Myth and Reality</u>, trans. Willard R. Trask (New York: Harper and Row, 1963), pp. 5-6.

2. <u>Ibid</u>., p. 91.

3. <u>Ibid</u>., pp. 192-93.

4. Martin Buber, <u>Israel and the World: Essays in a Time of Crisis</u> (New York: Schocken, 1948), p. 32.

5. Eliade, <u>Myth and Reality</u>, pp. 111-13.

6. Mircea Eliade, <u>Images and Symbols: Studies in Religious Symbolism</u>, trans. Philip Mairet (New York: Sheed and Ward, 1969), p. 73; see the entire discussion, pp. 67-91.

7. Abraham Joshua Heschel, <u>The Sabbath: Its Meaning for Modern Man</u> (New York: Farrar, Straus and Young, 1951), pp. 16, 100-01.

8. Mircea Eliade, <u>The Two and the One</u>, trans. J. M. Cohen (New York: Harper and Row, 1965), pp. 85-88. He notes "beliefs, myths and unsystematized ideas that are at the same time archaic and modern, pagan and Christian" (p. 88). One could add that they are both biblical and nonbiblical.

9. Paul Ricoeur, <u>The Symbolism of Evil</u>, trans. Emerson Buchanan (Boston: Beacon Press, 1967), p. 242; see the entire discussion on pp. 232-78.

10. See Martin Buber, <u>Good and Evil: Two Interpretations--Right and Wrong, Images of Good and Evil</u>, trans. Ronald Gregor Smith and Michael Bullock (New York: Scribner's, 1953), p. 66.

11. <u>Ibid</u>., pp. 63-66.

12. <u>Ibid</u>., pp. 118, 124.

13. <u>Ibid</u>., pp. 100, 116.

14. Martin Buber, <u>The Prophetic Faith</u>, trans. Carlyle Witton-Davies (New York: Macmillan, 1949), pp. 85-94; the selections quoted are from pp. 88 and 90; the section continues beyond the creation story to include a discussion of Cain and of the Tower of Babel; since these texts are treated more fully in <u>Good and Evil</u>, the following summary of Buber's views will draw on that work.

15. <u>Ibid</u>., p. 131.

16. See <u>ibid</u>., pp. 64-66.

17. <u>Ibid</u>., p. 64.

18. Martin Buber, <u>I and Thou</u>, trans. and intro. Walter Kaufmann (New York: Scribner's 1970), p. 130.

19. Ibid., pp. 98-101.

20. See the discussion by Theodore Dreyfus, "Understanding the Term 'Umkehr' in the Philosophy of Martin Buber [Hebrew]," Daat 9 (1982): 71-74.

21. Buber, Good and Evil, p. 142.

22. Ibid., p. 95.

23. Ibid., p. 120.

24. Buber, I and Thou, p. 98.

25. Ibid., p. 101.

26. Nahum N. Glatzer, "Aspects of Martin Buber's Thought," in Modern Judaism 1:1 (1981), pp. 1-16.

27. Ibid., p. 11.

28. E.A. Speiser, Genesis, Anchor Bible (Garden City, NY: Doubleday), p. 19. See the entire discussion of the creation stories on pp. 5-28, and also pp. liii-lviii.

29. Martin Buber, On Zion: The History of an Idea, foreword Nahum N. Glatzer; trans. Stanley Godman (New York: Schocken, 1973), pp. 10-11.

30. See the suggestive and controversial analysis provided by the feminist scholar of biblical archeology Carol L. Meyers in her Discovering Eve: Ancient

Israelite Women in Context (New York:
Oxford University Press, 1988), pp. 89–
108.

31. See Robert A. Oden, The Bible Without
Theology: The Theological Tradition and
Alternatives to It (San Francisco:
Harper, 1987), p. 104; see the entire
essay pp. 92–105. Oden's alternative to
theological interpretations of the Bible
leads him to emphasize the literary
implications of the mythic genre.

32. See Buber, Good and Evil, p. 124.

33. Buber, Israel and the World, pp. 99–100.

34. Buber, Israel and the World, pp. 73–99.

35. Buber, Good and Evil, pp. 67–68.

36. Buber, On Zion, pp.3–18.

37. Buber, Good and Evil, pp. 67–68.

38. Ibid., pp. 68–70.

39. Ibid., pp. 74–77.

40. Ibid., pp. 70–77.

41. Ibid., pp. 77–80.

42. Ibid., pp. 81–89; compare The Prophetic
Faith, pp. 90–91.

43. Buber, The Prophetic Faith, p. 89.

44. Ibid., p. 88.

45. Buber, <u>Good and Evil</u>, pp. 125-29.

46. <u>Ibid</u>., pp. 130-31.

47. Buber, "Foreword" to <u>Good and Evil</u>; compare Eliade's statements about the "fall" and "nostalgia for Paradise" in his <u>Myths, Dreams, and Mysteries</u>, pp. 59-72.

Chapter 5   The Exodus

THE SOCIAL MEANING OF MYTH

Buber's analysis of Genesis 1-3 focuses on the experience of one person, of an individual whose I-You meeting illuminated the life of an entire Jewish community. Other thinkers focus on the social setting of religious myth even when they recognize the importance of an individual's experience. Such a focus often occurs when theorists seek to explain the connection between myth and ritual. These theorists, as Robert Segal suggests, study "the social function of myth ... the public active role it plays in society."[1] Theodor Reik, for example, understands the myths in Genesis as references to an ancient ritual. Following the reconstruction offered by Sigmund Freud, Reik claims that psychoanalysis reveals "the truth of myth" and explains its relationship to ritual. Myths, he suggests, preserve memories from ancient times. The memories

so preserved recall both an actual social
event and the human response to that event.
Freud studied the interpenetration of myths,
expressed as totemism and ritual, taking the
form of prohibitions and taboos. He
suggested that both refer back to a primal
act of civil patricide. An ancient human
"horde" murdered its father and, coping with
the guilt of this act, created myths and
rituals to justify, legitimate, and
sublimate the deed. The various religious
traditions persisting until modern times
still retain traces of this original act.
"The totem religion," Freud explains, "had
issued from the sense of guilt of the sons
as an attempt to palliate this feeling...."[2]

Freud's fascinating reconstruction of a
psychological condition leaves the
connection between totemic beliefs and
totemic practices unclear. What Claude
Lévi-Strauss, one of the most profound
anthropological analysts of totemism, sees
as the "difficulty arising from the fact
that so-called totemic institutions include
not only the conceptual systems we have
chosen to consider but also rules of action"
remains obscure in Freud's analysis.[3] Reik
remedies this problem by looking
specifically at rituals. While he takes
Freud's pyschological interpretation of myth
as a point of departure, he also engages in
what he calls "archeological psychology"
that discovers the rituals for which myth
serves as a script. Those rituals express
the psychological truths from which humanity
tries to hide.[4]

Applying this approach to Genesis, Reik offers a theory of the meaning of the "tree of the knowing of good and evil" that interprets the entire story as the script of a great ritual. The ritual of initiation, celebrated by the circumcision of the initiate, reveals its psychological meaning through this myth that grows out of it. Reik builds his case from the same material that Buber uses for his: the correspondence of name between <u>adam</u> and <u>adama</u>, the problematic meaning of the "tree of the knowing of good and evil," and the tasks assigned humanity after eating from that tree. Despite these resemblances, however, Reik's reconstruction of the myth differs radically from Buber's by focusing on its social and psychological meaning.5 While Buber and Reik differ about the Genesis myths, they do not differ so radically as one might suspect. The modern Israeli biblical scholar, Benjamin Uffenheimer, follows Buber in distinguishing biblical myth from pagan myth precisely because of its communal ideals. He argues persuasively that the myths surrounding creation, kingship, and Mosaic leadership reveal how Israel's religious egalitarianism differed from the social authoritarianism of other ancient Near Eastern religions.6

Uffenheimer rightly refers to Buber's analysis of biblical myth, and indeed, Buber discusses how myth can arise from the memory of an event experienced by a group. He claims that ancient Israel's most distinctive myth--that of its covenant with God--derives from just such a social event.

For Buber, the nation as a whole rather than
the isolated prophet underwent "decisive
religious experience." Only as a member of a
people does each Jew understand the meaning
of Jewish religion.7 Buber traces the
stories of Israel's formation, of Moses and
the revelation given to the people, and of
the covenantal experience of the Jewish
people back to the memory of an originating
communal act, just as he traces the Genesis
myths back to a primary personal event. He
designates the question of whether the
memory "originated from its historical
actuality or signifies only a late illusion"
"decisively important." He tests the "truth"
of these social myths by the historical
accuracy of their portrait of communal
experience.8 This approach offers an
alternative to the myth-ritualist
interpretation by emphasizing the social
orientation of the Israelites as a
confederacy under the kingship of God.

Buber considers the entire story of
ancient Israel, from its beginnings in
Egyptian slavery through its national
development, a mythical narrative. The
story of Moses, found in the Bible from
Exodus through the end of Deuteronomy,
purports to be the history of the Israelite
people. The hero Moses arises from
obscurity to a position of great power,
leads his people out of bondage, provides
them with laws and leaders, and finally
brings them to the boundaries of the land in
which they will settled and establish a new
nation. To call such a story "myth"
suggests that the concrete events in a

nation's history, particularly as reflected
in the biography of a single individual,
stimulated a social response that demanded
more than factual reporting. References to
divinity throughout the stories of those
events suggest the reaction of those who
experienced them as a transformation of
their communal sense of identity. Buber
usually calls this story "legend" rather
than "myth." He has, however, called
"legend" "the latest form of the Jewish
myth." He contrasts the "god of pure myth"
to the "god of the legend" and then contends
that the latter "is the myth of I and Thou."
The terminology may confuse an unwary
reader. Buber does not contrast legend and
myth as such; rather, he elevates legend as
the most authentic kind of myth because it
focuses on the human deed, on the lives of
people.9   Buber considers the story of
Moses such a legendary myth, one recalling
the discovery of God's kingship by Moses,
the people, and the nation.

KINGSHIP OF GOD IN BIBLICAL MYTH

When, in 1955, Buber published a third
edition of his 1932 study, The Kingship of
God, he emphasized that the "History of
religion, like all of history, can only be
carried on scientifically by connection of
individualities and generalities."10 Unlike
those who emphasized a generalized "nature
myth" that dominated the ancient Near East,
Buber studied the unique in Israelite

society and religion. Although he traces
the evolution of its religious forms and
recognizes their relationship to the general
social background, he refuses to see
Israelite religion as merely one example of
a generic type. He points to the "religio-
historical peculiarity of Israel" as
manifested in its myths and in its social
organization. Each stage in Israelite
religious development grows out of a
specific societal and historical
experience.11 Buber's explanation of his
purpose in writing the book reflects his
later thinking. By 1955, he had completed
his work on the Psalms, the Prophets, and on
Genesis. Nevertheless, he had already
suggested his final views when working on
the idea of the divine kingship in 1932.
Then he remarked that he envisioned a three-
volume work beginning by tracing myth back
to its historical past, continuing by
focusing on "the genuine historical life of
faith," and concluding by hinting that only
messianic faith legitimates claims for
national leadership (a view directly aimed
at the Nazis and their self-proclaimed
nationalism). He justified this threefold
approach by contending that "Myth is the
spontaneous and legitimate language of
expecting, as of remembering, faith."12

    Buber hoped to guide the study of
biblical religion from a preoccupation with
"antiquities" to a realization of how the
events celebrated by myth point forward to
new events in the present. That
preoccupation continued unabated. In his
preface to the second edition of the book,

Buber rejects the search for the influences
on Moses, particularly the attempt "to
derive the religious achievement which is
connected with the name of Moses from
Egypt."13 In such a theory the "social"
element in biblical myth refers to its
indebtedness to its social environment.
Buber accepts the reality of cultural
borrowing, but he finds it irrelevant for
discovering the unique social structure of
ancient Israel. Buber's contribution to
biblical studies lies in his reshaping the
nature of the questions asked about the
relationship of religion to society. He
initiated "a wholly new line of Bible
scholarship," which others call "a witness
to the religion of Israel," and which might
provide a new direction to biblical
scholarship.14 The explication of the story
of Moses shows how myth recapitulates a
nation's historical experience and prepares
it for a continuing communal task.

Throughout his explanation of biblical
religion Buber characterizes ancient
Israel's social structure as that of
covenantal community. Three concerns unite
such a community: theocratic loyalty to the
deity; charismatic leadership, often
justified by an appeal to the holy war; and
bureaucratic routinization, by which
institutions dilute the original power of
religious insight. Yahweh, Israel's God,
calls the people into existence. The nation
therefore derives its self-identification
from its view of God. Buber argues that
this does not mean, as the French
sociologist Emile Durkheim might suggest,

that the divine personifies the community's own spirit of unity. Instead, he claims, God as King of the tribe "represents the power which transcends it, happens to it, which <u>changes</u> it, even historicizes it." The history of the people becomes its story by association with the people's God.15 Buber sometimes calls this kind of social organization "theocracy" but usually prefers to focus on sociologist Max Weber's theory of charisma to explain that social order.

Weber connects ancient Israel's creation of a theocracy to its experience during the Babylonian exile. Until that time leaders contended against one another, basing their claims on different sources of authority. Priests relied on bureaucratic authority derived from their training, skills, and specific abilities. Prophets claimed authority from an immediate "charisma," or influx of a divine power. Kings legitimated their power by appealing to the dynastic principle; they inherited their right to rule. The exilic prophet Ezekiel, however, "paints a panoramic image of the good society and ... mints his visions into an intellectually constructed utopia." He turned to the idea of "theocracy" as a rational ordering of society under an elite of religious experts. Religious expertise will replace priestly, prophetic, and royal leadership.16

Buber focuses on the same tensions in leadership as Weber. He disagrees with Weber about the origin and meaning of theocracy. He locates its origins at the

earliest period of Israelite life. From the
very beginning, he claims, only religious
experts ruled; only God's word determined
how the nation organized its lives. At
first, the kings, priests, and prophets
understood themselves only as instruments of
the divine. The idea that God rules through
human beings, however, entails a problem.
From that standpoint only prophets should
rule since they alone manifest the charisma
of divine selection. Kings and priests gain
authority from tradition, not from an
immediate act of God. Even prophets,
however, have no clear right to power since
they must demonstrate the legitimacy of
their claim to charisma. Beyond this, not
everything a prophet says springs from
charismatic inspiration. At times, prophets
speak for themselves. How are their
utterances as mouthpieces of divinity to be
separated from their personal views? Buber
begins with the idea that only God can rule,
but then he points to three questions
derived from that idea: the problems of
determining which leader actually speaks for
God, of discovering a means of legitimating
institutional leaders such as kings and
priests, and finally of distinguishing
between divine and human rulership.17

Buber thinks that covenantal
organization solved these problems by
providing criteria for deciding what was and
what was not a legitimate expression of the
divine will. He investigates the "kingly
covenant" made between God and Israel at
Sinai. He claims that this covenant refers
to a unique event, different in essence from

the covenants found in Genesis and those
made with later kings. He suggests three
basic elements in it. First, the covenant
establishes a new relationship between
Israel and God: they are now bound in a
political unity. This aspect of the
covenant establishes a new relationship
among the Israelites themselves. They are
now equals--each a priest before the Lord.
Priesthood requires a certain regimen of
behavior governing social, political, and
personal life. The second aspect of
covenant elaborates on that regimen of
behavior by providing a social legislation
combined with "the conception of a divine
ownership of the soil." Because they have a
unique relation to God and to one another,
Israelites have mutual duties and
obligations toward the land on which they
live. Finally, the covenant reaffirms a
theological presupposition: God accompanies
the Israelites. The people and its leaders
share the sanctity of the divine.18 Before
studying Buber's use of these views in
analyzing the Bible, it is necessary to
review the biblical record itself.

MYTH, RITUAL AND MOSES

Modern biblical students have, since the
nineteenth century, recognized the composite
nature of the first five books in the Hebrew
Scriptures. Following clues left by
repetitions of key phrases, by strange and
uncongenial combinations of symbols and

metaphors, and by duplicate accounts of identical events, scholars unravel the variegated sources of the biblical text. Digging into the prehistory of the text, these "archeologists of literature" depict a bewildering array of sources that transforms even the most essential and basic motifs of biblical religion into puzzles and problems. The idea of covenant--a concept that many thinkers consider central to biblical theology--represents such an example.19 The story of Israel's enslavement from Egypt, its escape from slavery, and its receiving of a covenant at Mount Sinai dominates the Pentateuch from Exodus through Deuteronomy.

That narrative provides a "master story" for biblical religion itself.20 The Bible presents the idea of covenant clearly and unmistakably; echoes of the concept resound throughout the entire biblical corpus. The biblical passages describing the covenant event itself, however, include some strange features. Exodus 24, for example, appears as a depiction of the final covenant ceremony in which Israel received its divine commission. That chapter in particular seems fraught with difficulties.

The chapter begins with God's summoning of Moses, Aaron, Aaron's sons, and the seventy elders to worship Yahweh; it continues with a very different portrayal of the covenant event and only returns to its original picture in verse 9. Verses 3-8 clearly interrupt the flow of the narrative. Even these verses show signs of a complex development, as a review of their content reveals:

> Moses came and reported all the words of the Lord to the people, so they answered unanimously: All the words which the Lord has spoken we will do. So Moses transcribed all the Lord's words. He arose forthwith in the morning and built an altar at the foot of the mountain and twelve pillars, representing the twelve tribes of Israel. He sent young men of the Israelites to offer burnt offerings and to sacrifice whole offerings of oxen to the Lord. Moses took half the blood and put it in basins and half of the blood he threw on the altar. He took the book of the covenant and read it before the people who replied: All that the Lord has spoken we will perform and obey. Moses took the blood and sprinkled it upon the people, saying: Behold the blood of the covenant which the Lord has made with you in accordance with all these things.

This passage requires detailed decoding to reveal its true meaning. Such decoding begins by noticing the double report of the people's confirmation of the divine pact (vv. 2, 7); the strange reference to the "young men" (rather than to the Aaronide priests or the elders mentioned earlier in chapter 24); and the strange proliferation of symbols, the most obvious of which are the twelve pillars, the book of the covenant, and the blood of the covenant.

Reference to a blood covenant requires explanation since it occurs nowhere else in the Pentateuchal narrative with reference to the Sinai experience. When this symbol is made central, a strange story emerges: that of the confirmation of Israel's covenant with its God, an event occuring when a special substance, blood, sanctifies the actions of young men. This tale exemplifies a common theme in many cultures: young men pass into adulthood through an initiation ritual using symbolic materials justified by a myth. The particular complex of blood symbolism, a specific ritual, and a mythic story appears elsewhere in the Exodus narrative. While the blood symbol remains constant, however, the myth and ritual associated with it vary from passage to passage.

The ritual of Passover, described in Exodus 12-13, places the blood covenant in a familial context. God, as part of the divine plan to free the Israelites from slavery, determines to slaughter every first-born male. The Israelites escape this slaughter by offering a sacrificial substitute for their own first-born sons. They mark their obedience to this ritual by smearing the doorposts of their homes with sacrificial blood, and God then "passes over" each Israelite home. Thereafter each Israelite family memorializes this event by a family ritual. The myth tells how each family escaped the fate of the Egyptians; the ritual focuses on each family's obligation for sacrificing the first-born of their flock. Exodus 13:14-15 summarizes the myth and its ritual without mentioning the blood symbolism, which is present only by implication:

> And when in time to come your son asks you: What is this? You shall say to him: By force God liberated us from Egypt, from the state of slavery. When Pharaoh continually refused to free us, the Lord slaughtered all the first born in the land of Egypt, whether human or cattle. Therefore, I sacrifice all the males that first open the womb to the Lord, but all the first born of my sons, I redeem.

Whereas the myth and ritual associated with Sinai emphasize the communal and national aspects of the blood covenant, the myth and ritual of Passover focus on personal experience--more specifically, familial experience. While the Passover ceremony itself takes place in a community setting, Exodus 12:48 describes a private ritual: that of circumcision, a rite that determines who may and may not participate in the Passover celebration. The circumcision rite reflects still another view of the blood covenant, mythically associated with the story of Moses as narrated in Exodus 3-4. That myth constitutes an essential part of the larger saga of Moses, Israel's liberator, and only incidentally records the ritual performance of circumcision.

According to the tale, Israelites, enslaved by the Egyptians, suffered great

persecution, including attempted genocide.
their people as a whole. In the course of
this persecution Egypt's royal family
eventually took in a baby Israelite as a
foster child. That baby, Moses, grew up in
a royal setting, but on maturity asserted
his solidarity with his enslaved people by
murdering an Egyptian taskmaster. The
consequences of that act forced Moses to
flee Egypt and find refuge in a wilderness
country, Midian, where he intermarried with
the natives. After a period of exile, Moses
returned to Egypt as the liberator of his
people. This stage of his life culminated in
a personal religious experience reported
ambiguously in Exodus 4:24-26. The deity
apparently attacked Moses and was
propitiated only by an act of circumcision
carried out by Moses' Midianite wife,
Zipporah (the text does not make clear
whether Moses or Moses' son is the object of
this operation). This strange and startling
circumcision story of Exodus 4 occurs as
Moses is about to begin his public mission
and must move from the private sphere of an
individual to the sphere of national
leadership. The myth suggests that the
ritual shedding of blood overcomes a
person's alienation and enables him to join
his national group. While the myth locates
the ceremony in conjugal privacy, it
recognizes the initiatory aspect of the
ritual with Zipporah's proclamation that
Moses is her "bridegroom of blood because of
circumcision" (Exodus 4:26).

The stories of Moses' circumcision, of
the Passover sacrifice before the Exodus

from Egypt, and the blood ritual at Sinai all focus on blood as a link between God and the Israelites. Despite the different myths or narratives, then, the rituals belong to a single tradition: that of the blood covenant. How did the symbol of a blood covenant become linked to three such different myths and rituals? Buber's interpretation of this text contrasts with that given by psychoanalyst Theodor Reik. A second and equally important alternative is suggested by W. Robertson Smith, whose pioneering comparison of the text with other Semitic rituals reveals the sociological significance of blood covenants. Comparing these three views illuminates Buber's distinctiveness.

THE SOCIOLOGY OF THE BLOOD COVENANT

W. Robertson Smith's analysis of blood covenant demonstrates its social dimensions. Smith focuses more on rituals practiced than on religious stories and symbols. From his perspective, the stories follow the rituals; the symbols gain meaning from their usage. Thus blood takes on symbolic meaning only by its traditional usage in a ritual. These rituals serve social needs and develop in response to communal motivations. Smith recognizes the importance of scholarly studies of particular rituals and myths. His main concern, however, lies with "a circle of cultivated and thinking men and women ... interested in everything that throws light on their own religion."21 The myths of modern religions and the explanations of rituals often differ dramatically from those of primitive or pre-modern religions.

According to Smith, the rituals themselves, however, retain residues of earlier stages demonstrable by meticulous historical analysis. While Smith agrees that "In principle there was all the difference in the world between the faith of Isaiah and that of an idolater," he studies "The conservatism which refuses to look at principles, and has an eye only for tradition and usage."22 He shows his audience how a similar conservatism produced survivals of primitive religion within their own faith. Smith concentrates on rituals because modern religions preserve in them the oldest remnants of early religion. He rejects the primacy of mythology for a similar reason. He sees myth as a later apologetic, an explanation, after the fact, for these older strands in new religions. Such myths "are the falsest of false guides as to the original meaning of the old religions."23 Smith's concern for disclosing the primitive within the modern leads him to analyze rituals as the most important data in Semitic religion.

That orientation toward the modern West, even when facing the Ancient Near East, shapes Smith's explanation of the covenant in ancient Israel's tradition. He considers the covenant idea a development from primitive times. Early worshippers, he

explains, unified their social community by
uniting with their deities and strengthened
their tribal group by assimilating the power
of their gods. They turned to magical
ritual to accomplish this feat. Sharing
some sacred substance such as food,
clothing, or part of one's own body created
a "living bond of union between the
worshipers and their god." Surveying the
data from Semitic religions, Smith concludes
that this union occurs through a ritual
sacrifice, usually of blood but sometimes of
hair or even milk. Thus covenant represents
a common life growing out of a shared bodily
existence.24

In its present form the Exodus narrative
focuses on the nation as a whole, on its
communal experience, and Smith, while
recognizing the various covenants of blood
in the Bible, assimilates them all into this
social explanation. He posits that Israel
once celebrated a great blood covenant
ritual and explained it by the Exodus myth.
Later generations no longer remembered the
magical significance of the blood covenant
and invented a narrative explanation for it.
They remembered the association of blood and
communal identity but rejected the primitive
aspects of the ritual. Smith uses this
hypothesis to develop a theory about the
creation of the narrative in Exodus 24.

The biblical text clearly emphasizes
that the blood sacrifice cements the
community and unites its various members.
Smith remarks that the place of the ritual
sacrifice, the erection of symbolic pillars,

the sprinkling of blood on covenantal participants, and the technical term "young men" applied to those participants all parallel general Semitic customs. He contends that when later generations forgot this meaning they reinterpreted the sacrifice as a celebration of revelation, as a symbol of the communal unity which they now associated with the Book of the Covenant ascribed to Moses.25

Smith argues, however, that originally this ceremony established a blood connection between the community and its deity. The mythic explanation of the ritual lay in the identification of all who shared a common blood. The Exodus story transformed this ceremony into a tale of how a common history created a communal identity. The story, then, preserves an accurate memory of the function of the ritual but misrepresents the means by which the original ritual accomplished its function.

Smith's approach to the biblical narrative offers many attractive features. He weaves together many similar biblical passages and helps explain how they fit into a single pattern. His interpretation of the story, however, lacks completeness. He never explicitly shows how one version of the myth grew out of another or how one ritual action replaced another or the motives for mythic changes.

REIK'S PSYCHOLOGICAL APPROACH

One can resolve the problems raised by Smith's analysis by reducing the various biblical rituals and myths to a single meaning. The different stories and the rites expressing them appear as variations on one constant but repressed theme. The repression accounts for the necessarily complex and allusive nature of the differing accounts. In studying covenant narratives, just as in studying Genesis myths, Theodor Reik follows this approach, explaining each of the covenant descriptions as a subtle evocation of a primal psychological reality. While acknowledging the difference between the myths and rituals of the various biblical passages, Reik interprets each of them as oblique references to a single psychological event: a young man's resolution of the Oedipal dilemma.26 While Smith sees biblical covenant as a sociological act, Reik sees it as a conversion of primal psychological reality into the language of national folk culture. The ideology of the chosen people, for example, only appears as a social theory. In fact, it reproduces the psychological experience of initiation into maturity.

Thus Reik reduces most biblical myths to a single purpose: they point to the ritual of circumcision and its psycho-social origins in primal history. Reik explains the story of Abraham's near-sacrifice of Isaac as a similar myth that originally (although not in its present form) described

an initiatory rite of circumcision. He
interprets the various covenantal accounts
as variant myths associated with the same
ritual of circumcision.

Often the biblical text seems to support
his arguments: Passover must be preceded by
ritual circumcision; Moses must engage in
circumcision before fulfilling his task in
Egypt; Joshua must circumcise the Israelites
as a sign that they accept the divine
covenant. At other times, however, the
communal celebrations that Reik traces back
to the ritual of circumcision seem to have a
tenuous link, if any at all, with that
rite.27 Reik explains the circumcision
story concerning Moses as a symbol of
national experience based on a private,
individual experience. He associates the
attack on Moses, with its clear reference to
circumcision, with a puberty ritual of
initiation. He explains that Israel
conceived of itself as a chosen people
because it shared this secret ritual. This
sense of election, perhaps derived from
Midianite tradition, provided ancient Israel
and later the entire Jewish people with an
"extraordinary pride and self-confidence"
that enabled the Jews to survive agonies and
tortures.28

Although Reik acknowledges Freud's
insights concerning the typical myth of the
hero found in the Moses story, he disagrees
with Freud. The only true protagonist of
the Exodus story, he thinks, is the Jewish
people as a whole. Moses as individual
stands for the entire nation; the election

of the hero represents national chosenness.29 Reik thus differs significantly from his teacher. While giving an approving nod to various social theories, he actually reduces the story of the Jewish people to a projection of an individual's experience. The shape of the Exodus story today, he thinks, really projects onto the Jewish people what was originally a personal rite of initiation. The public ceremony merely masks its origins in private rituals of initiation.

Reik considers the biblical account of Passover and its rituals a similar transformation of an individual's psychological history into a national epic. He concludes that "the exodus account comes closest to a report of a puberty festival."30 The sacred meal associated with Passover seems to him similar to celebrations found in the secret societies and mystery cults that evolved in other cultures. The Passover ritual, in this view, recapitulates in different language the same lesson found in the story of Moses: circumcision marks a man's entrance into adult society. For Reik, Moses uses Passover as a "revolutionary" initiation ritual. Faced with the need to unite a group of slaves, Moses created "a leap back into a more primitive form of initiation" that extended the "secret society" to include the entire people. Passover thus uses primitive rituals for a "regression to simpler forms of initiation" that democratized social life.31

Reik discovers a parallel history behind the covenantal narrative. Exodus 24 does not mention circumcision, and Reik admits that "there is neither manifest trace nor tradition of a puberty festival or rituals in the biblical reports." Nevertheless, he argues that the covenant ceremony described presupposes a "primitive blood covenant between the young people and their totemistic guardians." The biblical story includes key elements in such an initiation: forms of intimidation, purification ceremonies, and teachings. He suggests that this evidence points in the same direction as the other stories that do focus on circumcision. "The origin of the blood covenant," he declares, "is to be found in the initiation into the secret societies of brotherhoods between members of different tribes."[32] As with the Exodus stories, so the covenantal covenant narrative developed through a long pre-history from a psychological event: maturation.

Reik's studies in "psychological archeology" trace the development of the biblical story as an evolutionary process. The earlier phases of the tradition included a "half-historic" memory of the departure from Egypt. This memory "became amalgamated" with the initiation ritual of a secret society. As Israelite society became more democratic, "the initiation was now displaced from a generation to all members of the tribe." By this time the story had "arrived at the origin and home of oral tradition." The ritual "returns to certain collective experiences which reappear in various forms as the motifs of a symphony reoccur in later elaboration." The themes found in the circumcision of Moses and in the Passover echo throughout the story of the Sinai Covenant.33

In this way Reik unites the various elements in the Moses story and points backward to primitive initiation rituals and circumcision. Myth, whether focused on primal individuals, on a great hero, on national rituals, or on the formation of the national identity, derives from a single reality: the rituals of initiation. Thus Reik, like Smith, acknowledges the social evolution of the covenantal ritual but argues that this evolution merely hides a more original reality, one found in depth psychology: initiation into maturity.

BUBER AND THE EXODUS

Martin Buber's view, based on his covenantal interpretation of Israel's myth of divine kingship, moves beyond both Smith and Reik. Buber highlights the prophetic aspects of Moses as presented in the Bible. From this perspective, Moses succeeds not because he possesses some personal charisma but because he fulfills an appointed task. Although Moses creates a nation, Buber denies that he deserves esteem as a great politician. Although Moses transforms society and implements a broad social agenda, Buber refuses to call him a social reformer. Moses' success transcends

its individual parts to culminate in the
establishment of a people dedicated to God's
ideals.   Just as Moses' task goes beyond any
set boundaries of social, political, or
religious functions, so Moses' new view of
God transcends any simple definition.   That
transcendent view of an all-embracing faith,
Buber contends, marks the distinctiveness of
Moses' achievement.

The story of Moses provides "the
substantiation of a ruling by God that shall
not be culturally restricted."   This
comprehensive character distinguishes Moses
from all later prophets, who transmit the
same message but in a more limited and
focused form.   Mosaic leadership
demonstrates by its comprehensiveness the
eclectic concerns of Moses' God.34   Moses
accomplishes his primary role by pursuing a
task that surpasses that of either the
priest or the prophet.   As Buber imagines
it, Moses' special task lay in establishing
the kingship of God, thus setting the
framework for all future Israelite religion.
Moses represents, in this reconstruction,
what Buber considers a true "biblical
leader."   While Israel had kings, priests,
and prophets, Buber refuses to call them
leaders merely because they occupied an
institutional position of power.   True
leadership grows out of election and
includes an imperative for innovation:
"Only those who begin are then comprised
under the biblical aspect of leadership."
Moses' beginning stems less from his stature
as "Israel's liberator" or from the stories
surrounding his youth than from his

contribution to Israelite religion. His
innovation occurs in "the history of the
wandering in the desert" and encompasses
what might be called his failures.
According to Buber, Moses leads the people
because he provides them with a new goal.
Even when he fails, he leads because "his
work survives in a hope which is beyond all
these failures."35

As in Genesis, so in Exodus, Buber
traces the biblical myth to Moses'
biography, not merely to history. The story
of Moses, he thinks, records the life
stations of a leader whose personal stamp
remains visible even in later extensions and
exaggerations of his story. The myth of
Moses' birth records a moment of discovery
in which he learns both the alienation of
Egyptian culture and the need to surpass it
through an act of liberation. The means to
such liberation, however, elude him. Buber
suggests that this lack stems from an
incomplete self-transformation. When,
initiating the second stage of his life
(Exodus 3-4), Moses flees to Midian, he
still appears as an Egyptian, not a Hebrew.
The flight to Midian represents a return
home. Superficially, that flight only
furthers Moses' estrangement from his
people. He leaves Egypt and abandons his
people physically no less than spiritually.
The biblical text testifies to the
alienation Moses felt at this time: he
identifies himself as an Egyptian and names
his son "Gershom" to indicate that he is a
stranger in a strange land. For Buber,
however, precisely this flight away from

himself draws Moses back to himself: "Moses
came back to his forefathers by way of his
flight."36 The revelation at the burning
bush symbolizes this transformation by
declaring that the God of his fathers
appears to him.

Buber interprets Moses' encounter with
God at the burning bush as a symbolic
statement of this success even amidst
failure. God commissions Moses to lead the
Israelites from bondage to freedom. Moses
approaches that task as either a priest or a
prophet. He expects the people to ask him
for proof of his divine appointment. He
therefore asks this God for his "name" and
expects to be tested not with the riddle of
pronouncing an unpronounceable set of sounds
but "with its 'genuine' pronunciation, its
magic applicability." Priests often use
such magical knowledge to perform their
rites. Denying this request, God provides
Moses with a new conception of divinity: the
God whose name means the one who is always
present, whose invocation merely indicates a
divine intimacy and cannot include a
"conjuring." This new view of deity
provides "His people the assurance which
they need and which frustrates every magic
undertaking, but also makes it superfluous."
Israel can trust Moses not because Moses
possesses divine power but because Moses
shows them that they can trust their deity.
Moses' intuition, however, takes hold in
Israel only slowly. Later prophetic voices
must reaffirm it. Amos, Jeremiah, and
other, later prophets extend the idea
of divine kingship originally begun by

Moses, "the maturity of knowledge manifesting itself in them really only completes what was already there germinating in obvious vitality." Moses stands as a unique link. His desire to know God's name ties him to the priests, but the nature of the name he receives separates him from priestly religion. The declaration of divine kingship in the later prophets unites them with Moses, but he stands apart from them as the first to enunciate that principle.

Moses displays a distinctive leadership, acting neither as priest nor as prophet but as one who initiates Israel into the knowledge that God alone rules over them.37 The significance of this initiation derives as much from the terror and resistance awakened within Moses as from the intellectual content transmitted. According to Buber, the experience at the bush overwhelms Moses with a sense of identification: the same God who addressed his father now addresses him.38 Intimacy and familiarity do not overcome Moses' doubts. Here Buber notes Moses' "resistance offered to the mission," which Buber takes to represent "the most intimate experience of the prophetic man."39 Moses meets the ancestral deity who, like Moses, has been alienated from his people. Moses must overcome a double sense of estrangement: he has been alienated from Israel; God, in allowing Egyptian enslavement of the Hebrews, has become alienated from the people. Moses struggles with this alienation and overcomes it only

by accepting God's new name. The duality
within Moses recorded by the myth suggests
why Israel needs prophets throughout its
existence. Prophets reaffirm the experience
mythically reported in the Moses story: an
individual feels both repelled and compelled
by the divine. An event in which God calls
a person to service includes both a positive
attraction and a negative reaction. The
hero must acknowledge both.

The necessity for prophetic voices
points to the defeats that Buber attributes
to Moses. Moses provides a pattern, a hope,
and an ideal. He leads not by succeeding
but by offering a goal toward which the
people slowly grope. The memory of Moses
preserved by tradition maintains a pure
vision of the Kingship of God. Buber thinks
that Moses himself recognized this feature
of his leadership and regarded himself not
as a unique individual coming only once but
as the one entrusted with the task, who as
long as that task has not been fulfilled in
its entirety must return again and again --
not as the same person or the identical soul
"...but precisely as the one continuing the
fulfillment of that task, no matter what
else that person or soul may be."40 The
significance of Moses, then, surpasses his
historical success. The story of Moses
moves beyond reporting past events to
conveying the importance of those events.
Telling about Moses entails telling about
his visionary ideal.

Buber never explicitly calls the Moses
story "myth." At times, he seeks to

explicitly reject such a designation. By
his own definition, however, the story
qualifies as myth. It preserves the memory
of a spontaneous response to an I-You
meeting. It evokes that meeting and enjoins
others to enter such meetings themselves.
Buber imagines the "historical" Moses and
seeks to "come nearer" to him by "testing
and selective work on the text." By so
doing, he recreates the "myth" of Moses to
awaken moderns to the possibilities of human
meeting. Buber claims to discover within
the "sacred legend" and "sacred history" of
Moses "the indwelling story of faith which
inheres in them."41 This discovery arises
from Buber's understanding of the Moses
story as Jewish mythology.

BUBER'S VIEW OF MOSES

    The story of Moses, including the ritual
developments so important to Reik, seems to
Buber to center on three events: the early
life of Moses reveals the impact caused by
an awareness of the divine presence; the
instructions to the Israelites concerning
the Passover identifies the effect of law as
formative of Israel's cultural reality; and
the covenant at Sinai provides the
foundation for the social egalitarianism of
Israelite community.42 Buber examines the
story of Moses as a mythic evocation of
these values of covenant community. Buber
claims that Exodus 4 recalls and preserves a
crisis in Moses' development as a religious

leader. The tale not only records that crisis but helps others cope with similar experiences. Buber acknowledges that the tale includes echoes from an earlier tradition. He accepts the incident as an example of "divine demonism."43 Buber, however, claims that the experience at the core of this story emphasizes the importance of absolute faith rather than of God's demonic power. God "claims the entirety of the one he has chosen." The symbolism of circumcision, he continues, reinforces this interpretation.

While the events in Exodus 4 demand a literal circumcision, Moses himself complains of having "uncircumcised lips" in Exodus 6. Buber comments on this "absence of liberation which is clearly not organic but penetrates to the core of the soul." Both literal and figurative demands for circumcision point to a single truth: the awareness of inadequacy plaguing any religious leader. Moses experiences what the Israelites and Jews will experience again and again: those who seek to bring liberty to the world find themselves unequal to the task. What Buber calls "the tragedy inherent in revelation" finds expression here. At the close of his personal odyssey and at the beginning of his national mission, Moses realizes the challenges and limitations of the religious task. The experience of circumcision for Buber merely illustrates in deed the same existential reality as the story tells in words: a leader's response to an overwhelming task.

This equal consideration of act and story, of ritual and myth, distinguishes Buber's method from Reik's. While Reik contends that the story points back to a primal human ritual, Buber traces it to a leader's melancholy recognition that the divine call to create a holy people demands more than any one person can fulfill. Reik takes the act of circumcision in Exodus 4 as the basis of his interpretation of Moses' early career. He sees the story as a mask or disguise hiding the true meaning of the ritual. Buber disagrees. Both the ritual and the myth are inadequate but necessary expressions of a reality experienced in life. They do not disguise a primal event but testify to an event that words and deeds can never fully capture. Reik seeks to penetrate a mask; Buber seeks to explain the inexpressible.

COMMUNAL RITUAL IN EXODUS

Buber's sensitivity to the human event behind rituals enables him to move more easily than Reik from the psychology of the individual leader to the group psychology of Israel as a whole. Reik's exegesis of the Exodus oscillates between a Freudian reconstruction of early human history and his own reconstruction of an initiation ritual creating a sense of community and chosenness uniting ex-slaves into a coherent community. Because Exodus refers to Israel as God's son and treats the people of Israel as a single entity, Buber can defend the application of his "biographical" account to a social group no less than to an individual. The Exodus narrative reflects the collective encounter of the people of Israel with their God; for Buber, this means that it describes in mythic terms an I-You meeting that transcends daily experience. The transition from individual to group consciousness in the story marks the significance of the event. In the I-You meeting each Israelite discovered that personal identity also included a relationship with the Jewish people as a whole.

Moses' own experience exemplifies that change. Moses learns that he must demand of Pharaoh to "let my son go that he may serve me." Buber takes this verse as a clue to how Moses enabled Israel to understand itself even while laboring under Pharaoh's oppression. Israel learns to call its God and king "father" because it discovers its own identity in relationship to that God. At first, the idea may have grown from the story of "a mythical procreation" (the I-You meeting is conceived of on the analogy of biological birthing; God brings forth the nation as a mother brings forth her child), but it developed into the concept of "adoption." Buber affirms the reality of the concrete event to which the believer testifies by telling a myth. The meeting with divinity as father "embodies itself in a concrete event, which continues to operate concretely." The event that formed Israel's national consciousness and continued to maintain that consciousness was experienced as a relationship with divinity, a relationship in which God gave birth to the people.44 Insofar as the myth of Moses conveys this reality of divine fatherhood, it recapitulates the event of the individual's discovery of this truth: Moses discovers how God acts as a parent with human beings. The biblical narrative progresses beyond this relationship to use it as the model for God's interaction with the Israelite people as whole.

Buber traces the development of Israel's view of God through several transformations. It begins with an analogy between the relationship of God to Israel and that of a father to a son. It then evolves into the idea of God as a king, at first understood as merely an exalted father and then recognized as a political administrator. Buber claims that Israel experienced God not only as parent but also as the director of its institutions. Israelites considered themselves part of a divine experiment in which God would use this nation to provide humanity with "a living example of a true people, a community." The rhythm of exile and return pulsating through Jewish history contributes its sense of destiny and importance. In the history of Israel "national and human elements have always been merged."45 God requires this national body as an experiment in righteousness. While individuals perform righteous acts, only a society establishes the structure of righteous communal life.

Israel's meeting with God led to the development of laws and institutions, leaders, and forms of government. Reflecting on that fact, Israel's prophetic thinkers concluded that God could only have in mind the creation of an exemplary nation. God as King demands a kingdom, an "entire nation ... (to) demonstrate a life of unity and peace, of righteousness and justice to the human race."46 The myth of divine kingship reflects the moment when each person in Israel recognizes that the meeting with God also includes an obligation for political action. Buber's understanding of myth as a reflection on an event draws attention to how an event in an individual's life can reinforce social meaning. He suggests that Israel, collectively, discovered that: "We can only work on the kingdom of God through working on all the spheres of man that are allotted to us."

The rituals of Israel's political life reflect not the need for initiation into a separate "adult" brotherhood but rather a more general social truth: people serve both God and the community by recognizing that the community itself has a task that serves God.47 This view of Israel's God begins when God appears to Moses as master of natural events, able to transform water into blood, sticks into serpents, and healthy flesh into leprous skin, and as the concerned director of history who seeks liberation for the people of Israel.

Buber shows how this story reaches its culmination in the Passover celebration.

While Reik interprets that ritual as but one
more, redundant echo of an initiation
ritual, Buber shows how it represents a
growing consciousness within Israel's self-
understanding. Reik cannot explain why the
various relics of a primal initiation
ceremony occur in such profusion and
diversity in the biblical story. Buber,
however, offers a clear schema for
understanding the transition from
circumcision (the key ritual in Moses'
personal drama) to the Passover ritual (the
first communal ceremony in Israel's national
history). Through that ceremony the
covenant with God established by the
circumcision takes on a social meaning, and
Israel discovers its communal identity,
receives divine instructions about its
purpose, and gains assurance of God's favor.
These rituals affirming covenant enable
Moses to create Israel's self-conception and
delineate its communal selfhood.

     Biblical scholars suggest a long and
complex history behind the description of
the Passover ritual in Exodus 12-13.48 Reik
traces the story back to an ancient puberty
rite, ignoring the broader context in which
the tale now appears. Buber grants that the
ritual description incorporates ancient
forms that may well include "a preliminary
form of the blood covenant." He claims,
however, that the context in which the
author imbedded these relics of an older
ritual transforms their meaning. When these
old ceremonies became part of the new
tradition, the new purpose altered their
significance. The sharing of a communal

meal seems, to Buber, the central Passover
ritual; the people learn that through such
simple an activity as eating they can create
community. Moses "reintroduces the holy and
ancient" ceremony of the sacramental meal
both as a sociological institution uniting
the people and as a sign of the new nature
of the social unit, as a symbol of Israel's
special characteristic: the consecration of
life to a divine purpose. Since the
covenant event transforms the people of
Israel, Moses' new ritual of the covenant
evokes that occasion and invites the
Israelites to undergo such conversion anew.

From this perspective the myth
transforms a sociological ritual and a
totemic symbol into an opportunity for
personal conversion. Buber thinks that the
blood ceremony as used in Exodus conveys a
new idea: the ordinary human activity of
eating acts as a communal sacrament. The
normal human function of nourishment,
undertaken in a distinctive ritual setting,
changes "by the participation of the whole
community to the level of an act of
communion." Viewing the ritual from this
perspective suggests that it works by
engaging every community member in a common
activity. The annual repetition of this
ritual recreates that unifying spirit. The
festival taking shape each year celebrates
not "pious remembrance, but the
ever-recurrent contemporaneousness of that
which once befell." The feast of Passover
evokes a continual reality: a community
grows out of shared activity.49

Buber's interpretation of the laws of
Passover takes its symbols, rituals and myth
as expressions of a deeper reality: an event
in which the nation became self-conscious.
Taken together, these symbols, rituals, and
myth stimulate the performance of common
actions by community members. The symbols
evoke deep human emotions. The myth recalls
how history shaped a common response to
those emotions. The rituals offer a new
opportunity for such shared acting. Unlike
Reik, Buber refuses to translate different
myths into coded references to a single
psychological event. He takes each myth as
a recollection of a different historical
event; he interprets every ritual as an
opportunity for a new historical event.
Using this approach, Buber offers his own
interpretation of the Sinaitic blood
covenant.

BEYOND SOCIOLOGY: BUBER AND SMITH

Buber emphasizes the sociological
function of Israel's rituals. So, too, does
W. Robertson Smith. Smith, unlike Buber,
claims that ancient Israel's blood rituals
evoked a "magical" power. Rather than being
understood on a realistic or empirical
level, they operated on unseen, supernatural
forces. By participating in the "blood
feast," the Israelites shared in the life
force of their deity. Buber agrees that
Israel associated its birth as a nation with
its relationship to God. He denies that

this idea defies common sense. For Buber, "the current system of cause and effect becomes, as it were, transparent and permits a glimpse of the sphere in which a sole power, not restricted by any other, is at work." What appears to Smith as magic seems to Buber an expression by the people of Israel of how their deity encompassed all spheres of life. The rituals associated with Israel's exodus combine a respect for the historical and the natural: "What is shown us of nature is stamped by History" and while "Nature always points to History," "History always contains" elements of creation. Buber consistently refuses to admit magic into biblical thought.50

Smith's approach, from Buber's perspective, misses the essential meaning of Israel's evolutionary history. Not only did Moses' personal covenant experience become transformed into a social one; that social experience became the basis for a sense of universal mission. In the story of the covenant made at Sinai the people recorded still another transformational event: an event in which each person discovered not only a national destiny but also a task for humanity as a whole. Buber explains the covenant ritual at Sinai in Exodus 24 as testimony to a social, political, and religious transformation. Sometime in their history, according to Buber, the Israelites progressed from a state of chaotic and amorphous individualism to one of cultural self-consciousness; then, later, they changed and developed into a nation with a self-conscious political goal and

purpose. They understood this progression
in religious terms: only a relationship
with God could have catalyzed such a
momentous transformation. The people no
longer represented separate individuals or
even a cultural community. They now shared
a sacred mission as partners with God in a
divine program of world redemption. Buber
describes how the people celebrated this new
reality through a ritual, a "cult act"
transformed into a "pre-state" ceremony. He
interprets the symbolism of Sinai in terms
of national, social, and personal
obligation. God acts as a melekh, a king
who establishes the goals, boundaries, and
tasks appropriate for a nation. Israel acts
as a people, a loyal citizenry that accepts
the obligations imposed on it by legitimate
leaders.

Myth, as Buber understands it, records a
primal discovery and offers that record as
an invitation to its repetition. The
account in Exodus 24, then, describes the
memory on the basis of which Israel
repeatedly entered into relationship with
its God.51 This approach explains not only
the significance of the specific symbols,
rituals, and myths in each biblical passage;
it also provides a rationale for the
retention of all three. Each complex of
symbol, myth, and ritual represents a stage
in Israel's development. The circumcision
ritual, combined with the myth of Moses'
encounter with the deity and the blood
symbolism, reflects a leader's experience of
overcoming alienation through a sense of
task. The myth of the Exodus, the ritual of

the Passover, and the blood covenant of sacrifice in Egypt evoke the shared activities by which a community comes into being. Finally, the unique blood covenant of Sinai, its myth of covenant affirmation, and its national ritual record the dedication to task by which a nation became self-conscious.

The three stories of covenantal ceremony in the Bible reflect three stages in ancient Israel's religious evolution. One myth celebrates a moment of discovery during which an individual intuits the demand given by a God who transcends personal desires. A second myth recalls the need for some mark of social or cultural identification, some tangible or concrete sign of belonging to a group. A final myth evokes the highest ideal: an egalitarian community united not by force or necessity but by dedication to a great purpose and goal. Like Smith and Reik, Buber sketches the evolution of a ritual. Unlike them, he considers that development motivated by religious growth, by the evolving spiritual consciousness of the Jewish people.

Buber's analysis of the three blood rituals in Exodus reflects his view that ancient Israel developed its symbols, rituals, and myths to convey their reflection on an I-You event that shaped the nation. Together, these symbols, rituals and myths reflect an event that united and molded traditional rituals into a new synthesis that created a national identity that surpassed either individual experience

or mere shared communal living. This
synthesis recognized the human need for
images and symbols but transcended that need
by creating rituals, symbols and myths to
reaffirm the kingship of the divine.52
Buber finds in Israel's religiousness a
recognition of the forces working against
the ideal of God's kingship and an antidote
to them. The symbol of Moses himself
reflects this recognition. Unlike either
priest or prophet, he unites within himself
all aspects of communal life. Called to
realize "the unity of religious and social
life in the community of Israel," Moses
himself rises "above the compartmental
system of typology."53 Different authors
unravel the strands of the blood covenant,
its myths, and rituals differently. Reik
and Smith offer a simpler paradigm than
Buber's but also explain fewer of the
complexities of the text.

THE EXODUS TODAY

Beyond exegesis, however, each theorist
suggests a modern significance to the
biblical myth. Buber considers myth an
invitation to modern response. As a myth,
the story invites the people of Israel to
follow the same path as did Moses: moving
beyond human weakness, social necessity, and
the class interests of competing social
groups. Reik imagines myth reminding
humanity of a single common guilt: the
murder of the father as recreated in each

person's psyche. Telling the myth enables moderns to cope with their own maturation process and their own sense of guilt. Smith takes an even more restricted view of the modern purpose of his analysis. He seeks to show how modern religious practice owes its form and nature to more primitive sources. Of these three goals--that of reconstructing and evoking a primal experience, that of revealing a primal psychological reality, and that of tracing the sources of modern practice--Buber's task is far more ambitious, complex, and sophisticated. The reader may wonder whether the biblical rituals or their myths effectively achieve the goal Buber assigns to them. Smith's theory of sociological function and Reik's of psychological origin are limited, and thus often more acceptable than Buber's Nevertheless, while Buber's expansive vision may leave readers with more doubts about his particular argument for particular rituals, his approach does offer a synthesis and explanation for the variety of myths, rituals, and symbols maintained in the text. Such an explanation at least points in a more productive direction than the reductionism of either Smith or Reik.

NOTES

1. Robert A. Segal, "In Defense of
   Mythology: The History of Modern
   Theories of Myth." Annals of Scholarship
   I:1 (1980), p. 39; see his entire
   discussion of the "myth-ritualist"
   interpretation on pp. 39-43.

2. Sigmund Freud, Totem and Taboo:
   Resemblances between the psychic lives
   of savages and neurotics, trans. and
   intro.   A. A. Brill (New York: Random
   House, 1946), p. 187.

3. Claude Lévi-Strauss, The Savage Mind
   (Chicago: University of Chicago Press,
   1966), p. 129.

4. See the discussion in both Theodor Reik,
   The Creation of Woman: A Psychoanalytic
   Inquiry into the Myth of Eve (New York:
   McGraw-Hill, 1960), and his Myth and
   Guilt: The Crime and Punishment of
   Mankind (New York: Grosset and Dunlap,
   1957).

5. See Reik, The Creation of Woman,
   especially, pp. 24-31, 102-19; and Myth
   and Guilt, passim.

6. Benjamin Uffenheimer, "Myth and Reality
   in Ancient Israel," in S. N. Eisenstadt,
   ed.,   The Origins and Diversity of Axial
   Civilization (Albany, NY: SUNY Press,
   1986), pp. 136-67.

7. Martin Buber, <u>Israel and the World: Essays in a Time of Crisis</u> (New York: Schocken, 1948), p. 169.

8. Martin Buber, <u>Kingship of God</u>, 3rd ed., trans. Richard Scheimann (New York: Harper, 1967), p. 15.

9. Martin Buber, <u>The Legend of the Baal Shem</u>, trans. Maurice Friedman (New York: Schocken, 1955), p. 13.

10. Buber, <u>Kingship of God</u>, p. 48.

11. <u>Ibid.</u>, p. 53.

12. <u>Ibid.</u>, p. 14.

13. <u>Ibid.</u>, p. 27.

14. See Maurice Friedman, <u>Martin Buber's Life and Work: The Middle Years, 1923-1945</u> (New York: Dutton, 1981), pp. 133-37.

15. Buber, <u>Kingship of God</u>, p. 97.

16. Max Weber, <u>Ancient Judaism</u>, eds. and trans. Hans H. Gerth and Don Martindale (Glencoe, IL: The Free Press, 1952), p. 366.

17. Buber, <u>Kingship of God</u>, pp. 136-62.

18. <u>Ibid.</u>, pp. 121-35.

19. See the discussion in Steven T. Katz, <u>Jewish Ideas and Concepts</u> (New York: Schocken, 1977), pp. 156-62; compare my

Covenant and Community in Modern Judaism
(Westport, CT: Greenwood Press, 1989) in
which I compare Buber's view with those
of other contemporary Jewish theologians
such as Richard L. Rubenstein, Abraham
Heschel, and Mordecai Kaplan.

20. See Michael Goldberg, Jews and
Christians: Getting Our Story Straight
(Nashville, Abingdon, 1985); compare
Will Herberg's exploration of the
existential implications of the Exodus,
its association with covenant, its
echoes of earlier biblical tales, and
its meaning for modern Jews. Herberg,
however, steadfastly claims that the
Hebrew Bible emphasizes history, not
myth. Although I have learned much from
Herberg, and although my summary of the
Exodus story draws on his writing,
especially in Judaism and Modern Man: An
Interpretation of Jewish Religion (New
York: Harper, 1951), pp. 261-72, and his
Faith Enacted as History: Essays in
Biblical Theology, ed. and intro.
Bernard W. Anderson (Philadelphia:
Westminster, 1978), pp. 32-42, my point
of departure differs radically from his.

21. W. Robertson Smith, The Religion of the
Semites: The Fundamental Institutions
(New York: Schocken, 1972), p. vii.

22. Ibid., p. 5.

23. Ibid., p. 19.

24. Ibid., pp. 312-23.

25. Ibid., pp. 157, 211, 318, 344, 417.

26. See Reik, The Creation of Woman especially pp. 11–13, 141–49; and Myth and Guilt, pp. 46–79, 416–30.

27. See Theodor Reik, Mystery on the Mountain: The Drama of the Sinai Revelation (New York: Harper, 1959), especially pp. 87–96.

28. Ibid., pp. 140–49.

29. Ibid., pp. 16–18.

30. Ibid., p. 90.

31. Ibid., p. 176.

32. Ibid., pp. 121, 91, 66–69, 157.

33. Ibid., pp. 184–87.

34. Martin Buber, Moses: The Revelation and the Covenant (New York: Harper, 1946), pp. 185–86.

35. Buber, Israel and the World, pp. 123, 125.

36. Buber, Moses, pp. 37–38.

37. Buber, Kingship of God, pp. 104–7; compare Moses, pp. 48–55, and The Prophetic Faith, trans. Carlyle Witton-Davies (New York: Macmillan, 1949), pp. 27–30.

38. Buber, Moses, pp. 44–45.

39. Ibid., p. 47.

40. Buber, Moses, p. 200.

41. Ibid., pp. 18-19.

42. See Buber, Moses, pp. 121-35.

43. Ibid., pp. 56-59.

44. See ibid., pp. 65-66; The Prophetic Faith, pp. 5-6.

45. See Martin Buber, On the Bible: Eighteen Studies, ed. Nahum N. Glatzer (New York: Schocken, 1968), pp. 86-87; On Judaism, ed. Nahum N. Glatzer (New York: Schocken, 1967), p. 139.

46. Buber, Israel and the World, p. 186.

47. Martin Buber, Pointing the Way, ed. and trans. Maurice S. Friedman (New York: Harper, 1957), pp. 137, 217.

48. See John van Seters, "The Place of the Yahwist in the History of Passover and Massot," Zeitschrift Für Die Alttestamentliche Wissenschaft 95 (1983): 167-82; "The Plagues of Egypt: Ancient Tradition or Literary Invention?" Zeitschrift Für Die Alttestamentliche Wissenschaft 98 (1986): 31-39.

49. Ibid., pp. 70-73.

50. Buber, Moses, pp. 74-79.

51. Ibid., pp. 114-15; compare Kingship of God, pp. 121-35, 200-3, notes 1-22 (with explicit references to W. Robertson Smith in notes 3, 8, 22).

52. Buber, Moses, pp. 147-61; see especially the statement on p. 150, repeated on p. 156 about Moses' overwhelming "moment" in which the new cult come into existence.

53. Ibid., p. 186; compare pp. 182-90.

Chapter 6   Buber And Hasidic Myth

HASIDISM IN JUDAISM

While Buber shares his interest in the
Hebrew Bible with several theorists of myth,
his investigation of the seventeenth century
Jewish mystical movement hasidism
represents a pioneering effort in
elucidating an obscure mythic tradition.
Hasidism arose as a specific response to
challenges faced by Jews in the modern
world. The changes of modernity, beginning
with thinkers such as Spinoza and Voltaire
and continuing through the French Revolution
and the political reaction to it, brought
about two great movements in Jewish
religious life: that of the haskalah, the
Jewish Enlightenment, which sought to
incorporate modern science, philosophy, and
nationalism into Judaism, and that of
hasidism, a pietistic movement that
popularized personal devotion, enthusiastic
worship, and mystical reflections.1

Traditionally, scholars trace hasidism back to Rabbi Israel ben Eliezer, called the Baal Shem Tov, an eighteenth century Jewish leader in Poland known mostly from writings collected by disciples and late legends. Rabbinical Jewish leaders, known as mitnaqdim, or opposers, resented the popular approach of hasidism. These leaders utilized the weak weapons they still possessed--namely, moral argument, the ecclesiastical ban, and ostracism--to discredit the new movement. These weapons failed to attain their ends since rabbinic leaders lacked the political or social power either to enforce the ban or to impose moral sanctions on those who disobeyed them. Thus hasidism grew in popular appeal, not the least because it employed new kinds of religious propaganda such as stories, witty sayings, and new rituals. The Jewish community split between those supporting and those opposing the new movement. Although at first that division mirrored class tension, the Rabbi Dov Baer, who succeeded the Baal Shem Tov, emphasized the elitist and intellectual approach of the rabbinic tradition. He emphasized ecstatic worship, deep study of traditional Jewish lore, and creative exegesis of traditional texts--thus combining the forms of rabbinic religion with the new religious expression that had popularized the movement.

The hasidic leader, the zaddik, formed a charismatic center for hasidism. Both the Baal Shem Tov and Dov Baer emphasized the importance of the zaddik for the welfare of his community. Because the zaddik understood the mysterious powers of divinity in the world, he could guide each of his followers on the right path of religious life. As the movement grew, more and more leaders created their own independent spheres of influence. Rivalries divided one hasidic group from another. One faction, begun by Shneur Zalman of Ladi (1746-1812), synthesized mystical with rabbinic learning. By the nineteenth century, hasidism had united with rabbinical Judaism in a stand against the threat of modernity and the Enlightenment.

Rabbi Abraham Joshua Heschel suggests that the hasidic teachers revived an audacious Jewish impudence that had fallen into disrepute: they claimed that the leader intervenes with heaven for the sake of his followers. Hasidic teaching focuses again and again on the ability of the zaddik to manipulate heavenly powers for earthly purposes.2   One of the most exceptional talents of the zaddik lay in his ability to transform the raw material of daily life into spiritual substance. Jewish mystics both before and after the hasidim sought to redeem this fallen world.

According to these mystics, the creation of the world precipitated a crisis during which divine sparks of holiness were exiled in bodily existence. These holy sparks, trapped in corporeal matter, require uplifting; only when all sparks return to their heavenly source will redemption occur. A complex system of correspondences between human deeds and supernal reactions helped mystics navigate between the mundane and celestial realms. Hasidism accepted this theory and emphasized the mundane aspects of the human task. Human duty lies in redeeming just those material and corporeal elements that confront each person. The zaddik performs this duty through a devotional attachment to God, called in Hebrew <u>devekut</u>. They achieved this cleaving to God while accomplishing the simplest and most ordinary tasks. While the zaddik provides the clearest model of such devotion, every Jew must seek to fulfill this duty, at least by appealing to a zaddik for help. The redemption of the ordinary, daily experiences of every person moves beyond the hasidic leader to the individual hasidim and their duties before God.3

Hasidism believes that sanctifying everyday experiences brings cosmic redemption. Before the rise of hasidism, Jewry erupted into two major messianic movements: that of Sabbetai Zevi and that of Jacob Frank. Jews responded to the call of a messiah who promised them new hope in the seventeenth and eighteenth centuries. Scholars debate how directly hasidism responds to these two movements. Certainly stories about the leaders of hasidism make reference to both messianic figures. Many commentators argue that hasidism has "neutralized" the messianic spirit evident in earlier Jewish sectarian groups. Hasidic writings still hope passionately for a messianic fulfillment: they exalt the expectation of a return to the Land of Israel and of the liberation of the Jewish people from its exile. Nevertheless, they focus on the incremental nature of the redemption and the ordinary tasks rather than the extraordinary deeds that can hasten its coming. Hasidism preserves messianic longing but deprives it of the destructive power that Sabbetianism and Frankism exerted on the Jewish people.4

Buber as a theorist of myth contributes more than either a general theory or new insights to a well-known mythical tradition. He applies his theory of myth to a relatively ignored tradition to illuminate human mythology generally. Buber's exegesis of hasidic myth focuses on these three characteristics of hasidism: the centrality of the zaddik, the hallowing of everyday life, and the neutralization of messianism.

BUBER AND THE HASIDIC STORY

Most scholars see the centrality of the zaddik as the most characteristic aspect of hasidism. Buber attributes the vitality of myth in hasidic stories to the I-You relationship between a zaddik and his disciples. Hasidic stories about the zaddik point to the purpose of human existence: the meeting of an I and a You. Myth, Buber comments, "conveys the meaning of life" by narrating an incident and thus evokes the meaning of life generally through presenting a particular person in life. Buber claims that hasidic myth accurately reports

meetings between people that attest to
life's significance. These myths show how a
true leader helps his followers enter into
authentic human relationships. Buber argues
for the centrality of the zaddik as a
defining feature of hasidism from its very
beginning. The zaddik helps each hasid grow
into a meeting with others. The hasid
experiences this vitalization of his
potential as miraculous and therefore tells
stories about the zaddik as miracle worker.5

Hasidic legend offers these myths in its
anecdotes about the leaders of its movement
and their miracles. Buber's explication of
these stories continually shows how the
zaddik provides direction and purpose for
the hasidim. Hasidic myth, then, acts as a
positive force advocating human choosing.
By contrast, Buber suggested that myth as
used by messianic pretenders such as
Sabbetai Zevi and Jacob Frank prevents true
choosing. Such leaders merely "play" with
myth and thus fail to suggest how myth
reflects a genuine meeting between people.6
He thereby distinguishes between valuable
and dangerous uses of myth.

HASIDISM IN MODERN JUDAISM

This difference between the hasidic use
of myth and its use in other Jewish
movements suggests to Buber how myth
sometimes seeks to replace religion. While
religion depends on myth, myth may also

defeat religion by substituting the image
pointing to a lived experience for that
experience.7 The abuse of myth, however,
can lead to an equally disastrous reaction.
When leaders separate theory from practice
or reject imagination and focus purely on
thought and reason, they fall prey to self-
aggrandizement and spiritual isolation.8
Buber considers this double danger not only
illustrative of hasidism but also typical of
a continuing tension within Jewish religion.
Judaism as a whole reflects a struggle
between myth, which points to spontaneous
events, and religion, which limits and
confines response to appropriate times and
places. While it might appear that religion
wins its battle against myth and converts it
to a static symbol, substituting
manipulation for dialogue, Buber rejects
this conclusion. Hasidic myth represents
one in a continuing series of victories for
the mythic impulse in Judaism.9 Hasidic
myth arises in response to the myth of
earlier Jewish mysticism, myth that had been
converted into static religion by various
messianic movements and eschatological
philosophies. It replaces such philosophy
with a model of human reciprocity that for
Buber remains true to biblical Judaism and
its mythic tradition--the tradition that
shapes Jewish religiosity at its best.
Hasidic myth liberates kabbalistic myth and
returns it to its pristine purity.10

Buber argues that hasidism achieves this
return because it remembers the importance
of concrete events of daily life. Hasidic
myth points to a relationship that empowers

the ordinary Jew. The zaddik's power
enables a hasid to emulate the master's
ability to transform the mundane into the
supernal. Myth testifies to the
transformational power of I-You
relationship, together with the sense of
direction it provides. Hasidic stories
emphasize daily activities because those
activities express mythically the truth that
human meeting occurs through everyday life.
While the content of stories often appears
to be supernatural, Buber attributes this
characteristic to mythic form. Since people
experience their daily events as miracles,
they tell them using superlative language.
Despite this language, Buber claims,
legendary anecdotes narrate commonplace
events perceived as miraculous. His own
writings, he tells his readers, seek to
preserve both the sense of miracle and the
corporeal basis for the story.11

Buber recognizes that any event might
become the kernel of a miracle tale. The
superficial narrative merely carries the
mythic intention and does not exhaust it.
Myth, some might argue, substitutes
supernaturalism for empirical studies and
causal logic. Buber disagrees: Jewish myth
describes the normal causal experiences but
perceives them as "supracausally
meaningful." An empirical description of
events may accurately catalogue what
happened but overlooks its true
significance. Telling a story in a purely
empirical way obscures its truth, and
therefore "the Jew of antiquity cannot tell
a story in any other way than mythically."12

Accurate presentation of what occurs depends upon inclusion of its mythic component. As Buber interprets it, the true lesson of hasidic myth--that even the simple Jew had a concrete task to perform--represents another reflection of I-You relationship. The emphasis on the everyday suggests that religious life requires community, not isolation. While the zaddik aids in bringing redemption, he cannot achieve it alone. The stories of the zaddik merely point to a potential within the hasid. They do not show the zaddik effecting redemption alone. Buber summarizes the hasidic teaching on redeeming the world as the view that "each man can work on its redemption but none can effect it."13 This view of the messianic teaching of the zaddik provides a key to the mythic veracity of hasidic stories. Buber affirms the mythic vitality of stories which maintain a real dialogue between God and humanity.

In later hasidism, however, the zaddik became more and more estranged from his hasidim. As that happened, the stories obscured the line dividing the human leader and the divine leader. The zaddik, like Sabbetai Zevi and Jacob Frank, identifies himself with God and through that identification tries to hasten the redemption of the world. Just as God includes within the divine divinity both good and evil, male and female, so the zaddik unifies all within himself and "redeems" evil by participating in it. The messianic impulse leads to a sympathetic magic applied by a mystic who joins himself

with evil, thereby hoping to influence God
to do the same. Buber feels that
transforming the likeness between the divine
and the human into "an essential identity"
threatens the basic affirmation of God's
"unconditional superiority." The search for
redemption, when carried out by theurgic
attempts, or attempts seeking a magical
effect by imitating the object to be
manipulated, seek to force God to hasten
the time of salvation, leads to a radical
emphasis on human power. Such an emphasis
undermines the truth of myth, a truth that
requires dialogue with divinity rather than
its manipulation.14

Buber shows how hasidic stories of
redemption avoid this temptation to magic.
He acknowledges their messianic and
redemptive intention but explains their
meaning as myths reporting an event of
genuine meeting. When stories focus on
redemption, they point to the human part in
the messianic task. Hasidism reaffirms a
traditional Jewish emphasis on the
importance of each person's deeds. The
hasidic story thereby elaborates "the
traditional belief that God wants to win
through man the world created by him."15
Understood mythically, the stories respond
to the reality of I-You meeting, in which
each partner finds self-confirmation.
Hasidic stories testify to events in which
human beings recognized, with surprise,
their own power.

While hasidism produced a variegated
literature, its stories represent a unique

contribution to Jewish literature.16   Buber
concentrates on these stories because he
finds them peculiarly important in the
modern world. He claims that they speak
with particular relevance today. Modern
Jews, like those in the seventeenth century,
need reassurance of their own potential.
Hasidic stories respond to the modern crisis
of self-confidence by providing a dramatic
personal example of human achievement. They
perform a mythic function because they
indicate an event in which people, through
relationship to others, make a difference in
the world.17   Contemporary scholarship
often debates whether hasidic legends
actually reveal a self-conscious literary
intention or merely reflect folk beliefs.
Certainly the late flowering of hasidic
writings such as the tales of Rabbi Nahman
of Bratzlav and the Hebrew version of the
stories about the Baal Shem Tov bear the
marks of literary sophistication.18   Buber
finds such debate irrelevant because even
late myths point both back to a meeting
experienced as a miracle and forward to new
meetings thus being "a help for our concrete
life."19

BUBER'S CHANGING VIEWS OF HASIDISM

    Buber's own understanding of hasidism
developed as he himself changed from being
fascinated with the occult and mysterious to
an engagement with "I-You" reality.
Curiously, Buber's own struggle with

language and his efforts at expressing
Jewish myth seem a mirror image of the
development occurring within hasidism
itself. Hasidism often confused myth with
religion: it was most revolutionary when it
reintroduced spontaneous myth into the
structures of Judaism. Beginning as a
revival of obscured aspects of Jewish
religiosity, it ended by capitulating to the
formal rabbinic religion it had once
challenged. Buber's development, working in
an opposite direction, began as a
Westernized attempt to create a modern form
for the hasidic myth and ended by allowing
mythic truth to speak for itself unadorned
by artificial artistry. He retains his
Western perspective and admits that hasidic
tales often appear incredible. While
recognizing that some parts of the narrative
and some narratives in their entirety strain
belief, he still notes that some events took
place "but were apparent only to the gaze of
fervor" and that others "cannot have
happened and could not have happened in the
way that they are told." This
impossibility, however, applies only to the
description of external occurrences.20 The
true event for Buber occurs as a human
meeting of dialogue, and he claims that
hasidic myth points directly back to such an
event. Buber finds confirmation of this
view within the hasidic tales themselves.
They, too, testify to their mythic
significance even while remaining on a more
mundane level.

Maurice Friedman characterizes Buber's
growing understanding of myth as a growing

sensitivity to "the unique event responded
to with one's whole being."21   This
statement recognizes an important part of
Buber's approach to hasidism. Buber
considers hasidic stories more than a
fascinating relic from the Jewish past. He
presents their modern relevance as part of
his own message. He describes his function as
that of a "lateborn interpreter" who explains for
others the myth that "has entered into the
lived life of seven generations."22 He
serves this function by drawing attention to
the event at the heart of every hasidic
tale. He challenges readers to see that the
story uses exaggerated language to express
an overwhelming experience. The story may
seem fantastic. It only seems so because
the author tries to "outstrip all
imagination." The superlative and
supernatural elements of hasidic tales
disguise the factual events they describe,
events that Buber understands as occurring
when two persons meet as an "I" and a
"Thou."23

Buber's explanation of why Rabbi Israel,
the founder of hasidism, took the name of
the Baal Shem Tov emphasizes this mythic
imagination as a contrast to previous Jewish
mystical leaders. Buber focuses on the
personality of Rabbi Israel as an example of
a modern human being, of "personal wholeness
which leads to the spontaneous response
rather than to conscious imitation."24 The
Baal Shem Tov treated disciples as human
beings--teaching, healing, and helping them
develop as persons, not merely offering them
magical wonders. Buber focuses on the name

given this leader, a name that can be translated in one of three ways. The term "Baal Shem" means, literally, "Master of the Name." Used of miracle workers, it implies a magical mastery of certain demonic powers who must serve those who know their names. Many such magicians sprung up during the time of the rise of hasidism. Rabbi Israel, one might assume, followed in this tradition. Only he possessed a particularly powerful name: the "Shem Tov" or the "Good Name"--that of the divinity itself.

Another way of interpreting the title, however, applies the adjective "good" not to the name but to the man: he was a "good" Baal Shem, a wonder worker who acted for the benefit of his followers. A final interpretation, however, appeals more to Buber. The term "shem tov" by itself may be translated as "good repute." The name Baal Shem Tov refers to a person of good reputation. Rabbi Israel possessed a good name of his own; his power stemmed from his personality.25

Buber points to a famous anecdote to support this contention. One of those who opposed hasidism did so out of antagonism to magic. He struggled against the use of amulets and magical instruments designed to coerce the supernal world. When confronted by an amulet of the Baal Shem Tov, he angrily tore it apart. Yet instead of finding either a demonic name or a heavenly name inscribed on it, he found the name Rabbi Israel the son of Sarah. The Baal Shem Tov's healing power came from his

personal relationship with those needing
help. Buber draws a conclusion from this
story about the Baal Shem's power of
healing: it took place because of a trusting
personal relation. The amulet was not magic;
it was "nothing but a sign and pledge of the
personal bond between the helper and the one
who is given help, a bond based on trust."26

Hasidic sources reveal a different
meaning. According to them, the Besht
continues a tradition of his predecessors.
The variant forms of this story show that at
times it emphasizes the Besht's power of
magical coercion and his skill at defeating
others who practiced similar arts. Perhaps
most startling of all, however, is the
variant that claims that the Besht
discovered this mode of amulet writing from
one of his predecessors: Rabbi Naftali
HaCohen. The Besht hears that Rabbi
Naftali's amulets have great power. He
inspects them and finds that they contain
only Rabbi Naftali's name. At that point
the Besht decides to imitate this practice.
Buber misrepresents the historical
continuity of the Besht and the other
practical magicians of his time.27 Such a
criticism, however, misses Buber's main
intention. Buber invites readers to share
the insights of hasidism so that they, too,
can build a life on trust and personal
living. He tells the stories of the Besht
to communicate an event faithfully, not a
historical reality. Buber writes of his own
experience, "I had found the true
faithfulness more adequately than the direct

disciples, I received and completed the
task, a late messenger in a foreign
realm."28 Buber's renditions faithfully
reflect the mythic event: a meeting of human
beings enabled by the zaddik. Walter
Kaufmann shows more sensitivity to Buber's
own intention when he suggests that "what
we hear as we read is what Buber heard."29
Buber's telling of hasidic stories succeed
because it flows from his insistent honesty,
an honesty that the direct disciples, in
their zealousness, set aside in favor of
retaining a static symbol of their master's
teachings.

EXAMPLES OF HASIDIC MYTH

The best illustrations of how Buber
applies his theory of myth to hasidic tales
come from his explicit exposition of texts
rather than in his anthologies of tales. He
uses a hasidic story as the point of
departure for explaining the meaning of
myth. His anthologies of hasidic tales
offer a rich resource of myths (even if
Buber sometimes calls them legends) on which
he can draw in his more analytic writings.
Buber reflects on his personal reaction to
the stories, their relationship to other
stories in world literature, and their
importance as myth. His connected series of
essays, "The Way of Man according to the
Teachings of Hasidism," provides clear
examples of Buber's method. In each of
seven chapters he begins with a legend,

expounds its meaning as a reflection of I-You relationship, and supplements the legend with corroborating evidence.30

Buber reports on one tale that bothered him when he first heard it and that only gradually took on positive significance. A disciple of the hasidic teacher, the Seer of Lublin, once took upon himself a week of fasting to teach himself discipline. At the end of his self-imposed period of discipline he went to meet the Seer at the house of study. On his way, however, he passed a well of water. An overwhelming thirst assailed him. Try as he would, he could not overcome the temptation. He went to the well, about to break his fast. At the last moment he thought to himself, "Should I now lose everything for which I have labored all week?" He strengthened his resolve and left the well. As he left, however, he felt a swelling of pride, a sense of satisfaction at having resisted temptation. Sensing this impulse, the disciple changed his mind and returned to the well. Certainly the sin of pride would outweigh any gain that he had attained through fasting. Determined to break his pride, the disciple returned to the well of water and dipped the ladle into the bucket. No sooner had the fresh water come out of the well, however, than the disciple lost all desire to drink. He returned the ladle, still filled to the brim, back to the well and continued on his way to his master. The master looked at the disciple, shook his head sadly, and declared, "Patchwork."31

Buber's interpretive essay recalls how he once wondered at the harshness of the master's response. The disciple's intentions in each case seemed laudable. Learning discipline, breaking the back of pride, responding to the call of the situation at hand--all appear valuable tasks. Reflecting on the Seer's rebuke, however, Buber remarks that he realized that the essential task lies behind each of these individual ones. The master sought to teach the disciple the secret of devekut, of cleaving to God while performing mundane actions. That secret lies less in the particular deeds done than in the unified intention motivating any act. The Seer tried to inculcate a "unity of the soul," a unity that the disciple's patchwork behavior ripped apart. Buber comments that such unification of the self and intention must occur <u>before</u> action rather than in the midst of it. Why, however, did the Seer need to teach the disciple this lesson in so dramatic and painful a way? Buber concludes that only this confrontation would instruct the disciple both in the ideal to be pursued and in the possibility of attaining that ideal. The disciple had experienced failure after failure. What else could he conclude than that he had been programmed to fail? Through the human contact of the Seer's rebuke the disciple discovered his own potential. The Seer communicated a disappointment that also conveyed an expectation: the Seer declared the disciple's work "patchwork" because he knew that the disciple could achieve a unified soul. Through this meeting with the Seer

the disciple learned that "the man with the
divided, complicated, contradictory soul is
not helpless." The story points to the
value of a leader who refuses to accept
compromise and therefore teaches his
followers their unsuspected abilities.32

Taken as a historical anecdote, the
story is puzzling. When Buber read the
story only at its literal level, he could
not understand the master's response to the
disciple. Then he looked more deeply. He
found the myth of I-You relationship at the
heart of the tale. The master teaches the
student that every meeting, even one as
painful as a rebuke, may initiate the same
reaction, entering into I-You meeting.
Teaching through the example of a
relationship itself enabled the student to
know the possibility of personal
unification, of transcending the
multiplicity of the phenomenal world through
moving beyond I-It manipulation to I-You
living. What the student failed to
accomplish in his own patchwork, the master
teaches through an apparent rebuke. Because
Buber sees I-You meeting as the true
significance of the hasidic concept of
devekut, he can decode the Seer's response
to his pupil in terms of this basic reality.
Understood that way, the story mythically
evokes the possibility of human meeting.
Applying his view of myth to the story,
Buber translates the Seer's rebuke into an
existential meeting. The tale recalls that
meeting and its consequences and relates
them in terms that, however cruel, have the
power to reawaken such meeting once again by

those who read its myth truly. The word here, according to Buber, represents a call to action. Buber sees the actions demanded as personal and moral. The disciple learns to unite his life rather than merely practice religious disciplines.

This emphasis on personal and moral response leads Buber to deemphasize traditional Jewish law and practice. Thus Buber tells of a hasidic master who once opened the prayerbook of Isaac Luria during the worship of the Days of Awe but who never glanced inside it. When questioned by his disciples, he narrated a tale about the Baal Shem Tov. Once a poor farmer and his family served a great Christian lord. Times became hard, and the farmer and his wife both died, leaving their young son, Nahum, an orphan. Raised by Christians, the boy knew nothing of Judaism. Once, however, exploring his adopted home, he came across the possession which his parents had left behind: a prayershawl, prayer bands, and a heavy prayerbook. Day after day, Buber relates, the boy would secretly go to that room and gaze at the letters in the book "until the eyes of his mother emerged." When the High Holy Days arrived, the boy felt drawn to the synagogue and learned that the day was holy. Aware that he could not pray himself, the boy "took his mother's book, laid it on the desk," and declared, "I do not know what to pray ... but here, Lord of the world, you have the whole prayerbook." No one knew what to make of that event, but "the Baal-Shem knew of this happening and he spoke of the prayer with great joy." After the

holiday he taught the boy "the pure and
blessed truth."33

The story emphasizes the importance of
intention rather than traditional practice.
Buber acknowledges the importance of deeds
but does so in a non-traditional way. He
tells how Rabbi Hayyim of Zans complained to
Rabbi Eliezer that "My hair and beard have
grown white, and I have not yet atoned."
Rabbi Eliezer responded, "You are thinking
only of yourself--start thinking of the
world." Buber's essay comments that this
anecdote teaches the necessity of moving
beyond the self and contrasts this approach
to that of Christianity. The Jew must be
preoccupied with the welfare of the world;
personal salvation is not the highest aim
but merely a tool by which humanity helps
God's creation become "the kingdom of God."
The story emphasizes an important aspect of
Buber's view of hasidism. Hasidic
messianism focus attention on improving the
world rather than on improving the self.34
The theme of redeeming the world without
becoming self-absorbed plays an essential
role in Buber's exposition of hasidism. The
story at hand, however, involves more than
just this idea. The tale evokes a human
meeting. Rabbi Hayyim tortures himself
about his lack of atonement. Finally, he
gathers enough courage to approach Rabbi
Eliezer and, as in the previous tale,
receives what can only be considered a
rebuke. Buber's ability to move beyond this
rebuke to an exploration of messianism and
the need to redeem the world derives from
his reading of the tale as a myth. Between

the story itself and Buber's exegesis lies its mythical content.

The story, read as myth, reflects an event occurring between Rabbi Hayyim and Rabbi Eliezer. In their meeting Rabbi Hayyim discovered the purpose of his life, the meaning of his soul searching. The story recasts that experience into a story about two men confiding their dearest secrets to each other. Buber intuits this mythical basis in the tale. Rabbi Eliezer calls Rabbi Hayyim "my friend," a term that shows that human companionship provides life's meaning. This response enables his friend to discover that repentance points beyond itself to an act performed for the good of the world as a whole. Through his meeting with Rabbi Eliezer Rabbi Hayyim realized that he had been wasting his "soul-power" on self-reproach when he should have used it to find "a way of fulfillment of the particular task for which he, this particular man, has been destined by God."35 God's concern with the world becomes each person's concern to fulfill a particular duty toward the world. The myth tells this as a story. Hasidic teaching couches this idea in philosophical language. Buber moves from the story back to the myth and presents a new teaching couched in his I-You language about redemption in response to the event.

Buber takes a simple story that glorifies ignorant prayer and develops it into a commentary on human life. A person begins as an orphan and stranger: we do not know our parents or our tradition. Yet we

do find relics of it here and there. The
words of those relics loom before us as an
abyss. We do not understand them; we
grapple with tradition but cannot comprehend
it. If we grapple honestly, good will come
even of our ignorance. The boy who
responded to the power of the letters and
admitted his lack of knowledge finally
deserved the teachings of the Baal Shem Tov.
Like the boy, every Jew seems to journey
toward his original purpose. Every Jew
faces the task of converting the evil and
tragedy of his situation into the basis of
good and human growth. The story in Buber's
version moves beyond the experience of Jews
in particular to encompass every human
story. While in its earliest form the story
functioned as part of hasidic polemic
against the tyranny of an intellectual
elite, for Buber it reveals the deepest
human struggle. The audience of this tale,
whether Jewish or not, recognizes the
potential locked within the "evil" and
problematic aspects of life. Ignorance may
seem a sin, but it can become a blessing;
human beings seek the relics of their
identity to derive some meaning from their
existence. The relics provide more than
meaning; they also offer a sense of
direction. That direction, once discovered,
leads to greater knowledge, unlocking
potential not even suspected before. The
story awakens the thirst for realizing one's
possibilities in the world by its mythic
force.

Buber presents a modern audience with an
opportunity to discover the message of

hasidic truth: its testimony about I-You
meeting and its invitation to similar
meetings in human life today. Buber's
anthologies of hasidic stories narrate tales
so that readers may respond to their
meaning. They offer selections from
legendary anecdotes that directly addressed
Buber, that are written in such a way that
they also address his audience, and that
provide introductory interpretations to open
the texts for readers so that they may
respond spontaneously to them. One story
relates how Rabbi Shneur Zalman, the founder
of Habad hasidism, confronted a skeptical
non-Jew.36 The tale explains that the
opponents of the hasidim, the Mitnagdim,
reported the Rabbi to the Russian
authorities. Their machinations succeeded
in having the hasidic leader imprisoned.
The jailer, a deeply religious non-Jew, took
advantage of the presence of this holy man
to begin a theological discussion. In the
midst of the discussion the jailer demanded
of the Rabbi an explanation of a puzzling
passage in Genesis 3. After Adam and Eve
have disobeyed God and eaten from the
forbidden fruit, they hear God walking in
the garden. Frightened, they hide
themselves. God calls out to the man, "Man,
where are you?" The jailer wonders why God,
whose omniscience should include the
knowledge of where the humans have hidden,
needs to ask that question. The Alter
Rebbe, as the hasidim call Shneur Zalman,
gives an answer directed to the personal
life of the jailer: God determines a life
pattern for each person. Again and again,
the deity calls out to that person: you have

lived just so many years; where are you on
the road that I have set for you; how much
have you accomplished so far toward the
goal that I have established for your life?
According to the tale, the Rebbe mentioned
the exact age of the jailer, who trembled at
these words.

Taken at face value, the story tells a
historical anecdote: how the hasidic master
defeated a rival in theological debate.
Buber recognizes this style of anecdote as
an ancient genre going back to rabbinic
literature. He emphasizes, however, that
the hasidic version transforms the basic
genre. The Alter Rebbe refuses to be drawn
into a purely intellectual discussion and
converts it into a conversation about how
one should live and whether a person has
succeeded in fulfilling life's tasks. While
the jailer addresses Rabbi Zalman with
theological, abstract questions, the founder
of Habad responds with direct, personal
answers. Thus Buber comments: "An
impersonal question which, however seriously
it may be meant in the present instance, is
in fact no genuine question but merely a
form of controversy, calls forth a personal
reply or, rather, a personal admonition in
lieu of a reply."37 Buber suggests
throughout his analysis of this story that
its content lies in this personal
admonition: human beings must begin by
analyzing where they are and how far they
have come on the road allotted to them. The
tale addresses each person, just as the
Alter Rebbe addressed the jailer and demands
self-searching personal introspection.

Although the story of the Alter Rebbe
makes explicit reference to the divine,
Buber sometimes indicates a more subtle
religiosity in hasidic myth. Hasidic
stories present variations on traditional
religious themes that point toward the I-You
meeting they intend to celebrate. Thus
Buber characterizes the hasidic master,
Rabbi Zushya, by the general category of the
"holy fool," known throughout popular
religious literature. At the same time
Buber stresses the peculiar trait of Zushya
as "separate but not separated" from other
people and examines his characteristic love
of others.38 Such introductory words point
the reader toward Zushya's personality,
toward the human being at the heart of the
myth. The introduction, however, does not
illustrate Buber's own responsive reaction
to the myth that addresses him. Buber's
exposition of hasidic myth takes this extra
step. When explaining the Besht's ideal of
a zaddik who fulfills the command to love of
others, the command to love the neighbor as
the self, Buber refers to Zushya. According
to the legend Buber relates, Zushya once
shamed a sinner in the presence of his
teacher. The teacher thereupon "blessed"
Zushya with the ability to see either only
the good in all people or the sins of others
as his own. In the context of Buber's
argument this illustration points to the way
teachers inculcate the true love. By taking
on themselves the sins of others, the
leaders unify the human community. In this
way, Buber comments, the hasidic saying
supplies "what is lacking" in other

traditions: one must include the other in the unity; then one has a good influence on him. People today can learn from this lesson. They will recognize their neighbor's needs and be able to love their neighbor when they can emulate Zushya and include the neighbor in a unity of meeting.39

Buber insists that this emulation can occur only through a human relationship and not through thought alone. The hasidic myth transmits more than a mere message. It also evokes the core event that stimulated the message. Love of neighbor goes back to a human meeting that enabled Zushya to love his neighbor. Buber's exposition of the story of Zushya's ability to see only the good in a sinner connects his ability to identify himself with sinners to his own lack of compassion. Tracing the story back to its mythic roots means looking for the I-You meeting it reflects. Zushya learned from his teacher that when an I and a You meet, they share responsibility and blame. The story, then, has mythical significance because it evokes an event by which Zushya discovered the true meaning of love.

262 **BUBER AND HASIDIC MYTH**

NOTES

1. See Raphael Mahler, <u>Hasidism and the Jewish Enlightenment</u> (Philadelphia: Jewish Publication Society of America, 1985); the pioneering work of Simon Dubnow, <u>History of the Jews in Russia and Poland</u>, 2 vols. (Philadelphia: Jewish Publication Society of America, 1946) remains a valuable resource.

2. Abraham Joshua Heschel, <u>A Passion for Truth</u> (New York: Farrar, Straus and Giroux, 1972), pp. 69–72; compare Samuel H. Dresner, <u>The Zaddik</u> (New York: Abelard Schuman, 1960).

3. See Gershom G. Scholem, "Devekut, or Communion with God," in his <u>The Messianic Idea in Judaism and Other Essays on Jewish Spirituality</u>, trans. Michael A. Meyer (New York: Schocken, 1971), pp. 203–27.

4. See the discussion throughout Scholem.

5. See Martin Buber, <u>Tales of the Hasidim: The Early Masters</u>, trans. Olga Marx (New York: Schocken, 1947), pp. 5–6; see Buber's Hebrew version, <u>Or HaGanuz</u> (Jerusalem and Tel Aviv: Schocken, 1957), and <u>The Origin and Meaning of Hasidism</u>, ed. and trans. Maurice Friedman (New York: Horizon Press, 1960), pp. 27–28.

6. Buber, <u>Origin and Meaning of Hasidism</u>, p. 34.

7. <u>Ibid.</u>, pp. 50-54, 153.

8. <u>Ibid.</u>, pp. 63, 434.

9. Buber, <u>The Legend of the Baal Shem</u>, trans. Maurice Friedman (New York: Schocken, 1955), p. 11.

10. See Maurice Friedman, <u>Martin Buber's Life and Work: The Later Years, 1945-1964</u> (New York: Dutton, 1981), pp. 58, 283.

11. Buber, <u>The Early Masters</u>, pp. vi-ix.

12. Martin Buber, <u>On Judaism</u>, ed. Nahum N. Glatzer (New York: Schocken, 1967), pp. 104-6.

13. Martin Buber, "Replies to My Critics," in Paul Arthur Schilpp and Maurice Friedman, eds., <u>The Philosophy of Martin Buber</u>, The Library of Living Philosophers, vol. XII, (La Salle, IL: Open Court Press, 1967), p. 739.

14. Buber, <u>Origin and Meaning of Hasidism</u>, p. 236.

15. <u>Ibid.</u>, p. 50.

16. See Joseph Dan, <u>The Hasidic Story--Its History and Development</u> [Hebrew] (Jerusalem: Keter, 1975).

17. Buber, <u>Origin and Meaning of Hasidism</u>, pp. 42-45.

18. See Yoav Elstein, <u>Maaseh Hoshev: Studies in Hasidic Tales</u> [Hebrew] (Jerusalem: 1983), pp. 63–125; compare the writings of Joseph Dan on hasidic and Kabbalistic story in his two works, <u>The Hasidic Story</u> and <u>The Hebrew Story in the Middle Ages</u> [Hebrew] (Jerusalem: Keter, 1974).

19. Buber, <u>Origin and Meaning of Hasidism</u>, p. 71.

20. Buber, <u>The Early Masters</u>, p. 1.

21. Maurice Friedman, <u>Martin Buber's Life and Work: The Early Years, 1878–1923</u> (New York: Dutton, 1983), p. 415.

22. Martin Buber, <u>Hasidism and Modern Man</u>, ed. and trans. Maurice Friedman (New York: Horizon Press, 1958), p. 41.

23. <u>Ibid.</u>, p. 33; compare Buber, <u>Between Man and Man</u>, trans. Ronald Gregor Smith and Maurice Friedman (New York: Macmillan, 1965), p. 203.

24. Friedman, <u>The Early Years</u>, p. 120.

25. Buber, <u>The Early Masters</u>, pp. 11–12.

26. <u>Ibid.</u>, p. 13.

27. See the variants collected in Israel Jacob Klapholtz, <u>All the Stories of the BESHT</u> [Hebrew] I (Bnai Berak: Mishor, 1989), pp. 236–38.

28. Buber, <u>Hasidism and Modern Man</u>, pp. 61-
    62.

29. Walter Kaufmann, "Buber's Religious
    Significance," in Paul Arthur Schilpp
    and Maurice Friedman, eds., <u>The
    Philosophy of Martin Buber</u>, The Library
    of Living Philosophers, vol. XII. (La
    Salle, IL: Open Court Press, 1967), p.
    677.

30. Buber, <u>Hasidism and Modern Man</u>, pp. 123-
    76.

31. <u>Ibid.</u>, pp. 146-51.

32. <u>Ibid.</u>, p. 149.

33. Buber, <u>The Legend of the Baal-Shem</u>, pp.
    92-97.

34. <u>Ibid.</u>, pp. 162-67.

35. <u>Ibid.</u>, pp. 163-64.

36. See <u>Ibid.</u>, pp. 130-34.

37. <u>Ibid.</u>, p. 132.

38. See Buber, <u>The Early Masters</u>, pp. 26-27;
    my rendering based on the Hebrew in <u>Or
    HaGanuz</u> differs from Olga Marx's
    translation that says "Zushya does not
    sequester himself; he is only detached."

39. Buber, <u>Hasidism and Modern Man</u>, pp. 253-
    54.

Chapter 7   Myth as Language

SILENCE AND SPEECH IN HASIDIC MYTH

Understanding Buber's approach to hasidic legend as an application of his theory of myth puts in perspective the criticisms often brought against him as an interpreter of hasidism. Other scholars tend to approach hasidism in a reverse manner from Buber. They look at the particular case of hasidism as an illustration of a previously held general theory. Gershom Scholem, the foremost modern scholar of Jewish mysticism, studies hasidism as another example of Jewish mysticism, comparable with earlier forms of Jewish mystical or gnostic religion.1 Scholem evolves a general theory of mysticism. He explores how different Jewish movements exemplify this theory, how mystical symbols, rituals, and philosophies develop in specific historical contexts. Scholem, as much as Buber, seeks to universalize his discoveries. He

investigates the sociological and
psychological dynamics of mystical thinking
and applies these general theories to the
specifics of Jewish mysticism, including
that of hasidism. Scholem attacks Buber for
relying on hasidic stories but ignoring the
esoteric teaching informing them.2

Scholem claims to have discovered several
flaws in Buber's method. First, by de-
emphasizing the teachings that even Buber
admits draw heavily on pre-hasidic kabbalah,
Scholem charges that Buber overlooks
hasidism's continuity with Jewish
gnosticism. Buber transforms hasidism into
an existentialist theology only by
artificially severing its connection with
the magical tradition at its roots. Second,
Scholem charges, Buber's concentration on
the story substitutes evidence from a later
period for more original testimony. Since
the stories Buber analyzes all come from at
least fifty years after the beginning of
hasidism, Scholem claims that they cannot
represent the original hasidic tradition.
Third, Buber, according to Scholem, imposes
a modern and alien meaning to the texts he
studies, suggesting that his view of
hasidism is "tied to assumptions that derive
from his own philosophy of religious
anarchism and existentialism," lacking any
basis in the texts themselves.3 Finally,
Scholem objects to Buber's universalization
of hasidic religiousness as a general
example of I-You meeting. He insists on
distinguishing between the a specific
religious tradition and the category
in which it falls. These criticisms,

however, need to be understood within the context of a deeper division between Scholem and Buber: their different views of language and silence.

A popular theory, recently challenged by Joseph Dan, a contemporary scholar of Jewish mysticism and a disciple of Gershom Scholem, traces the evolution of hasidism as a rapid progression from early vitality to degeneration. According to this view, hasidim begins with the charismatic message of Israel Baal Shem Tov in the early eighteenth century and then deteriorates into a nearly idolatrous reverence for the hasidic masters, the zaddikim, by the end of the nineteenth century.4 While Martin Buber questions some tenets of this theory, he accepts the thesis of a general, arc-like trajectory in its development. For example, he hails Rabbi Mendel of Vorki for developing the art of silence, an art Buber considers appropriate for Rabbi Mendel's age of hasidism's decline. Early hasidism had kept words alive, had vitalized religious language. In its stage of deterioration, however, hasidism lacked that power of invigoration. Words became barriers to the life proclaimed by hasidic leaders: "The time for words is past," Buber comments, "It has become late."5

While Buber lauds Rabbi Mendel for understanding the needs of his age, he castigates other zaddikim who fail to recognize the demand for silence. Rabbi Israel of Rizhin, whom Buber admits baffles him, developed an aphoristic style,

delighting in the power of words. Buber
charges the rabbi with self-indulgence.
While admitting Rabbi Israel "certainly a
genius," he comments on the arrogance
preventing Rabbi Israel from serving as "the
vessel and the voice of the religious
spirit."6 Even this self-indulgent leader,
however, sometimes divines the truth.
Struggling to understand Exodus 20:21-22,
Rabbi Israel intuited an important lack in
his own aphoristic style. Although renowned
as a conversationalist whose use of language
gained him followers and fame, Rabbi Israel
recognized the limits of words. Exodus
20:21-22 distinguishes between a sacrificial
altar made of earth and one made of stones.
God prefers the former but will accept the
latter if the stones are rough hewn and not
of fashioned stone. Rabbi Israel, according
to Buber, applied this verse to worship of
God. God, he stated, preferred silence, but
if words are used, they should be
unfashioned, spontaneous, and unrefined.7
Despite his own affectation of "beautiful
speaking," Rabbi Israel admitted that God
has no love of such speech and desires
unsophisticated, rough hewn words, if not an
abandonment of speech altogether. Buber,
like Rabbi Israel, considers silence greater
than language. For Buber, language
"displaces rather than reflects the reality
being discussed."8 Buber's approval of
Rabbi Israel's silence and his rejection of
Rabbi Israel's aphorisms reflect his view of
language and its limitations even more than
his evaluation of the development of
hasidism and its historical phases. Buber
himself imitates the masters of silence and

moved from the "easy word" of beautiful speaking in his early writings to speaking truthfully in a stammering language that acknowledges the limits of any spoken word.9

GERSHOM SCHOLEM AND BUBER

Gershom Scholem, who, in contrast to Buber, focuses on hasidic theory more than hasidic story, offers a different evaluation of Rabbi Israel of Rizhin. Indeed, Scholem once challenged Buber on his lack of interest in that Rebbe. Scholem pointed to the "unfathomable" words of Rabbi Israel concerning the messianic time: in those days people will quarrel not with one another but with themselves; in those days the world will no longer have images since the image and its object will bear no relation to one another. These ideas, Scholem claims, demonstrate how mystics "fathom the unfathomable." Buber, however, shows no interest in such paradoxes and claims not to understand them. Scholem sees in such statements "the real phenomenon of hasidism, both in its grandeur and in its decay...."10

Scholem disagrees with Buber to such an extent in his positive evaluation of this last phase of hasidism that despite his usual neglect of hasidic tales, he actually turns to a story of Rabbi Israel of Rizhin at the conclusion of his <u>Major Trends in Jewish Mysticism</u>. According to the tale, the Rabbi of Rizhin once faced a crisis similar to that faced by his predecessors. He recalled that when the founder of hasidism, the Baal Shem Tov, confronted the problem, he combined magical technique (theurgy) with an appeal to God and thus resolved the crisis. When a later disciple encountered the same challenge, he no longer knew the entire process of magical actions. Nevertheless, he performed what he knew and uttered his prayer to God, and this sufficed. The Rabbi of Rizhin, however, only remembered the story and knew neither the theurgy nor the prayer. By telling the story, he accomplished the purpose. The tale by itself achieved the miracle aimed at by the theurgy.11

Some interpreters of hasidism suggest that the tale shows how a decline in theurgy may increase the need to rely on purely human powers of redemption. They emphasize the inherent spiritual strength of storytelling as a religious act. Moshe Idel, in a recent study of Jewish mysticism, challenges this view and claims instead that the story replaces theurgy with personal mysticism, with the union of the narrator to the divine addressee of the story.12 Perhaps Buber intuits this insight and therefore demurs from the general acclaim given the story. He never reproduces the tale and expresses his disapproval of Rabbi Israel. Buber exalts hasidism because it rejects personal mysticism and engages instead in an evocation of the lived reality that language only partially reveals and usually conceals too well.

Perhaps this recognition explains a rather strange interchange between Scholem and Buber. Once, Scholem remarks, he asked Buber why he disliked Rabbi Israel, and Buber responded that he did not "understand" this teacher.13 This response conceals more than it reveals. What Buber did not "understand" lay in the human qualities of the teacher; the artificial "cleverness" of Rabbi Israel seemed somehow inauthentic to him, less an expression of mythic reality than a crystallization and fossilizing of "religion," an example of dead form replacing living religiosity. Those comfortable with how religion simplifies the complexity of life may well be attracted to the Rizhiner. That very sophistication, however, repels those who look to myth as an invitation to response.

The different approaches to language separating Buber and Scholem shape each thinker's view of Jewish myth. Buber's paradigm of language as a secondary reflection on an immediate experience parallels his definition of myth. For Buber, Jewish myth records, inadequately but faithfully, an event in human experience. While the stories of the hasidim seem to tell about ideas and values, Buber claims that they actually point to a living event; they suggest that only a life, not a doctrine, expresses truth.14 Even when Scholem's disciples tend to agree with Buber in discerning the importance of stories about zaddikim, they reject his use of I-You philosophy as a way of interpreting the

mystic power in the tales. Thus Joseph Dan
combines Buber's emphasis on the value of
hasidic narrative with Scholem's insistence
on their theological content. He suggests
that the stories are simultaneously
symbolizations of the cosmic theories found
in classical Jewish mysticism and myths
seeking heroic models in times of crisis.15
Such an attempted reconciliation of story
and theory, however, misses the dramatic
dichotomy between Buber and Scholem on the
meaning of language. The two disagree not
merely about the meaning of hasidism but
more importantly about how myth expresses
truth.

BUBER AND HASIDIC LANGUAGE 16

The key to Buber's approach lies in his
contention that "All speech, therefore, is
answering, responding."17 Speech arises in
response to a human experience. It
translates into tangible symbols a reality
that originally occurs in the relationship
between one person and another. Myth for
Buber serves as the language for religious
experience. As language responds to daily
experience, so myth responds to
extraordinary experience. Just as language
must be decoded by comparing the linguistic
symbol with the referent to which it points,
so myths must be traced back to their
originating events. The truth of language
depends on its accuracy in reporting events
in the world. The truth of myth depends on

its accuracy in reflecting its event that
gave rise to its creation. Just, however,
as language does not exhaust the reality
within which human beings live, so, too, for
Buber myth does not exhaust the religious
reality from which it originates.

    Buber's view of myth as the language
that inadequately points to a religious
event pervades his study of hasidism. He
seeks to evoke the kernel of a "memory that
can nonetheless outstrip all imagination."18
Emphasizing the human value of this memory,
Buber finds the value of myth in its effect
on people, not in the message it transmits.
Buber opposes distilling myth into knowledge
rather than into life. In this vein Buber
claims that "genuine religious movements" do
not create philosophies of life but
reinforce each person's ability to live that
life. Religious myths evoke the possibility
of living rather than transmit a message
about the meaning of existence.   These
myths focus not on "the solution of the
world mystery" by providing diagrams of some
external reality. Instead, Buber contends
that myths "equip" people "to live from the
strength of the mystery." Since myths shape
the way people live rather than how they
think, Buber insists that they do not
"instruct about the nature of God" but
rather point each person to the path on
which God can be met. Buber interprets
myths the way he interprets all language: as
an inadequate suggestion of a fuller truth,
the truth of human living.19 Buber's
argument rests on the claim that myth
derives from reflection on an event. God's

voice meets people in every situation in a
unique and singular way. On reflection, the
variety of voices arising from these moments
takes on a unity and becomes the expression
of the single voice of the Lord of the
world. Myth expresses that intuition in
language and provides a key by which to
reflect on new situations and on the voices
arising from them.20

Since Buber's writing about language and
myth resembles that of Ernst Cassirer, a
contrast between the two illuminates Buber's
distinctiveness. Both Cassirer and Buber
recognize the "God of the moment" as the
immediate reality meeting people from "some
entirely concrete and individual, never-
recurring situation." Like Buber, Cassirer
distinguishes between the image of that
momentary God created by language and the
reality of its immediacy. Both Cassirer and
Buber turn to poetry rather than philosophy
to discover the "origins" of language.
Trying to convey his understanding of
religion, Buber provides what he calls "a
gauche comparison." Understanding a poem,
he suggests, occurs immediately as a reader
suddenly grasps the meaning behind the
poet's words. Continued study of one poet,
however, prepares readers so that their
immediate meeting with the poem takes on
greater fullness and significance. "In such
a way," he claims, "out of the moment Gods
there arises for us with a single identity
the Lord of the voice, the One."21

Buber differs significantly from
Cassirer. Where Cassirer's momentary gods

dissolve into the remembered image, Buber's
point beyond themselves to "the One." This
difference grows out of the way Buber thinks
language and religion are related to each
other.   Language not only reflects upon
truth but draws attention to it.   While
language objectifies, it also addresses.
Language moves between "speaking about" and
"speaking to."   Language uses signs to point
backward at an immediate experience;
religion uses myth to point backward to a
meeting with God; language calls reality
into being again and again; religion invites
a renewed I-You meeting with the divine in
which "the All reveals itself as language,"
thus completing the circle.   The dynamic
interplay of the immediacy of meeting with
the language reflecting that meeting seems
to Buber a double activity: while language
does suggest the ultimate "One," it also
legitimates and justifies the individual
selves making up the "All".   Thus language
stimulates diversity, even while confining
it.   Language and myth point backward
toward their origins in experience and
beyond themselves to a renewed contact with
the fullness of original experience.22
Language flows from a unique meeting that
cannot be replaced by any "experience."

SCHOLEM AND HASIDIC MYTH

Scholem's view of myth generally, and of
Jewish myth in particular, differs radically
from Buber's.23 Scholem trusts language. He

emphasizes that the word represents a "real" entity: it points to an actual thing in the world. According to Scholem, mystics portray a real world that consists solely of language. Struggling to find a new way of expressing the ineffable deity, mystics devise a new reality, a reality they construct through words. In that new language, Scholem contends, "the divine things are at the same time the divine words." Words become images; language and spiritual reality become one. In the mystical system "Only that which lives in any particular thing as language is its essential life." Scholem's approach to Jewish mysticism reflects his understanding of it as language. He tries to decode its symbols and translate them from one vocabulary into another. When Scholem decodes mystical myth, he shows how it creates a new language that participates in the divine truth to which it points.24

Scholem, unlike Buber, offers no definition of myth. He prefers to let the data establish their own self-definition. His long article on "Myth and Kabbalah" gathers copious examples of symbols forming a mythic vocabulary to show how mystics conveyed an ineffable experience in concrete images and evocative symbols. By producing such a compendium of symbols, Scholem shows how myth attempts to transmit a concrete intuition of the divine through the medium of language. Symbolism reflects upon the mystical experience and transforms experience into concrete reality. Myth linguistically portrays the divine being.25

Philosophers, he believes, misunderstand
reality by reducing it to rational concepts.
While, he claims, the philosophical approach
demands that knowledge fit into an
intellectual framework, mystics reject that
framework and thereby grasp reality more
truly. Scholem argues that mystics express
in myth and symbol what philosophers can
only call "ineffable," that is to say,
inaccessible to their systems. He thinks
that philosophers err because they identify
reality with what is expressible in their
special terms. Mystics see more clearly and
therefore create a language adequate to the
full scope of truth, the language of myth.26
In so doing, they create a vocabulary that
evokes the world it portrays. For Scholem,
mythical language serves the mystic as
rational language serves the philosophers.
In both cases, language refers to an
experience in the objective world that
bridges apprehension and experience.
Scholem, much like the early gnostics,
identifies mystical secrets with a higher
truth than that which philosophers perceive
and interprets myth as a specially coded and
mysterious language that only the initiated
can understand.27 Myth presents humanity
with a singular gift: a more complete
reality than that which philosophy gives.

MYTH, REVELATION, AND PHILOSOPHY

Buber's emphasis on living response
leads him to understand the relationship of

myth and philosophy differently from
Scholem. Not only myth but also philosophy
arises in spontaneous answer to a divine
call. Both philosophy and myth are
secondary reflections on a primary
experience. Language, whether conceptual
and philosophical or mythic and mystical,
testifies to a reality beyond itself for
Buber, the reality of revelation. Buber
understands by revelation not a specific
message but "that meeting of the divine and
the human in which the human has a factual
share." He claims that philosophy still
plays a role in interpreting that meeting.
Revelation, as he understands it, "summons
reason" to a twofold task. First, reason
must help expound the implications of
revelation. It must aid in converting the
immediacy of meeting into an on-going path.
Second, however, reason must heed the
challenge of revelation. It must "be
stirred and renewed by it."28 Not only
should students of myth and philosophy
beware of reductionism; they must recognize
that both myth and philosophy lie open to
the demands growing from the event that gave
them birth: a revelation about reality.

Scholem confronts the challenge of
revelation in a distinctive way. He
suggests that revelation as traditionally
received represents an alternative truth to
that advanced by Jewish mystics. The
mystic mediates between the raw material of
a personal revelation, which points to an
extraordinary and untraditional view of God
and God's demands as presented in
tradition.29 The mystic engages in a

process of translation: the language of
myth translates an esoteric revelation into
a more public language. When, however, the
translation appears too idiosyncratic or
free, then tradition acts to keep it within
comprehensible boundaries. This balancing
act, however, brings a tension with it.
Scholem considers "the mystical sphere" a
"meeting-place" of primitive mythology and
developed revelation. That paradox combines
an elevated theory of religious life with
"revival" of naive mythic symbols.

The mystic for Scholem intuits truth on
a different plane from ordinary Jews.
Mystics then explain that truth in terms of
the norms governing traditional Jewish
behavior. While the Jewish mystics seem to
affirm traditional ways of expressing
religious truth, Scholem shows how they use
the expressions and literature of rabbinic
Judaism as a point of departure to convey a
new message. The content of the message is
revolutionary; the descriptive terms they
use are traditional. Mystical myth succeeds,
Scholem thinks, just because it combines
"the spiritual heritage of rabbinical
Judaism" with "the main forces active in
Judaism."30 Scholem understands this
success as linguistic conquest. Jewish
mystics create a religious vocabulary by
which to describe their experience of
reality. They do not, as philosophers
strive to do, evolve a new language, but use
the old language in a new way. Philosophers
transform a people's understanding of God.
Mystics communicate the reality of God,
presenting rather than explicating truth.31

Scholem's dichotomy forces a choice
between philosophical and mystical
approaches. Myth differs from philosophy by
using old language in a new way rather than
by inventing a new language. Buber
disagrees and suggests that while sometimes
explaining and sometimes asserting, language
may also convey an opportunity. Language
sets the choice of how to live before each
person. The major distinction among
believers, Buber claims, is that between
those affirming a commanding God and those
denying such a God. A person can believe
that God creates and sustains the world
without feeling an obligation to that deity.
When a person recognizes God as a concerned
other making demands of humanity, then
belief leads to responsive living.
Religions differ not in their affirmation
that God is real but in their views of
whether the deity interacts with humanity or
remains aloof from it. People differ not
because one is a theist and the other an
atheist but because of their acceptance or
rejection of an obligation to the divine.32
Myth for Buber conveys the reality of choice
by confronting each person with the
necessity for decision. Buber holds that
myth succeeds only when, like language, it
evokes the reality that created it and when,
by stimulating speech, it enables people to
become more fully human.33 This emphasis on
reality, not language, testifies, as Maurice
Friedman suggests, that "More important
than Buber's having developed a philosophy
of the word is the fact that he became and

remained a person of the word, of the lived word that is spoken."34

RABBI NAHMAN OF BRATZLAV

One early confrontation between Buber's and Scholem's understanding of myth arose over Buber's free renderings of the tales of Rabbi Nahman of Bratzlav.35   How might Buber's view of myth as language compare with Scholem's when tested against those tales? Rabbi Nahman of Bratzlav (1772-1812), a great grandson of the Baal Shem Tov, fascinates modern scholars of literature, psychology, and religion. He stood against the stream of his times, opposing rationalists, secularists, and rival mystical leaders. Caught up in the controversies of his day, he created a literature that continues to exercise an influence over his followers.36 He sought a broad audience and popularized pithy sayings, often inventing such sayings based on his unique reading of primary materials. Finally, he chose storytelling as the most effective means of popularizing Jewish teachings. The thirteen major tales which he composed distill his religious message and illuminate his teachings. Arthur Green, a recognized scholar of hasidism in general and of Rabbi Nahman in particular, realizes this aspect of the tales and therefore partially sides with Buber against Scholem on the importance of hasidic stories in understanding hasidic religion.37 It remains questionable, however, whether the meaning of those tales in fact agrees more with Buber than with Scholem.

Rabbi Nahman himself provides a key to help decode the meaning of his stories.38 Nahman understood stories as responses to the needs of the hour. Rabbinic literature often quotes Psalm 119: "It is time to work for the Lord since they have voided His Torah." When Jews disobey God's laws (when they void His Torah), then extraordinary measures must be taken. Some early rabbis interpret the verse differently: when it is time to work for the Lord, then you are permitted to void His Torah! Rabbi Nahman interprets the verse in this way, justifying his use of folklore and popular literature as a necessary strategy in a time of crisis. Rabbi Nahman uses stories to adapt transcendent teachings to the chaotic world in which we live. "After evil decrees were issued against the world," Nahman writes, "prayer was forced to disguise itself as story." Nahman uses stories as an external expression of exalted spiritual realities and claims that they effect a reparation on the upper worlds when usual means such as Torah and Prayer fail. For him, Jewish stories have redemptive value, just as popular conversation elevates ordinary people by linking them to the knowledge of the zaddik, the righteous leader. When a zaddik reveals secret meaning, he multiplies peace in the world, clothing the hidden light of truth in a strange garment. Nahman claims that a zaddik fulfills three tasks: gaining knowledge of true piety (fear

of the Lord), revealing the means of gaining
such piety, and transmitting that piety
through the telling of stories. These
stories awaken people from their sleep to
service of God.

   In some ways Nahman's view of
storytelling supports Buber's contentions.
Nahman must hide religious truth within the
protective shell of myth. Myth serves to
preserve silence; its very artificiality
draws attention to its distance from
reality. Scholem can argue with equal
justification that Nahman's strategy
preserves the essential teaching: Nahman
merely disguises the form of expression, not
the content. Rabbi Nahman indicates the
multivalent meanings of religious symbols in
his stories. His myths draw from classical
sources and allude to them. His tales
intertwine biblical phrases with Yiddish,
the common language of Jews in his day,
echoing popular folklore while hinting at
references to traditional lore and rabbinic
teachings. Nahman insists again and again
that his stories constitute Torah and must
be linked to Judaism's normative books.
That allusiveness confirms Buber's
intuition. Buber claims that Nahman's
relationship to language emphasized dynamic
interaction. Nahman strove for the
mutuality in which speaker and hearer
dissolve into one. Thus Buber attempts to
catch the unspoken teaching of mutuality
whereas Scholem restricts himself to
collecting Nahman's words in a complete
bibliography of his writings.39

RABBI NAHMAN'S TALES

Nahman's own testimony can fit either Buber's framework or Scholem's. How does each interpretive structure suit particular tales? The first point of debate arises over the value of silence. Buber refuses to translate or analyze Rabbi Nahman's first tale. He considers it a "fairy tale," "unoriginal" and not part of Rabbi Nahman's religious contribution. The story itself seems to bear out this view.40 The tale describes the servant of a great king. The king had six sons and a single daughter, whom he particularly loved. Once, however, she angered him, and he cursed her saying "May the 'Not-Good' take you away." In the morning she was gone and no one knew where she was. The king's trusted servant went in search of her, encountering obstacles along the way. Even after finding her, he had to pass certain trials. Twice he failed in his purpose, once by eating an apple and once by drinking wine. Thereafter he enlisted the aid of three giants, one of whom summoned all the winds. One wind knew that the princess had been taken to a golden mountain and was held in a pearly castle. Equipped with magical means, including a purse that could not be emptied of money, the king's servant eventually succeeded.

While apparently made up of common folk motifs, the story actually portrays the mythic system about which Gershom Scholem writes. Scholem offers several renditions of this basic kabbalistic myth.41 He claims that mystical truth portrays a metaphysical reality as objective truth. According to this myth, the world began with a catastrophe: God's pure holiness shattered the shell of creation, and sparks of holiness became trapped in the shards of that shell. The first human, Adam, forfeited the opportunity to liberate those sparks, as did succeeding generations. Only the Jews who possess the tool of Torah as mystically understood can redeem creation from the effects of the original crisis. Mystical evocations of this myth provide blueprints for redemption. They point unequivocally to the primal crisis, its progression through history, and the techniques for achieving liberation of the sparks of holiness and restoring the world to its pristine purity.

Rabbi Nahman's first tale recapitulates that cosmic myth, thereby affirming Scholem's contention: just as language communicates truths about the world of experience, so myth conveys truths about reality beyond experience. With this in mind, Arnold Band, a noted scholar of Hebrew literature, points out that Rabbi Nahman makes use of a "simple folktale" to provide "model of the cosmic drama which filled Lurianic Kabbalah and obsessed Nahman and other hasidic masters."42 The story provides a blueprint for redemption. The princess represents the ideal world that was destroyed by human error: the foolish curse of the king. Only the lowly servant, modern Jews, can succeed in reversing this catastrophe by avoiding the major temptations of life: the taboo on eating recalls the sin in the Garden of Eden; the taboo on drinking recalls the sin of Noah after the flood; the detailed instructions given the servant parallel the laws of Moses; the three giants symbolize the magical forces aiding in tikkun or reparation by which a wise adept can liberate a fallen world. As a magician's guide to world redemption, the story confirms Scholem's advocacy of stories as magic rather than Buber's call for silence.

Even Band, however, recognizes the limitations of this analysis based on mystical cosmology. The tale lacks a real "closure." It ends by merely saying that the servant liberated the princess but does not describe the actual process of such liberation. "Nahman," he explains, "declined to describe the actual act of redemption."43 Nevertheless, Nahman hints at the higher meaning of the tale by claiming that it has so much power that "whoever heard it had thoughts of repentance."44 Yoav Elstein analyzes the mythical meaning of this story, discovering that while it does use the kabbalistic system as a background, it also evinces a deeper structure. The story develops through parallels and opposites to typify a basic human view of reality rooted in psychology rather than cosmology. Superficially, the story seems to emphasize the redemption of the lost princess. In reality, however, it sketches the yearning of the minister of the king. The story shows how self-discipline, prayer, and desire train a person in the worship of God. Nahman's tale may well be a tale of silence

since he extols not the attainment of a
human goal but the motivation that leads a
person to pursue that goal.45   This
perspective confirms Buber's understanding
of myth.   Although the myth may not
represent an I-You meeting, it acts as an
affirmation of human life rather than as a
magical attempt to manipulate cosmic
redemption.   While Scholem's literalist
approach to language appears to function
well, it cannot explain the truncated ending
of the tale or its focus on the yearning of
the king's minister.   Buber's identification
of the myth as a myth of human meeting fits
the narrative of the story better.

MYSTICAL MYTH

Buber may correctly understand the
purpose of Rabbi Nahman as a didactic author
but still misinterpret the myths used.
Scholem, at least, argues that Buber
distorts the stories by ignoring the
"Kabbalistic ethos" that, in his view "is
probably the most important legacy of the
Kabbalah to Hasidism."   He charges that
Buber's personal commitment to "religious
anarchism and existentialism" limits his
ability to discern the true meaning of Rabbi
Nahman's stories.46   Nahman's tale "The
Switched Children" seems a simple story in
which the "fairy tale" elements dominate.
The tale presents an opportunity for judging
whether Buber indeed pushes hasidic myth too
far.   The classic motif tells of two

children switched at birth who eventually
regain their original status. Whose view of
mythic language better captures Nahman's
intentions in relating this tale?47   The
tale begins with two switched infants: the
king's son grows up as a servant and a
servant's son as the prince. When the
supposed prince becomes the king, he cannot
hide his true nature. Rumors circulate
about the switched infants. The false king
persecutes the true king's son, who flees
into exile and drowns his feelings of
injustice in wine. No longer does he act
like a prince; he no longer even acts like a
rational human being; he wallows in his
desires and becomes like an animal. To earn
his living, he serves as a herdsman, and the
people call him "the cattle man," indicating
his decline into animal sensuality. Once
while keeping herd, however, two animals run
off; pursuing them without success, he loses
his way in a dark forest, he meets a "forest
man" who warns him, "Do not keep pursuing
your sins." Pausing, the king's son meets
his rival, who does not recognize him but
who instead retells the story, adding that
his conscience had bothered him because of
his treatment of an innocent person.
Finally, he recounts, he lost his way in
this forest and has wandered hungry and
thirsty for days. The false king sells
himself into bondage to the true king's son
for food and drink.

    As the story progresses, the two
travelers meet the forest man and spend time
with him. The true king's son learns the
song of the animals and increases his

domination over the servant's son. When,
finally, the two leave the forest, the
forest master gives the true king's son a
musical instrument which the prince
exchanges at the gates of a great city for
the ability to deduce one thing from
another. Using this knowledge, the true
king's son passes various tests to become
king over the city, where he restores order
to a chaotic kingdom. Once the order
returns, he states to his companion, "Now I
know that you are the servant's son and I am
the true son of the king."

Arnold Band calls this story "a study in
the discovery or rediscovery of self." He
shows how mystical interpreters explain the
story as "a dramatization on a personal
level of the process ... whereby the
cosmos is restored to the harmony" of its
primal creation. On the level of plot the
tale differs considerably from Rabbi
Nahman's first tale. On the mythic level,
however, the images point to the same
reality. The ordeals the true king's son
undergoes parallel those of the king's
minister in the previous tale. Redemption
occurs only after a primal fall. The true
son gains his appropriate status only by
learning to use magical instruments given
him as a reward for his actions and
perceptions. The process of cosmic
reparation takes place by stages. Scholem's
view seems confirmed. Despite superficial
differences, the images used by Nahman point
to a single myth: the myth Scholem
identifies in the later kabbalah.48

Other interpreters, however, see the
myth in psychological terms. Nahman's tale
may remind people of their inner division.
The two protagonists may mirror two internal
realities, two impulses within each person.
Joseph Weiss, whose pioneering work on Rabbi
Nahman's psychology lay the foundation for
future studies, claims that Nahman himself
identified with the "divided ego" of the
story. Weiss claims that Nahman focuses on
the problem of the alienated self and its
disastrous consequences. Yehudit Kuk, an
observant traditional Jew who presents Rabbi
Nahman as an idea for modern Israelis, seems
to agree with some of these conclusions.
She interprets the story as an allegory of
how each person transforms the evil impulse
into a force for good. While recognizing
the resemblance of the story to the
traditional kabbalistic symbols, she also
understands them in personal terms. In her
view the tale advocates traditional Jewish
values and practices: repentance, prayer,
the offering of animal sacrifices, and
Sabbath observance. Her analysis, however,
goes even further to see the tale as an
allegory about the people of Israel and the
nations of the world. Israel has lost its
way in the world. The other nations
dominate history and enslave the Jews.
Jews, according to Rabbi Nahman, can
reassert themselves only by moral actions
which transform society itself. Jews will
regain power only when they have created an
ordered world. The redemption of the Jewish
people as the prince among the nations will
occur only after the Jews rediscover their
royal task of restoring the divine pattern

intended by creation. This interpretation helps a reader decode references in the story as allusions to Israel's exile, its love of the Land of Israel, and the possibility of its return to a national home.49

As the diverse interpretations show, Nahman's story has a multivalent meaning. Whether Scholem or Buber correctly understands "the" mystical myth, Buber offers a better model of how mythic tales function in mystical writing. As Kuk and Weiss suggest, the stories evoke a multiplicity of responses. Buber's view of myth as a stimulus to I-You relationships allows for this variability; Scholem's interpretation does not. In this story of the switched children, Buber permits the text to speak for itself. He refrains from any major alteration of Nahman's story as such. Sometimes, however, he transforms his sources in modern ways to obscure clear references to gnostic or magical theories. Buber avoids such references because of his discomfort with magic as an alternative to religion. Critics often fault Buber for rewriting hasidic tales in his own image.50

SIMPLICITY IN HASIDIC MYTH

One of Rabbi Nahman's stories might appear to support Buber. The "Tale of the Clever and Simple Man" shows the superiority

of simplicity to the sophistication of
philosophy and magical theory. Nahman uses
the tale to show how philosophy leads to
doubt and suspicion. Piety depends on
simple trust rather than on an esoteric
intellectualism. Precisely this story,
however, exposes the dangers of Buber's
approach. The conclusion of the tale
depicts a confrontation between the
incarnation of evil, Satan, and a righteous
leader, called the Baal Shem. That title
reveals some ambiguity. Rabbi Nahman
clearly does not refer to his great
grandfather. The story, however, makes the
Baal Shem involved as more than a mere
magician. Perhaps Rabbi Nahman hopes that
his readers will learn that a leader who
appears only as a popular wonder worker
actually fulfills a more exalted function in
the world. The story conveys quite clearly
the magical power of the zaddik to protect
his followers from the machinations of the
devil. Buber omitted all references to
demonic power from the story. When, years
later, challenged on this point, he admitted
that he regretted much in his translations
of Nahman's tales. On this point, however,
he could see no alternative, even with his
new perspective. A modern author cannot
present evil in so magical a way.51

    Rabbi Nahman's tale tells of two
brothers, one clever and one simple, and as
in many folk tales, the simple son succeeds
while the clever son fails. The story
reaches its climax when the devil catches
the clever brother in his trap. The simple
brother's attempts to prove the reality of

Satan to his sophisticated sibling go
unheeded. Finally, however, the clever
brother acknowledges Satan's power, throws
himself on the mercy of a hasidic saint, and
escapes the devil's clutches. By admitting
the reality of evil, the clever brother can
grapple with it, in himself and in others,
and finally triumph. Only those who pretend
that evil does not exist fall into its
traps. Those who recognize its threat can
transform the evil impulse and use it for
good.

Retelling this story, Buber not only
omits the final episode but alters
apparently minor details to create a
psychologically compelling rather than a
magically oriented story. The original tale
emphasizes that the "wisdom" of the clever
son stems from philosophy. He studies
medicine, Latin, and then philosophy. Buber
merely states that he "grasped the wisdom"
of his teachers with penetrating acuteness.
Nahman's tale focuses on the clever man's
dissatisfaction with himself. Buber
transforms this attitude into an inability
to accept criticism from others. Finally,
Nahman reports that the clever brother
assimilated into the gentile world: at one
point he appeals to a gentile magistrate
against the Baal Shem. Buber omits all
reference to that theme of Jewish/non-Jewish
tension. Arnold Band suggests that the
story moves in three sequences, building up
to the final contrast between belief and
skepticism, in which the clever brother
finally accepts the hasidic saint. Buber
has altered not only some details in the

story but also its inner structure. Buber's
rendition of the story undermines this
carefully prepared literary architecture.
Buber's deviations from the original tale
suggest that Scholem correctly notes his
methodological limitations. Almost
intentionally, Buber avoids the esotericism
which permeates hasidism and specifically
the hasidic exaltation of the zaddik.52

Belief in the zaddik need not, however,
imply esotericism. Yehudit Kuk explains how
the zaddik enables each person to begin the
process of growing toward God. Both the
simple brother and the clever brother
experience the influence of the Baal Shem as
a moral force that reaches out to them as
people. The irreducible power of the zaddik
may lie in his human qualities, not in
esoteric magical skills.53 Joseph Weiss
suggests that the problem of "evil" for
Rabbi Nahman lay in the ambiguity of truth
and wisdom itself. On this reading, Nahman
supports the position of neither the simple
man nor the clever man. The story confronts
its readers with the basic problem of human
life: how to attain both wisdom and
belief.54 Human beings cannot live with
either simplicity or wisdom alone. In the
story the simple man does gain wisdom. In
the epilogue that Buber omits the clever son
seems to gain the faith of his brother. The
story offers no unambivalent response to
either wisdom or simplicity.

Buber has clearly altered the original
story. Nevertheless, his alterations convey
the sense of the myth. His contention that

the myth reflects an event of meeting rather than a set of cognitive principles explains the dynamics of the tale as well as Scholem's theory does. While Buber's uneasiness with magical elements in hasidism leads him to transform the story, his understanding of myth as evocative rather than denotative language enables him to remain true to the intention of the tale.

REDEMPTION IN HASIDIC MYTH

The three tales of Nahman use folklore and "fairy tale" elements to evoke a sense of fantasy.   Yet Buber's description of Rabbi Nahman's journey to the land of Israel evokes a contrasting realism.55 Several scholars agree with Buber's contention that Nahman introduces a major change in Jewish thinking about the land of Israel. Arthur Green, in his definitive study of Rabbi Nahman, comments that while he cannot accept Buber's method, he finds his basic point that Nahman "marks a new beginning of a realistic relationship with Erez Israel, in contrast to earlier oversimplification and romanticization," valuable and "worthy of consideration."56 In his anthology of hasidic stories Joseph Dan introduces the story of the journey by remarking on Buber's rendition. Dan also suggests that the story is "realistic despite hasidic attempts to symbolism."57   Hasidism, at least as Rabbi Nahman lived it, may have provided an

impetus to Zionism as a realistic political
movement.

Scholem's trust in language leads him in
an opposite direction. He refused to be
misled by apparently realistic hopes for a
restoration in Zion. In contrast to Buber,
Scholem distrusts a "Zionist" view of
hasidism. He emphasizes the role Israel
played as an idea in Jewish mystical thought
and contrasts that role to Israel's
potential as a real, physical place.
Buber's extension of Nahman's symbolism to a
political program seems erroneous. Scholem
thus notes that "The creative power of
Hasidism was centered on the mystical life,"
not on history. He avers that "the hasidic
movement, in spite of many modern
affirmations to the contrary, could do
without the Land of Israel."58 Where Buber
emphasizes the realism in the story as an
example of a full human life, Scholem
considers the "real" Israel of hasidism to
be a metaphysical one. Nahman himself seems
to understand the story in cosmological
terms. Later commentators discern
metaphysical implications in the story
similar to those in the thirteen more
"fabulous" tales. Comparing the narrative
given by Dan with Buber's suggests that
Buber has overemphasized the realism of the
tale.59 Buber's approach, however, finds
some confirmation in other sources. Buber
contends that Nahman considers the lived
human life central and therefore turns to
concrete experience. He remarks that Israel
itself stands for "simplicity" rather than
for complex symbolism. In short, he

concludes, "it is the true wisdom to taste
in one's bread all the pleasant tastes of
the world."60

Other interpreters unite the two
approaches. Meir Urian, an Israeli critic
who combines literary studies with
interpretations of hasidism, considers
Nahman the most "messianic" of all the
hasidic leaders. Nevertheless, he remarks
that Nahman believes that only by realizing
the concrete reality of the Land of Israel
can Jews truly understand its metaphysical
meaning. In the same way, Nahman argues,
the metaphysical status of a true zaddik
needs the confirmation and reality of a
concrete, living zaddik. Ironically,
Nahma n's own followers have abandoned such
a living zaddik in favor of the continued
metaphysical presence of Nahman even after
his death.61

The messianic element within Rabbi
Nahman's writings seems to echo that
metaphysical ideal. Scholem recognizes
Nahman's messianic leanings, even while
suggesting that hasidism neutralized their
political significance. From this standpoint
Nahman's stories symbolize redemption by
telling the tale of cosmic disaster
and suggesting the path to cosmic healing.62
Nahman himself emphasizes that his stories
have a messianic purpose: they bind Jews to
their true leader, the zaddik, the
righteous master, the rebbe. Why must an
individual be drawn to a zaddik? Rabbi
Nahman replies that people need guidance
and instruction if they are to accomplish

their task of redeeming a fallen world.
They need teachers who take the humanity of
their students more seriously than either
material goals or intellectual standards.
Buber explains this answer by suggesting
that Nahman told tales to awaken the hearts
of his disciples: "He wanted to plant a
mystical idea or a truth of life in the
hearts of his disciples." By doing this,
according to Buber, he addressed their need
and their individuality. Using the stories
for this address did not make them less
symbolic but "more inward."63 Naturally,
others disagree and accuse Buber of making
the stories appear too "psychological," thus
ignoring "both the stark kabbalistic
allusions of the Hebrew and the numinous
tone" of the original. In this case the
issue is whether the stories act as myth in
Scholem's sense or as revelation in
Buber's.64

BUBER'S POPULAR APPEAL

Buber's approach to hasidism reveals a
sensitivity to human needs. That
sensitivity may well explain the popularity
of his presentation of hasidic lore. Rabbi
Nahman himself understood the need for such
an approach and used his stories to bring
his followers closer to his ideas. Buber's
recognition of this pedagogy leads him to
oppose Scholem's construction of the
division between the hasidim and normative
Judaism. Scholem follows traditional

learning, which suggests that a tension
between the latent antinomianism of Jewish
mysticism and the legalism of normative
Judaism--between, as he called it, the
language of revelation and the language of
myth--created the controversy between
rabbinical authorities (mitnagdim) and the
hasidim. Buber identifies the tension as
one between the immediacy of the event of
revelation itself and the language
describing it. Rabbi Nahman's tale of "The
Rabbi's Son" bristles with the tension
between normative Jewish leaders and hasidic
mystics while relating a tragic story of the
delay of an imminent redemption.

     This story, Nahman's eighth tale, tells
of a young man's thwarted attempt to find a
teacher.   Unlike other hasidic stories of
its type, this one ends in tragedy.65 The
story describes the son of an anti-hasidic
rabbi who complains that his study lacks
soul. Persuaded that only a hasidic teacher
can help him, he pleads for his father's
permission to visit a hasidic master. His
father, however, seeks to dissuade him since
the hasidic rebbe lacks rabbinic
qualifications: the master ignores the
classic texts and, instead, tells popular
stories. This emphasis on the normative
tradition prevents the father from
understanding his son. When the son
perseveres in demanding to visit the hasidic
teacher, the father relents but places
conditions on the visit: if any unusual
obstacle prevents their journey, they must
turn back in the knowledge that God has not
looked favorably on their endeavor. Several

obstacles do arise. Twice the wagon breaks
down and cannot proceed. On their third try
they meet a merchant who persuades the
father that the hasidic rebbe is a charlatan
and fake. True to their agreement, father
and son return home.

   Father and son return home, but the son,
seeking fulfillment of something "lacking"
within his soul, despairs of his hope of
self-fulfillment and dies, a victim to his
father's blindness. The father, too, does
not escape the consequences of his deeds.
Night after night he dreams of his son, who
tells him to visit the hasidic master. On
his way the father meets the merchant who
had slandered the rebbe, and that man
identifies himself as none other than Satan.
Satan reveals that had the rebbe met with
the lad, then the messiah would have come
and redemption would have been complete.
The father's reliance on traditional norms
and on pragmatic considerations prevented
the realization of universal redemption.
When the father reaches the zaddik, he cries
out in despair for "those who are lost and
will return no more."66 On this ambiguous
note Rabbi Nahman concludes, but a pious
editor has added a warning about the
machinations of Satan and the need to avoid
satanic traps.

   Nahman's story displays a not unusual
metaphorical use of a generational conflict
to suggest the struggle between the forces
of good and those of evil.67 The cosmic
dimensions of that contest and its enduring
persistence may explain why this story,

unlike the three other stories, ends
tragically. From Scholem's perspective the
tension here resembles that between
revelation and myth. Revelation offers a
clear path, a sense of perfection. Myth, by
contrast, strives against imperfection,
against an unredeemed world. The story ends
tragically because the normative tradition
refuses to recognize the need to repair the
world and cannot penetrate the disguise of
Satan. Buber's telling of this tale
emphasizes compassion. Where Nahman tells
that the son sought to improve a personal
imperfection, Buber emphasizes a need to
look beyond self-absorption toward either
the world outside or the inner world of
imagination. Where Nahman has the son
consult with "two young men," who advise him
to go to a zaddik, Buber has him associate
with a group of hasidim who tell him that
the zaddik is neither learned nor holy but
rather compassionate. The son, on Buber's
reading, then identifies this compassion
with "the rung of the great light,"
anticipating what Nahman reveals only at the
end: when the great light and small light
meet, redemption will occur. This evasion
of the esoteric references in the story
culminates in Buber's description of the
final outcry in the story. For Buber, the
father, finally realizing the error of his
ways, cries out in anguish over his own lack
of compassion.

Buber's interpretation follows his own
intuition about the meaning of myth. If
myth and revelation equally report and
reflect on a formative event, tension arises

when the form replaces the reality it
represents. The father in the story focuses
on external truths: those found in books or
in experienced reality. He forgets that
both tradition and pragmatic values arise
only through a meeting between people.
Redemption occurs when that meeting takes
place. Recognizing his error, the father
cries out with his new knowledge, lamenting
the meeting that cannot now occur. This
view of the story clearly emphasizes the
psychological rather than the metaphorical
resonance of the characters and plot.
Nahman never states which of these purposes
his story serves. Readers, however, cannot
fail to find themselves confronted by the
choice facing the rabbi in the tale. Every
person encounters an ambiguous mixture of
tradition, pragmatism, and inner motivation
complicating personal choices. Nahman
himself may well have identified himself
with each character in the tale and told the
story to objectify and understand his own
predicament.68 Current readers can
identify themselves with characteristics in
each character, whether that contention
holds true or not. Buber's view of this
story as an example of a myth recalling and
inspiring an event in human decision making,
as a "word" pointing to a human meeting,
explains the details of the tale as
adequately as Scholem's.

The four stories considered prove as
amenable to Buber's view of myth as to
Scholem's. As examples of human
communication, they may represent language
either as a spiritual fact itself or as a

symbolic response to a spiritual fact.
Those who share Scholem's trust in language
will accept Nahman's stories as testimony to
a mythic reality. Those sympathetic to
Buber's linguistic skepticism will recognize
how the stories invite response on a variety
of levels. Buber reports Nahman as claiming
that people create words because they cannot
withstand silence. God offers a person
grace in "holy silence" until, unable to
"endure the power of silence," the person
"cries aloud."69 Myth represents such a
"crying aloud," and one's view of myth is
shaped by whether one seeks to find the
silence out of which the cry came or whether
one accepts the cry as the one authentic
reality. This multidimensional approach
provides a greater sense of universalism and
applicability of theory than does Scholem's
more restricted interpretation.

Perhaps just as importantly, Buber may
have captured a more accurate picture of
hasidism as a movement. A recent study on
hasidism by Yaakov Hasdai suggests a "social
link between and common origin of the
founders of hasidism and mitnagdut."70 The
hasidim triumphed not because they
championed the ignorant but because their
compassionate response to the needs of the
community proved more effective than that of
their opponents. Buber recognizes this
dimension of hasidism: its human concern
born in the mythic evocation of a moment of
meeting.

NOTES

1. See Gershom G. Scholem, <u>Major Trends in Jewish Mysticism</u> (New York: Schocken, 1946), pp. 325-50.

2. Gershom G. Scholem, "Martin Buber's Interpretation of Hasidism," in his <u>The Messianic Idea in Judaism and Other Essays on Jewish Spirituality</u>, trans. Michael A. Meyer (New York: Schocken, 1971), pp. 228-50.

3. <u>Ibid</u>., p. 247.

4. See Joseph Dan, "Hasidism: The Third Century," [Hebrew] <u>World Union of Jewish Studies Newsletter</u>, 29 (1989), pp. 29-42.

5. Martin Buber, <u>Tales of the Hasidim: The Later Masters</u>, trans. Olga Marx (New York: Schocken, 1947), p. 46.

6. <u>Ibid</u>., p. 16.

7. Martin Buber, <u>The Origin and Meaning of Hasidism</u>, ed. and trans. Maurice Friedman (New York: Horizon Press, 1960), pp. 147-48.

8. See Laurence J. Silberstein, <u>Martin Buber's Social and Religious Thought: Alienation and the Quest For Meaning</u> (New York: New York University Press, 1989), p. 65; compare the discussions on pp. 10-11, 53-70.

9. Maurice Friedman, <u>Martin Buber's Life and Work: The Early Years, 1878-1923</u> (New York: Dutton, 1981), pp. 304-18.

10. Gershom G. Scholem, <u>The Messianic Idea</u>, pp. 34-35, discusses Rabbi Israel's messianic sayings; suggests why those sayings provide the true data of hasidism (p. 248); and records the conversation between Scholem and Buber on the Rizhiner (p. 250). The entire essay, "Martin Buber's Interpretation of Hasidism," is of great interest and has been reprinted in Judah Goldin, ed., <u>The Jewish Expression</u> (New Haven: Yale University Press, 1976), pp. 397-418.

11. Moshe Idel discusses this story and its variants in his <u>Kabbalah: New Perspectives</u> (New Haven: Yale University Press, 1988), pp. 270-71, 397 n. 96. Gershom Scholem, as Idel notes, credits Shmuel Yosef Agnon with the story: see his <u>Major Trends in Jewish Mysticism</u>, p. 350; compare Shmuel Yosef Agnon, <u>Sefer, Sofer, Vesippur</u> [Hebrew] (Tel Aviv: Schocken, 1978), p. 349. Compare Yoav Elstein in his <u>Maaseh Hoshev: Studies in Hasidic Tales</u> (Jerusalem: n.p., 1983), pp. 54-57.

12. Idel, <u>Kabbalah</u>.

13. See Scholem, "Martin Buber's Interpretation of Hasidism," p. 250; perhaps Buber's lack of understanding stems from the very nature of the Rizhiner that appeals to Scholem.

Scholem characterizes this teacher as "nothing but another Jacob Frank who has achieved the miracle of remaining an orthodox Jew" (<u>Major Trends in Jewish Mysticism</u>, p. 337). Since Buber seeks to uncover genuine Jewish myth and "understands" as authentic only that which points to true I-You encounter, he clearly would find the incipient Frankism of the Rizhiner outside the realm of his interests. David Biale, in his critical analysis of Gershom Scholem, focuses on the contrast between Buber and Scholem: see the discussion throughout David Biale, <u>Gershom Scholem: Kabbalah and Counter-History</u>, 2nd ed. (Cambridge: Harvard University Press, 1982); see especially the chapter "Theology, Language, and History," pp. 112-46, reproduced in Harold Bloom, ed., <u>Gershom Scholem</u> (New York: Chelsea House, 1987, pp. 47-55).

14. Buber, <u>The Origin and Meaning of Hasidism</u>, pp. 61-62.

15. Joseph Dan, <u>The Hasidic Story--Its History and Development</u> [Hebrew] (Jerusalem: Keter, 1975), pp. 7-24.

16. Steven Kepnes explores Buber's use of language in a perceptive chapter in his forthcoming volume, <u>Interpreting and Narrative: From the Writings of Martin Buber</u> (Indiana University Press, 1991). I appreciate his sharing of insights with me before publication.

17. Friedman, The Early Years, p. 313.

18. Martin Buber, Hasidism and Modern Man, ed. and trans. Maurice Friedman (New York: Horizon Press, 1958), pp. 25-26.

19. Buber, The Origin and Meaning of Hasidism, p. 76.

20. Buber, Between Man and Man, trans. Ronald Gregor Smith and Maurice Friedman (New York: Macmillan, 1965), p. 15. Buber's language and some of his ideas resemble those of Ernst Cassirer, Language and Myth, trans. Susanne K. Langer (New York: Harper, 1946), pp. 34-42.

21. Buber, Between Man and Man, p. 15; compare Cassirer, Language and Myth, pp. 34-26.

22. Martin Buber, I and Thou, trans. and intro. Walter Kaufmann (New York: Scribner's, 1970), p. 151.

23. This difference occurs even though both thinkers seem to be influenced by Cassirer. Scholem follows Cassirer's trust in language and his contention that myth "transforms the spiritual dawn which takes place with the advent of language into an objective fact, and presents it as a cosmogonic process" (Cassirer, Language and Myth, p. 81). Scholem, like Buber, rejects Cassirer's reduction of myth to a philosophical

concept. On Cassirer and Scholem see
Biale, Gershom Scholem, pp. 67-68.

24. Gershom G. Scholem, Origins of the
    Kabbalah, ed. R.J.Zwi Werblowsky and
    trans. Allan Arkush (Philadelphia:
    Jewish Publication Society of America
    and Princeton: Princeton University
    Press, 1987), pp. 277-79, 285.

25. Gershom G. Scholem, On The Kabbalah and
    Its Symbolism, trans. Ralph Manheim (New
    York: Schocken, 1969), pp. 87-117.

26. See Scholem, Origins of the Kabbalah,
    pp. 406-7.

27. On Scholem's view of myth as a gnostic
    type of knowledge, see Biale, Gershom
    Scholem, pp. 51-70.

28. Buber, A Believing Humanism: Gleanings,
    trans. Maurice Friedman (New York: Simon
    and Schuster, 1969), pp. 113-14.

29. Biale, Gershom Scholem, pp. 125-27.

30. Scholem, Major Trends in Jewish
    Mysticism, pp. 22-23.

31. Ibid., p. 269; in the footnote here (p.
    412n.77) Scholem compares the
    kabbalistic view with Schelling's
    philosophy.

32. Buber, Hasidism and Modern Man, p. 226.

33. See the discussion in Friedman, The Early Years, p. 315.

34. Ibid., p. 317.

35. See Biale, Gershom Scholem, pp. 115-18.

36. See Dan, The Hasidic Story, pp. 132-58. For good background material see Martin Buber, The Tales of Rabbi Nachman (New York: Horizon, 1956); Arthur Green, Tormented Master: A Life of Rabbi Nahman of Bratzlav (New York: Schocken, 1981); Yehudit Kuk, Rabbi Nahman of Bratzlav: Comments on His Stories [Hebrew] (Jerusalem: Gersht Institute, 1973); Mendel Piekarz, Studies in Braslav Hasidism [Hebrew] (Jerusalem: n.p., 1972); Joseph Weiss, Studies in Bratzlav Hassidism (sic) [Hebrew], ed., Mendel Piekarz (Jerusalem: n.p., 1974).

37. Green, Tormented Master, p. 368.

38. See Nahman ben Simhah of Bratzlav, Sefer Ha Middot [Hebrew] (New York: n.p., 1976) pp. 91, 200, 269, and compare his Likutei MoHaRaN [Hebrew] (New York: n.p., 1969), I:1; and his Sippurei Maasiyot [Hebrew] (New York: n.p., 1969); Piekarz, Studies, pp. 94-95; see also his "The Concept of the Tale in Hasidism Generally and in Braslav Hasidism in Particular," pp. 83-131, especially pp. 108-22. See Arnold Band, ed. and trans., Rabbi Nahman: The Tales (New York: Paulist

Press, 1978), p. 307; see also pp. 133ff., 308.

39. See Dan, Gershom Scholem, pp. 318-19.

40. See Band, Nahman of Bratzlav, 55-61.

41. See Scholem, Major Trends in Jewish Mysticism, pp. 273-86; On the Kabbalah, passim; and The Messianic Idea, pp. 43-48, 186-96.

42. Band, Nahman of Bratzlav, p. 285; see the extended study of this story in Dan, The Hasidic Story, pp. 132-44.

43. Ibid., p. 287.

44. Band, Nahman of Bratslav, p. 55.

45. Yoav Elstein, In the Footsteps of a Lost Princess: A Structural Analysis of the First Tale by Rabbi Nachman of Braslav [Hebrew] (Ramat Gan: Bar Ilan University Press, 1984); see pp. 226-28; Compare Weiss, pp. 141-43.

46. See Dan's preface in Band, Nahman of Bratzlav, p. xv, and Scholem, The Messianic Idea, pp. 238, 247.

47. Buber, The Tales of Rabbi Nahman, pp. 95-113; compare the telling of the tale in Band, Nahman of Bratzlav, pp. 193-209; see the lucid rendering of the story into Hebrew in Kuk, pp. 81-95, and her penetrating analysis of its possible meanings on pp. 97-108.

48. See the discussion in Band, <u>Nahman of Bratzlav</u>, pp. 315-16.

49. See the various discussions throughout Kuk, pp. 97-108, 279-80 (these pages make the connection of the symbolism in the story with the land of Israel and the Jewish exile explicit), and in Weiss, pp. 161-63.

50. See especially Rivka Schatz-Uffenheimer, "Man's Relation to God and World in Buber's Rendering of The Hasidic Teaching," in <u>The Philosophy of Martin Buber</u>, The Library of Living Philosophers, vol. XII, Paul Arthur Schilpp and Maurice Friedman, eds. (La Salle, IL: Open Court Press, 1967), pp. 403-34.

51. For this discussion, the summary of Rabbi Nahman's original tale, see Friedman, <u>The Early Years</u>, pp. 102-5; see Buber, <u>The Tales of Rabbi Nachman</u>, pp. 71-94. The story appears in Band, <u>Nahman of Bratslav</u>, pp. 141-61; see also Kuk, pp. 181-203, 265-68.

52. Band's comments reveal the mystical allusions in the story as an allegory about belief in God; see Band, <u>Nahman of Bratzlav</u>, pp. 309-10; for criticism of Buber see Scholem, <u>The Messianic Idea</u>, pp. 240-42.

53. See Kuk, pp. 201-3.

54. Weiss, pp. 109-49, particularly pp. 124-25.

55. The difference may come from the fact that the narrative about Rabbi Nahman's journey originally appeared in Buber's survey of the idea of Zionism. Nevertheless, Buber eventually included the tale in his collection of Rabbi Nahman's tales and so must have seen a relationship between them: see Martin Buber, On Zion: The History of an Idea, trans. Stanley Godman (New York: Schocken, 1973), pp. 89-108; The Tales of Rabbi Nachman, pp. 179-214.

56. Green, Tormented Master, p. 27.

57. See Joseph Dan, ed., The Hasidic Novella [Hebrew] (Jerusalem: Bialik Institute, 1966), pp. 187-88; the story as presented here differs in several specific cases from Buber's rendition.

58. Scholem, The Messianic Idea, p. 202.

59. Thus Buber misrepresents Nahman's vacillation from a condition of spiritual exaltation to one of "katnut," or spiritual descent; compare the story in Dan, pp. 152-55, with Buber's version in The Tales of Rabbi Nachman, p. 195.

60. Buber, Tales of Rabbi Nachman, p. 214.

61. Meir Urian, <u>In The Circle of Hassidism and in the Paths of Our Time</u> [Hebrew] (Jerusalem: Rubin Mass, 1977), pp. 79-80.

62. <u>Ibid</u>., p. 179; see his entire essay, "The Neutralization of the Messianic Element in Early Hasidism," pp. 176-202. Compare Dan and Band in <u>Nahman of Bratzlav</u>.

63. Buber, <u>The Tales of Rabbi Nachman</u>, p. 44.

64. Band, <u>Nahman of Bratslav</u>, p. 43.

65. See Buber, <u>The Tales of Rabbi Nachman</u>, pp. 49-58; Band, <u>Nahman of Bratzlav</u>, pp. 133-38, 307-8.

66. In some translations the "he" who cries out refers to the rebbe; in others, to the father.

67. See Yoav Elstein's discussion of a similar conflict in a tale told about the Baal Shem Tov in <u>Maaseh Hoshev</u>, pp. 20-22.

68. See Weiss, pp. 155-56.

69. Buber, <u>The Tales of Rabbi Nachman</u>, p. 36.

70. Yaakov Hasdai, "The Origins of the Conflict Between Hasidim and Mitnagdim," in Bezalel Safran, <u>Hasidism: Continuity or Innovation?</u>, Harvard University

Center for Jewish Studies (Cambridge: Harvard University Press, 1988), pp. 27–45; the cited sentence appears on p. 44.

Chapter 8 Hasidism And Modernity

THE APPEAL OF HASIDISM TODAY

Buber shows how the message of hasidic stories confronts the problems of modernity. For him, the universal meaning of hasidism appeals to all people by giving evidence of how people today can live in I-You relationship. Buber's retelling of the older tradition accentuates this potential within it. Despite this new presentation, however, Buber's additions merge almost imperceptibly with the sources he uses. Novelist Meyer Levin comments that "the interpolations of Martin Buber have seemed so just as to become an integral part of the myth."1 That statement, however, may miss the real point. Buber's telling of the stories self-consciously illuminates the mythical elements in hasidism. The original stories by themselves often seem oriented to more modest goals. They seek to reinforce communal structures, to oppose legalistic Judaism, and to attract new disciples.

Buber knowingly reshapes the stories to
reveal their inherent but often latent
purpose. He contends that hasidism responds
to the great challenges modernity placed
before modern people, Jews and non-Jews
alike. His mythicization of hasidic
stories follows from his theory of myth.

Buber introduces his second volume of
interpretations of hasidism by commenting on
his conviction of hasidism's importance "for
Jews, Christians, and other men, and at this
particular hour more important than ever
before."2 Moderns face a peculiar crisis:
a crisis of religious belief and a crisis of
hope. After the collapse of traditional
systems of faith, they search for a living
religious life that seems somehow beyond
their reach. Hasidism responds to that
challenge by recognizing the challenge and
the crisis as a reality. Buber criticizes
the older Jewish leaders for seeking to
respond to new threats with antiquated
weapons. They issue pronouncements against
anti-traditionalism. They forbid reading
modern books or engaging in discussion with
"heretics." They define the modern world as
an evil temptation. Such strategies merely
perpetuate ancient ways; they do not renew
the life of the Jewish people. Hasidism
goes beyond rabbinic Judaism because it
recognizes the need of the times. For
Buber, only a new Jewish religiosity can
restore the vitality that modernity saps
from the veins of traditional Judaism. An
inner transformation of Judaism alone can
avert the threats being launched against
Jewish religion. Hasidism contributes a

realistic appraisal of the challenges
Judaism faced while rabbinic leaders avert
their eyes and refuse to see the magnitude
of the attacks waged against them.3

Buber notes two major personalities
whose lives and thought represent the threat
of modernity to Judaism: Baruch Spinoza,
both the first modern philosopher and the
last of the medievals, and Sabbetai Zevi,
the Turkish Jew whose messianic claims
stirred and confounded world Jewry.4
Spinoza exemplifies the modern challenge to
belief. His philosophy God strips divinity
of its ability to communicate with humanity.
Spinoza attempted to overcome the Cartesian
dualism between mind and body but, Buber
suggests, fell into a greater trap: that of
locating eternal reality outside of the
concrete lived moment of humanity. Buber
sees hasidism as responding to that
challenge with a new statement of God's
pervasiveness. God indeed pervades the
world but not as an absolute and
inaccessible power. God's presence promises
that any moment may become a sacred moment.
For hasidism, Buber claims, the idea of
God's eternal reality means that "the
concrete world of this moment of personal
existence" is always "ready to be a
sacrament...."5 Spinoza offers an "ethics"
of abstraction and distance from human
reality. Hasidism responds with an ethics
of daily involvement. Threatened by the
view of a God who unifies reality only by
removing it from human existence, modern
Jews turn to the world affirming ethics of
hasidism. Buber testifies that this ethics

drew him to hasidism even before he realized
it. He notes his early "premonition" that
no matter how he resisted, "I was
inescapably destined to love the world."6
Buber prepared his volumes on hasidism for
Jews and non-Jews who struggle with the same
premonition and for whom hasidism may also
prove a solace.

Some Christians take exception to such
"solace" offered by a Jew. They feel secure
in a truth that offers what appears to them
a more enduring comfort. Buber scandalizes
such Christians even further by contending
that Jews understand Jesus "from within"
better than "the peoples submissive to
him."7 Buber intends no disrespect.
Instead, he expresses a Jewish conception of
the modern dilemma. Jews confront a world
in which redemption seems impossible.
Messianic heroes inevitably lead their
followers into disaster. How can a modern
Jew live in a patently unredeemed world
holding fast to hope when traditional
messianism appears bankrupt and corrupt?
The experience of world Jewry with the
messianic debacle of Sabbetai Zevi in the
seventeenth century has left Jews wary of
religious answers to social and political
problems. Gershom Scholem suggests that the
Sabbatian messianic movement "helped pave
the way" for Jewish Enlightenment and the
reform movement in Judaism in the nineteenth
century.8 Despite this continuity, however,
Buber is correct in suggesting that new
Jewish movements could not use messianism as
their models. They learned from the failure
of Sabbetai Zevi that messianism leads to

disaster. Buber traces the false messiah's
transition from "honest self-assurance into
a pretended one" that "ended in apostasy."9
Jews had accepted the "false messiah" as a
sign of divine concern. When that sign
proved false, it appeared that God had
proved equally false. Bereft of trust, many
Jews abandoned hope. No longer trusting in
a heroic messianic figure to redeem them and
the world, they despaired of themselves and
their future.

Buber suggests that hasidism solves the
problem raised by failed messianic heroes by
pointing to the redemptive community rather
than a redemptive person. Hasidism trusts
that Jewish history does not require an
extraordinary intervention by God to bring
redemption. The hasidic message of
redemption involves all people working
together as partners in the work of
salvation. While the Sabbatian movement
focused on the personality of Sabbetai Zevi
and his personal biography, hasidism
emphasizes a chain of redemptive moments in
the life of the community.10 Hasidism's
answer to messianism, like its answer to
Spinoza, solves a modern dilemma.

REVIVING JEWISH RELIGION

Buber's retelling of hasidic myth evokes
its transformative power. Sometimes his
versions of these stories differ from the
original tale precisely because his make the

myth of I and You so clear. Hasidic
tradition delights in recording the
hostility with which the Baal Shem Tov's
brother-in-law, Rabbi Gershom, initially
misunderstood and resisted the message of
hasidism, only subsequently to be
transformed into an ardent disciple.
Describing the self-revelation of the Besht,
hasidic sources tell how a nameless disciple
of Rabbi Gershom, traveling to his master,
was forced to stop at the Besht's inn. Even
the piety of the Besht's wife could not
relieve his sense of discomfort. Compelled
by strange circumstances to stay the Sabbath
with the Besht, he discovered the Besht's
secret and became the emissary of the Besht
to the "sect of the Great Hasidim."11

  Buber retells this story very
differently.12 Buber personalizes the
disciple, calling him Rabbi Naftali. Rather
than being concerned with halakhic details
of Jewish observance, the disciple in
Buber's tale struggles to understand the
meaning of life. The delays that send him
back to the Besht arouse in him self-doubt
and questions about his place in the
universe. He looked within, and "it seemed
to Rabbi Naftali as if the chaos out of
which the world was created was his
soul...."13 The Besht exercises his power
by curing this spiritual malaise. He
enables Rabbi Naftali to make peace with the
world and himself. By the end of his
confrontation with the hasidic leader, "he
knew the man and the goal of the six days
(of creation)."14 Buber's story echoes the
searching and wondering found in the

original but expresses it in terms of human
life rather than in terms of Jewish
practice.

   While some hasidic tales focus on the
individual's search for religious life,
other stories reconstruct the ideal Jewish
community. A strange account of the Besht's
failure to save a group of Jews martyred for
their faith evokes the social dimension of
hasidic myth.15 The tale relates that Rabbi
David of Korostyshev fled to the Besht,
telling him that certain Jews lay under the
charge of a blood libel. The Besht assured
him that they would be saved, but instead
they were martyred. In anger, the Besht
appealed to the dead heroes to exact revenge
against their enemies. The martyrs asked
indulgence since they prefer death to life.
Even in their past life, they explained,
they had been touched by the "evil
inclination" since it had "touched our
thoughts just a hair." The sufferings
engendered by this taint of evil outweigh
all possible human sufferings. Were they to
be reborn, they might sin even more
grievously and thus suffer even more
punishment. Although the Besht did not
succeed in saving the lives of the martyrs,
the story succeeds in binding them to an
eternal, invisible, and powerful community.
Both the martyrs and those who read about
them accept the necessity and even the value
of their deaths. They share a negative
evaluation of this world of trial. They
acknowledge a common struggle against the
evil inclination. These values transcend
time and place. They unite the hasidim

despite the separations imposed on them by
historical events.

Buber changes the emphasis in this story
as he retells it by adding a prologue and
epilogue. He informs the reader that Rabbi
David "had begun a book which told how one
could serve God with his life." He fled
from the martyrs because they sought to
sanctify God with their deaths, not with
their lives. The incident taught him the
difficulty of sanctifying God in life rather
than death, and after it he "did not
complete his book."16 What changed his
mind? As Buber presents the dialogue with
the martyrs, the sin caused by the evil
inclination takes on concrete form. The
martyrs had allowed the evil inclination to
touch them and "force our spirits to bow."
They fear to return to earth since they must
"return to the world where we have no place
in which to rejoice in the Lord, and where
we breathe an air which is not the Lord's."
In such a place not only can they not serve
God with their lives, but the temptation to
bow their spirits grows even greater.17 The
martyrs appear in this version as proto-
Zionists, restless with their exilic
condition, desirous of their own land and
free air as the precondition of religious
living. The problem of Jewish life lies not
in serving God but in creating a space
within which to serve God joyously. The
communal task--in fact, the Zionist task--
takes precedence over the individual's
private quest. After learning this about
the martyrs, Rabbi David must abandon his
self-appointed task. One fulfills the human

task neither by submission to life nor by
submission to death. A person must choose
to change the conditions of living even
before choosing how to live or die.

Buber's retelling of hasidic tales
captures not only their view of religious
life and communal ideal but also their model
of personhood. Many modern commentators on
hasidism focus on its goals, its stories,
and its values even while recognizing the
inadequate representation of those goals and
values in actual hasidic communities. The
ideas themselves lead to an ethics that
encourages changing the conditions of human
life. The ethics of hasidism demands an
altruism that helps Jews diagnose their own
limitations and change their lives.18
Folklorist Pinchas Sadeh presents a story
culled from an early twentieth century
collection that illustrates this view of
hasidism. The story concerns the Baal Shem
Tov, a rich Jew, a poor but pious man who
always recites King David's psalms, and King
David himself.19 According to this tale, a
certain wealthy Jew observed all the laws
commanded meticulously. After completing a
particularly arduous commandment, the rich
Jew celebrated with a great feast to which
he invited rich and poor alike. One guest
was a poor Jew who served as water drawer,
distinguished only by his recital of the
psalms of David. When the bread was
distributed, the poor man could not restrain
himself and ate immediately. The rich man,
outraged that both the scholars present and
even the Torah itself had been disgraced by

this breach of Jewish law, rebuked the poor
man so that he left the house in shame.

Although the rich man forgot about the
incident, his normal study of Jewish law
left him restless that night. Leaving his
home, he found himself lost in a wilderness
until finally he came to a great mansion.
There he encountered David the King, arguing
with none other than the Baal Shem Tov.
They discussed the rich man's case--King
David demanding the death penalty for having
insulted one who recited David's psalms.
The Besht made a better argument: who would
gain from the rich man's death? Would it
not be better to have him summon everyone to
a great feast and make a public apology?
The rich man acts on that last proposal and
thereby saves his own life.
The dynamics of the plot depend on the
inability of communal life to approximate
the ideals of hasidism. The point seems to
be that while the rich often flout the
ethical vision of hasidic morality, that
morality prevails, at least in heaven. The
rich will learn the error of their ways. If
they continue to prevail, they do so in
hopes of their reformation. The ideal
remains powerful even when disconfirmed by
general practice. Heaven, at least, takes
the part of the poor and oppressed. Those
who affirm a legalistic religion eventually
discover its inadequacy to protect them.
Those who insult the defenseless may seem to
escape punishment. They will nonetheless
apologize and recognize the evil of their
ways.

Buber transforms this story into another
example of mythic evocation of I-Thou
meeting.20 As might be anticipated, Buber
ignores all references to traditional Jewish
law. The rich man is flawed by his
impatient nature, his thoughtlessness, and
his "noisy being." He insults the
waterdrawer merely for being slow in his
task, not for infringing on traditional
custom. Buber also changes the emphasis of
the Besht's defense of the rich man. David,
the Besht argues, should know the heart of
those who sin since he, too, sinned and
found forgiveness. David should recognize
the possibility of transcending one's nature
since the psalms are "the diamond bridge
which leads upward out of the valley of
depravity to the heart of God." Buber's
most important change of the story lies in a
continuing emphasis on human meeting. The
Baal Shem, he contends, knew about the rich
man's troubled life and "loved him from
afar" since he recognized the potential
hidden by his externally gruff nature. The
rich man, for example, loved and honored the
psalm singer because "It seemed to him as if
there lived in the song of the man the
stillness which so seldom visited him." The
Baal Shem wins from King David not an
alternative punishment but an acknowledgment
of the importance of forgiveness. He gains
that victory by reminding the King: "When
your song took me by the hand, I forgot
justice, and when it smiled at me, all
opposition disappeared within me." That
statement creates a bond of human meeting
out of which "there rushed upward a great
movement as when a mystery fulfills itself

and then sinks down." When two souls
understand each other so well that one can
help the other see itself, then redemption
begins. Buber does not need to emphasize
that ethics triumphs eventually. Instead,
he evokes several moments of human meeting
that are left incomplete. The Besht's
meeting with the rich man and the rich man's
reaching out to the psalm-singer never reach
fulfillment. Through the meeting of the
Besht and King David, however, both find
their meaning. Buber intimates that this
myth of the ideal flows from the mystery of
human meeting.

YOAV ELSTEIN'S CRITIQUE OF BUBER

The previous chapter discussed how
Gershom Scholem challenged Buber's accuracy
as a historian of Jewish mysticism. Yoav
Elstein, a more recent writer, informed by
both Scholem and by non-Jewish students of
myth like Mircea Eliade, the well known
historian of religions, criticizes Buber's
understanding of the phenomenon of myth.
Following Eliade, Elstein understands myth
as a recreation of primal time and hasidic
stories as reverberations of eternal themes
and continually recurring events. He denies
that the stories tell about a single
historical act. While a hasidic tale
appears to describe an event that occurred
once in human history, it really celebrates
a "metaphysical act," that is, an event
occurring on a cosmic level, echoed by

repeated events but not to be identified with any of them. Each apparent "historical event" actually approximates and illustrates an ideal event that is not physical but metaphysical. When Elstein studies a hasidic story, he traces its plot and themes as they are repeated throughout Jewish writings. While in practice he emphasizes these Jewish echoes in the hasidic story, he explicitly claims that the events described occur "to all people at all times."21

Unlike Scholem, who criticizes Buber from an unsympathetic vantage point, Elstein sympathetically challenges Buber's reading of hasidic myths. Elstein declares that he has no wish to enter into the debate between the "two mountains" of Scholem and Buber and implies that, like Buber, he considers hasidic tales a source of illumination of hasidic thinking. He often supplies Buber's rendition of certain tales in his footnotes.22 While he rarely explores the differences between his analysis of the original stories and Buber's, those differences cannot be ignored. If myth transmits a metaphysical message by pointing to the ongoing patterns that determine human existence, then Buber's search for an event is misguided.

Deciding between Elstein and Buber entails looking at how each presents hasidic stories and measuring that presentation by Buber's own standard. Buber's major program in presenting hasidic myth is oriented to that goal. He retells hasidic tales because they testify to the "overpowering objective

reality ... of the exemplary lives." He
seeks to show that "the teaching is there
that one may learn it and the way that one
may walk on it." His success must be judged
by whether or not he conveys "the stammering
of inspired witnesses." If Buber offers a
more compelling rendition of that stammering
than Elstein, then his approach offers an
equal, if not superior, opportunity for
moderns to appreciate and learn from
hasidism.23 The next section shows how
Buber sought to fulfill this task and then
asks whether Elstein's criticism actually
refutes Buber's attempt.

THE MYTH OF ETERNAL RETURN

Buber shares with other theorists the
contention that myth points people toward
their selfhood, that it provides direction
and meaning. He differs from many of them
in his view of the mechanism by which it
achieves this end. Modern Jews often seek a
"return" to self. Students of modern Jewish
life study the phenomenon of the "baal
teshuva," the Jew who rejects a secularized
modernity and embraces traditionalism.24
Buber recognizes this aspect of hasidic
stories: they interpret the meaning of
return to Judaism and suggest a way of
return. His interpretation of this motif,
however, differs considerably from that of
other commentators on hasidism and
highlights the distinctiveness of his own
theory about mythic meaning.

Elstein disagrees and considers hasidic myth exemplary of an "eternal" way. He claims that hasidic tales recapitulate other stories and echo traditional themes. Buber, by contrast, thinks that hasidic myth awakens a Jew to the moment of decision calling for an affirmation of human life. Buber thinks of Jewish "rebirth" as a renewed opportunity for human meeting, not the re-enactment of a primal event.25 Both Buber and Elstein agree that hasidic stories echo past events. Elstein, however, thinks of that echoing as a replication of some "eternal" event that lies outside of time and space. While Buber insists that myth points back to a historical moment, Elstein claims that it points to basic structures of human life that are always present in human society, even if not always recognized. The theme of return to a truth not previously recognized occurs often in hasidic tales. Both Buber and Elstein recognize the theme but treat it differently. Buber points to the continual accessibility of I-You meeting. The Besht, according to Buber, chooses an eternal cycle of rebirth as his appropriate task. The tales of the Besht recapitulate earlier motifs and stories because they point, as do those stories, to the same I-You reality.

Elstein, by contrast, interprets these hasidic tales as re-enactments of biblical stories of Joseph, David, and Solomon. He suggests that while appearances change, reality remains the same.26 The stories are myths not because they recapitulate the

Bible but because they use biblical motifs to suggest that what happened once upon a time continually reoccurs. Elstein insists that despite the folktale-like appearance of the narratives, they address a different question. Plot and character give way to theme and motif. The story exists not to entertain by relating a unique event but to demonstrate those patterns set in earliest times that still "apply to every man at all times." Elstein suggests that the stories are therefore metaphysical, not merely historical. They make an eternal pattern manifest in a particular time and place.27 Hasidic stories represent a Jewish version of a universal myth: history does not progress; life repeats itself by exemplifying an unchanging cycle. Arnold Band, a literary critic and scholar of hasidism, analyzes an important tale about the Besht that seems to confirm Elstein's theory. Band points to the first story describing a confrontation between the Besht and the powers of evil as an example of how an apparent folktale actually recapitulates themes drawn from throughout Jewish literature.28

The story begins with the Besht's youth, as his dying father passes on to the boy a legacy of faith and hope. As the Besht matures, however, he appears an unruly, untalented child, fit only for menial jobs. One such job entails leading children from their homes to the school, the beth-hamidrash. He fulfills this task, however, with great joy and power. He teaches the children to sing to God, and their song "rises more sweetly than the sacrificial smoke from the Jerusalem Temple." The text next inserts a verse from the Book of Job: "Then Satan came also among them."

The story uses the biblical verse to suggest that the events of the Besht's life parallel previous mythic narratives. The tale proceeds to explain how Satan took action against the Besht to prevent the children's songs from ascending on high. According to the story, the devil "transformed himself into a gentile sorcerer" with the power to become a werewolf. In this guise he frightened the children and prevented them from continuing their studies. The cessation of their singing recapitulates the historical destruction of the "continual offering ascending to God" of the Jerusalem Temple. The Besht, at first daunted, recalls his father's instruction not to fear anything since God is with him and decides to "fight with the beast and kill it in the name of God." He runs to the werewolf, hits it on the forehead, and kills it. The next morning, instead of an animal, people find the corpse of the gentile sorcerer lying on the ground. The story picks up immediately with the next stage in the Besht's career: the Besht next becomes the watchman of the beth-hamidrash.

Band identifies the mythic elements in the story with traditional Jewish themes. Like David battling Goliath with merely a slingshot, the Besht appears as an unlikely hero using song and faith against a powerful

adversary who commands an arsenal of magic.
Like Joseph, misunderstood and maligned by
those of an alien culture, he succeeds where
normal leadership fails. The parallel with
Job explains one of the puzzling aspects of
the tale. While Satan starts the action,
the ending ignores him. The demonic
symbolizes the eternal possibility that evil
interferes with the smooth functioning of
piety. The resolution of the problem,
however, remains fully human. As in the
story of Job, Satan falls out of the story,
thereby suggesting the purely symbolic
nature of this personification of evil. By
the tale's end the werewolf is but a gentile
sorcerer.29 The supernaturalistic and
magical elements of the story pale beside
the exaltation of the hero's faithfulness.
Finally, Band suggests that the contest
between the Besht and Satan anticipates a
climactic struggle between good and evil.
The story envisions a messianic battle won
by the power of good, symbolized by the
Besht. Oddly, however, this decisive
victory fails to lead either to a messianic
fulfillment or to an explanation of why such
fulfillment never occurs.

Band points out the problems with the
story as pure narrative. The story has no
satisfactory conclusion. The Besht remains
as unappreciated after his confrontation
with the werewolf as before. The
machinations of the devil continue unabated.
The Besht's victory wins no enduring
triumph. The story never describes the
children's return to their singing and moves
without pause to another incident in the

Besht's life. While flaws in a folktale, these defects are irrelevant to a mythic tale. As myth, the story merely echoes eternal themes. It need not advance to a climax, provide a resolution, or describe the consequences of its narrative. On one level the tale does seem to exhibit folk elements. On another level, however, these elements are merely outward disguises. Underneath the folk form lies the eternal message of myth that surfaces again and again. Thus the story takes place on two levels. On one level the Besht vanquishes a human enemy. On the other level the Besht replays the role of ancient Israel's great liberators, of whom David is the primary example. The enigmatic nature of the story signals to the initiated its real meaning. Band thinks that readers discover "two categories of knowledge and the means of achieving both of them."30

BUBER'S VERSION OF "THE WEREWOLF"

Buber's telling of this story begins with a prologue-like account of the Besht's legacy from his father. The Besht's father, before dying, informs his son of his destiny as a Jewish leader. The Besht, his father tells him, will struggle with evil at every stage in his career but need have no fear of evil. Despite this prologue Buber titles this chapter "The Werewolf," focusing on the Besht's first encounter with Satan. Indeed, Buber intimates that such encounters

characterize the Besht's entire life. The
Besht's father warns him not only that he
should trust in God but also that "the
Adversary will confront (you) in the
beginning, at the turning, and at the
fulfillment."31 Buber describes the process
by which the Besht discovers his own
function in the world. The Besht lives in
tension with the normative Jewish tradition
of his time. He rejects formalized learning
and flees from the schoolhouse to the world
of nature. Buber describes how the Besht
grew up with the "speechless modes of the
creatures" and recognized a power
independent of the learned tradition. Unlike
Band, Buber emphasizes the unique aspects of
the Besht's career. He refuses to see the
Besht as a mirror or echo of earlier
traditions but rather as a singular
individual, groping toward a meeting between
an I and a You.

   The Besht's function as a helper
conducting children to school represents a
further stage in his development. He learns
to communicate not only with nature but also
with children. He conveys the flame of
religious fervor to his charges, teaching
them to sing to God of their joy in living.
In so doing, he enables them to transcend
the limits of their daily living. His
influence breaks "through the thick smoke of
misery and confusion that presses down on
earth." Buber attributes this success to
the Besht's ability to affirm the children
as unique individuals with a value beyond
their routine existence. Buber interprets
the demonic response to this I-You meeting

differently from his sources. Those sources attribute Satan's concern to the fact that when children learn Jewish lore (torah), heaven rejoices. Buber, however, records that the Adversary "swelled up with disquietude and hatred," complaining that with such self-acceptance among humanity he would lose his function. I-You meeting threatens to sanctify everyday life; demonic success lies in desanctifying that life.

To reestablish his realm of terror Satan chooses an individual whose life seems bereft of sanctification. While the original tale focuses on aspects of evil within the person whom Satan chooses--he is a gentile and a sorcerer--Buber stresses that the human being chosen by Satan had been weakened by internal conflict. Buber describes him as a poor charcoal burner, alienated from other people, who when compelled to turn into a werewolf suffers deeply since "his simple heart writhed under the bitter compulsion." This werewolf symbolizes the cessation of I-You meeting, just as the singing children had symbolized its genesis. Faced with this challenge, the Besht, according to Buber, remembered his father's last words. Buber asserts that "now for the first time" he knew the significance of his Adversary and how, at the very beginning, he must confront the threat to true dialogue arising from alienation.

As the story develops, Buber reconstructs the contest between the Besht and the werewolf as a psychological event.

The Besht unites himself with the werewolf
penetrating its very soul. During the fight
"It seemed to him as if he were going
farther and farther" into the werewolf.
Band, probably correctly, sees the story as
a messianic contest. Buber, however,
understands the victory psychologically.
The Besht wins by converting the coal
burner's soul. When the coal burner is
found dead, Buber reports, "Those who came
across him were astonished by the great
peacefulness of his countenance." The Besht
liberates the coal burner from his unhappy
compulsion so that he can attain
reconciliation. Buber stresses the benefit
the Besht provides his erstwhile enemy. The
success of an I-You meeting presages not
social and political messianism but self-
reconciliation. The story points to the
moment at which meetings between an I and a
You creates a surprising peace, the peace of
self-affirmation despite the tribulations of
life.

This conclusion appears positive and
unambiguous. Buber, however, adds a
pessimistic note. From this moment on, he
remarks, "the boys forgot their singing and
began to resemble their fathers and their
fathers' fathers." This rendition honestly
transmits the ambiguity of the original
tale. This time, however, the focus shifts
from an unfulfilled messianism to the
transiency of I-You meeting. The Besht
discovers the flaw in his victory. He can
protect the children from the threat from
without but not from the threat from within.
Normal routine, no less than abnormal

morbidity, saps the strength of I-You affirmation of the human self. The lack of closure that Buber finds in the tale conveys his understanding of I-You meeting as continual renewal, not eternal repetition of primal patterns. In this sphere persons discover through meeting that their lives have meaning as "the ever-renewed preparation and hallowing" necessary to stimulate a lived moment of response. The Besht, for example, discovers that his is "not the hour of redemption, but of a renewal." In this first encounter with Satan the Besht learns purpose of his existence: he is to proceed through life "being addressed and answering, addressing and receiving answer." The continuing stories chart his progress through these dialogues.32 Buber's interpretation of this story as myth differs radically from Band's. Unlike Band, he refuses to divide the story into an external and an internal meaning, a superficial tale for the folk and an esoteric tale for the elite. By replacing esotericism with a lesson for modern life, Buber creates out of his sources a genuine myth of the I and the Thou.

PURIFICATION FROM POLLUTION

Buber's approach unravels aspects of the story that lie outside Elstein's definition of myth. One central hasidic concern focuses on ritual and magic. Buber accepts the challenge of showing how this apparently

supernaturalistic and unrealistic aspect of
hasidic myth actually responds to universal
human concerns. Many cultures establish
rituals to they dispel demons and other
spirits and thereby ensure prosperity and
fertility. Sometimes these rituals initiate
a struggle against the demons; sometimes
they provide sympathetic magic imitating the
motions of a flock or of sowing a field;
often the rituals entail a public ceremony
with bells and magical incantations.33
Hasidism includes references to such events.
In one hasidic tale the Besht seems to
reenact a purification ceremony.34   When
pollution increased in the world, the Baal
Shem set out to defeat it in concert with
another hasid and a certain ignorant but
devout shepherd called Moses. The story
describes the shepherd's devotion in two
different ways. At first, as the Baal Shem
Tov observes him, the shepherd addresses God
in a simple prayer: I cannot serve you as
you need to be served, but if you had a
flock, I would shepherd it for free. This
peasant's prayer resembles other hasidic
stories that emphasize the value of
sincerity rather than form as the mark of
true worship. A second description,
however, seems far stranger and closer to
mythic images. On approaching Moses, the
Baal Shem Tov notes how he serves God simply
by leaping about and crying out to God. The
shepherd's piety, on this account, consists
of magical ritual, of a "homeopathic"
action: an action imitating natural forces
undertaken to ensure fertility and
prosperity. Theorists studying this part of
the story would note its affinities to

magical rites, popular theurgic customs, and general rituals of purification. Because some taint pollutes the land, agriculture suffers. The magician restores purity and productivity by simulating the action of a fully healthy natural world.

The tale moves quickly from this theurgic emphasis to traditional Jewish law and lore. As the story progresses, the Baal Shem Tov teaches the shepherd the Hebrew alphabet, the story of how enemies destroyed God's Temple, and the technique of how certain prayers would help bring redemption. At this point, the story transforms an originally magical myth into a reinforcement of traditional religion. While in its primal form the story exalted folk customs, as a developed tale it cautions against such unconventional practice. Instead of magic, the shepherd must learn the communal forms of devotion. The three leaders learn to merge their talents. Jewish tradition emphasizes that a quorum of three represents the minimum needed for worship. While some prayers do require the presence of one hundred people and others ten, three men constitute the smallest unit of public worship. Public recital of the blessing after meals, for example, begins with such a quorum. When three do not recite such blessings, God's name is profaned.35 Since the number three represents a community, or havurah, the additional person must participate in the ritual for its effectiveness. When the three do combine their actions, heaven seems responsive to their deeds. At this stage the myth exalts

communal power. What magic does not
accomplish, the united forces of a social
order achieves. Tradition succeeds by
synthesizing aspects of magic, study, and
mysticism.

The optimistic note sounded here,
however, soon changes to a pessimistic one.
The myth reflects a tragic reality:
pollution cannot be completely nullified.
Messianic fulfillment still lies in the
distant future. The tale explains this
tragedy by suggesting that the Devil took
action against the purification rituals and
thwarted the concerted efforts of the three
heroes. Satan succeeded in disrupting life
by creating a great fire in the neighboring
town. The leaders of the city responded by
ringing the bells of the town to assemble
people to help extinguish the fire. These
two elements, fire and bells, often
accompany rituals of purification and
expiation. They echo the original myth from
which the tale emerged, a myth of the
riddance of evil by rituals.

In the present tale, however, these
elements bode disaster. The sounds disturb
the performance of the ritual. When the
shepherd Moses hears the commotion, he
thinks the masters of the flock know he has
abandoned his sheep. Fearful for his job,
he runs back to the hillsides, and the Baal
Shem Tov reluctantly admits defeat. After
that defeat he and his companion escape
great harm only by dint of their holiness.
As in many traditions, so, too, here, the
failure to perform ritual magic correctly

entails danger for the magician. In its
developed form, the story concludes by
affirming the insufficiency of ritual
purification. Some temporary advantage
follows these rituals, but Satan grips the
world too securely to allow an absolute
absolution of pollution. This myth
describes a failed ritual and shows why
rituals fall into discontinuance: even the
most punctilious observance of a ritual
cannot reverse the corruption that is
humanity's inevitable fate.

Buber's rendition of this myth retains
its sense of pessimism but illuminates its
darkness by an affirmation of I-You meeting.
The story no longer entails ritual or
magical purification but rather an
acceptance of historical destiny. The myth
evokes moments of decision during which
people meet one another and discover how to
convert evil into good. In telling the life
of the Baal Shem Tov (but not in his <u>Tales
of the Hasidim</u>), he associates this story
with the Baal Shem Tov's death. The
differences in his telling of the tale show
how Buber evokes the mythic power of the
stories about hasidic leaders. Buber begins
by describing the Baal Shem Tov's struggle
against evil generally and against the
demonic threat of Jacob Frank's incarnation
of the Sabbatian movement in particular.
The Besht feels the hand of the demonic
angel on his shoulder and knows he must
prepare for battle. He turns to his
spiritual allies but finds them engaged in
equally important duties and releases them
to do their own work. Ascending on high

with his teacher Ahijah the Shilonite, the
Besht learns from Elijah that only Moses the
shepherd can help him in this struggle.36
The earlier myth focuses on a generalized
pollution, on an agricultural dilemma.
Buber's myth conveys the weariness of
contemporary Jews, the sense that all the
old allies have failed and that traditional
religious answers no longer satisfy modern
needs. The life of the Besht, however,
illustrates how one man may continue the
fight, seeking the one ally suited for him.
Buber, by this touch, emphasizes personal
dialogue. The original story focuses on the
three Jews needed for a basic quorum; Buber
replaces this with the two partners
essential for human meeting. He also
changes the reasons behind the Besht's
actions. They become modern ones: those for
immediate human encounter, for transcending
established religious institutions, and for
affirming personal paths to salvation.   As
myth, the story evokes the moment in which a
person discovers the need to transcend
tradition and find a single human partner.

After Buber's long introduction the
story continues much as in its original
version, mentioning the shepherd's simple
prayer and his active leaping. Buber,
however, avoids advocating traditional
religion. The shepherd in this tale does
not need to learn the Hebrew alphabet or
rehearse Jewish history. According to
Buber, the Besht appeals to Moses' love and
compassion for God. He "spoke of the
solitude of God and of God's presence that
is exiled...." The shepherd, moved by love

of God, seeks to fight the one who seduces
people away from God. The Besht then
proceeds to "instruct him in battle." The
earlier story understands traditional law
and lore as the best strategy for combating
pollution. Buber focuses on how people
become sensitive to the needs of others. He
replaces the demand for Jewish solidarity
and ritual correctness in the first story
with a demand for compassion for other
people. Where the original story points to
a myth of purification and identifies the
means of such purification, Buber points to
the myth of an I's meeting with a Thou and
concludes that this meeting requires a
commonality of sympathy.37 Again, Buber
reads the story as myth in his peculiar
definition of the term. The story points
backwards to an event in human experience:
human beings learn how to battle evil
through their compassion for others. In the
moment of meeting with others, they discover
a commonality of need.

As in the original tale, so in Buber's:
the devil must receive his due. Humanity,
at least in this unredeemed world, can never
achieve an unmitigated triumph. When the
struggle against the devil ensues, the Besht
and Moses seem to prevail. In desperation,
the demon appeals to God. He rules the
temporal world according to his right. God
responds "full and overfull with sadness,"
allowing the demon to revel in its
ignorance. The demon then strikes the city
with fire, and the bells ring. In Buber's
version of the story the shepherd hears the
bells and thinks immediately of his flock,

"which had been scattered unprotected over the mountain." Moses turns to his sheep, and the Besht must meet the angel of battle alone. This time, however, the Besht recognizes the angel as a more positive force: the prince of death and of rebirth.38 The myth, as Buber tells it, teaches compassion for the demon no less than for God. The moment belongs to the demon. The audience, together with the Besht, hears the anguish of the demon, sympathizes with its concerns, and turns from hostility to understanding. The myth of the I and the Thou expands beyond compassion for the common other. It includes compassion for the different other. The tale evokes a moment in which the Besht learned to affirm the truth and reality of the "evil one."

Still another moment follows the moment of compassion. While victory seems to belong to the demonic, the Besht actually learns otherwise. He discovers his own task in the example of Moses the shepherd. Just as the shepherd leaves the cosmic task to pursue the daily one, so the Besht begins his earthly task again and again. The decision facing the hero forces a choice between the single great battle and the ever different battles that arise from daily tasks. Buber presents the story as an exemplification of the myth of I and Thou, in which each person must meet the challenge of commonplace demands, choosing to face those recurrent tasks rather than expending energy on the one futile struggle. The Besht learns that he must continually renew his activities. The audience re-enacts that

learning, committing itself to performing
the common duties of humanity rather than
abandoning them for supernatural rituals
that seek to remove impurity in one single
blow.

Buber takes the raw material of a
purification myth and fashions it to express
his own insights. Whether or not the story
in its original form testifies to moments of
decision and their effectiveness, Buber's
rendering of it does so. Buber constructs a
tale in which readers can discover that the
daily challenges they face are no less
important than the "grand battle against
evil" told in myth. As transmitted, the
original tale seems confused and ambivalent.
Never fully contented with its popular and
magical sources, the tale meanders through
traditionalism and the exaltation of
community to an unsatisfying conclusion.
Buber's myth, however, develops logically
and carefully. Each moment leads to the
next so that the apparent failure in the end
merely confirms the value of I-You meeting
as an eternal possibility rather than as a
tactic in one great war. Buber's
interpretation of the hasidic myth points to
its modern possibility: it can teach moderns
how to live more fully; the significance of
the story transcends its magical or
supernatural elements. As in his other
interpretations of myth, so, too, in his study
of hasidism, Buber sacrifices literal
accuracy to allow modern readers an
opportunity to find answers to their own
questions. Buber's significance lies less
as a historian of hasidism than as an author

349 HASIDISM AND MODERNITY

whose works show how ancient stories reveal
possibilities for contemporary living.
Buber honestly conveys the fullness of life
and avoids theories of myth that he
considers too restricting. That the myth
conveying this message owes more to Buber's
creativity than to his hasidic sources does
not negate its value for contemporary
readers.

NOTES

1. Meyer Levin, <u>The Golden Mountain</u> (New York: Behrman House, 1932), p. xvi.

2. Martin Buber, <u>The Origin and Meaning of Hasidism</u>, ed. and trans. Maurice Friedman (New York: Horizon Press, 1960), p. 22.

3. <u>Ibid.</u>, pp. 40-42.

4. Buber. "Spinoza, Sabbatai Zvi, and the Baal Shem," in his <u>The Origin and Meaning of Hasidism</u>, pp. 90-112.

5. <u>Ibid.</u>, p. 97.

6. <u>Ibid.</u>, p. 99.

7. <u>Ibid.</u>, p. 251.

8. Gershom G. Scholem, <u>The Messianic Idea In Judaism and Other Essays on Jewish Spirituality</u>, trans. Michael A. Meyer (New York: Schocken, 1971), p, 84.

9. Buber, <u>The Origin and Meaning of Hasidism</u>, pp. 109-11.

10. <u>Ibid.</u>, p. 112.

11. See Dan Ben-Amos and Jerome R. Mintz, eds., <u>Shivhei HaBesht: In Praise of the Baal Shem Tov</u> (Bloomington: Indiana University Press, 1970), pp. 28-31.

12. Martin Buber, <u>The Legend of the Baal Shem</u>, trans. Maurice Friedman (New York: Schocken, 1955), pp. 62-72.

13. <u>Ibid.</u>, p. 68.

14. <u>Ibid.</u>, p. 72.

15. See Ben-Amos and Mintz, pp. 161-63.

16. Buber, <u>The Legend of the Baal Shem</u>, pp.73, 78.

17. <u>Ibid.</u>, p. 77.

18. See, for example, Reuven Bulka, ed., <u>Mystics and Medics: A Comparison of Mystical and Psychotherapeutic Encounters</u> (New York: Human Sciences Press, 1979), and Mordecai Rotenberg, <u>Dialogue with Deviance: The Hasidic Ethic and the Theory of Social Contraction</u> (Philadelphia: Institute for the Study of Human Issues, 1983).

19. Pinchas Sadeh, <u>Sefer HaDimyonot</u> [Hebrew] (Jerusalem: Schocken, 1983), pp. 47-48, 284.

20. Buber, <u>The Legend of the Baal Shem</u>, pp. 131-38.

21. See Yoav Elstein, <u>Maaseh Hoshev: Studies in Hasidic Tales</u> [Hebrew] (Jerusalem: n.p., 1983), pp. 41-62 and 130-31.

22. See <u>ibid.</u>, p. 49.

23. Ibid., pp. 21-26.

24. See Janet O'Dea Aviad, Return to Judaism: Religious Renewal in Israel (Chicago: University of Chicago Press, 1983); Saul Bernstein, The Renaissance of the Torah Jew (Hoboken, NJ: KTAV, 1985); and Michael Graubart Levin, Journey to Tradition: The Odyssey of a Born-again Jew (Hoboken, NJ: KTAV, 1986.

25. Buber, The Legend of the Baal Shem, pp. 12-13.

26. Elstein, Maaseh Hoshev, pp. 63-128.

27. Ibid., pp. 130-32.

28. See the story itself in Ben-Amos and Mintz, pp. 11-13, and for analysis in Arnold Band, "The Function of the Enigmatic in Two Hasidic Tales," in Joseph Dan and Frank Talmage, eds., Studies in Jewish Mysticism (Cambridge, MA: Association for Jewish Studies, 1982), p. 187.

29. Band, in "The Function of the Enigmatic," pp. 190-92.

30. Ibid., p. 193.

31. Buber, "The Werewolf," The Legend of the Baal Shem, pp. 51-55.

32. See Buber, The Origin and Meaning of Hasidism, pp. 28, 20, 236, 229, 91.

352 HASIDISM AND MODERNITY

33. See Theodor H. Gaster, The New Golden
    Bough: A New Abridgment of the Classic
    Work by Sir James George Frazer (New
    York: Criterion, 1959), pp. 53-54, 174,
    599-609.

34. See Micha Joseph Bin Gorion, "Moses the
    Shepherd," in his Mimekor Yisrael:
    Classical Jewish Folktales, ed. Emanuel
    bin Gorion and trans. I. M. Lask
    (Bloomington: Indiana University Press,
    1976), vol. 2, pp. 962-63.

35. See Mishnah Berachot 7:1; Babylonian
    Talmud 45a; Mishna Avot 3:3.

36. Buber, The Legend of the Baal Shem, pp.
    202-5, and compare Buber, The Origin and
    Meaning of Hasidism, pp. 24-112.

37. Buber, The Legend of the Baal Shem, pp.
    205-7.

38. Ibid., pp. 207-8.

Chapter 9   Evaluating Buber

HASIDISM AND MYTH

Theorists of comparative mythology draw
freely on Buber's work, even though they
often misunderstand his intention.   Thus
Eliade, for example, uses one of Buber's
tales to emphasize the importance of
learning about a culture other than one's
own.1   The story tells of Rabbi Eisik, son
of Yekel of Crakow.2   Rabbi Eisik
repeatedly dreamed that a great treasure
awaited him under the main bridge of Warsaw.
When he told his dream to others in his
hometown, they laughed at him.   Why should
he want to go to Warsaw?   His friends in
Crakow told him that anything he wanted in
Warsaw he could find at home.   His family
reprimanded him for intending to desert
them.   Despite all pleas Reb Eisik left home
for Warsaw.   The promptings of his dream
proved more powerful than rational argument.
The passion for self-expression urged him to

seek a higher good than that found in his
own home.

Once he arrived in Warsaw, Reb Eisik
could no longer remain isolated. He came
into contact with others who shaped his
life. Warsaw boasted numerous bridges. How
could he discover the correct one? After
careful investigation he settled upon one as
the likeliest to harbor his treasure. He
took a shovel and went to that bridge
intending to dig up his treasure.
Unfortunately, he could not proceed as
planned. Guards attended the bridge day and
night, allowing only authorized persons to
approach and scrutinizing passing strangers
carefully. Reb Eisik refused to despair and
maintained a vigil, hoping that the guards
would leave. Soon he became friendly with
some of them. They took note of him, shared
food with him, and began a conversation.

During one conversation a certain
captain inquired about his interest in the
bridge. Reb Eisik explained about his
dream and his hopes for a great treasure.
On hearing this explanation, the captain
laughed, saying that he too had such a
dream. In his dream a voice proclaimed that
he would find a treasure under the stove of
a certain Eisik ben Yekel in Crakow. The
guard scoffed at ever finding that treasure.
He declared that half the Jews in Crakow are
called Yekel and the other half Eisik, so
that he despaired of ever discovering the
right house. The guard told Reb Eisik to
return home because dreams only bring
trouble, never success. Reb Eisik heard the

story in respectful silence. Reb Eisik took
the guard's advice and returned to Crakow,
now knowing the location of his treasure.
When he looked under the stove, he took the
treasure meant for him. How did Reb Eisik
use that treasure? He realized that what
his friends had told him was true. Anything
that could be found in Warsaw could also be
found in Crakow--anything except Reb Eisik
and Reb Yekel. He and his father, the two
whose names according to the guard comprise
all the Jews of Crakow, make the city
unique. Reb Eisik had discovered himself in
Warsaw and learned the meaning of his
existence in Crakow: he was one of the Jews
whose existence identified the place. With
that new knowledge in mind he used his
treasure to affirm the meaning of his life:
he built a house of prayer, which he called
"Reb Eisik Reb Yekel's Schul." Reb Eisik
returned home and created a synthesis
between the old and the new. The treasure
which he discovered under his own roof only
because he abandoned it supplied the
resources for a new religious experience.3

   Buber interprets the tale as a
reflection of I-You meeting. The I-You
meeting between Reb Eisik and the guard in
Warsaw teaches him a perspective on his own
life. Buber remarks that each person has a
distinctive treasure but that the means of
finding it may be hidden. The story
suggests that self-discovery depends upon a
dialogue with others. The myth confirms
this: self-discovery lies in going beyond
oneself. The myth recalls the event
stimulating Reb Eisik's return to Crakow and

his creation of a new house of prayer.
Buber's own treatment of hasidic legend acts
as a similar myth. His responsive
interpretations of those legends point to
the event of human meeting to which they are
later responses. A study of Buber as
theorist of myth must take this I-You
approach to mythic meaning as its point of
departure.

MYTH AS COMMUNICATION

Many critics find Buber's ontological
conception of myth puzzling.4 Part of the
problem arises from Buber's view of myth as
communication. Many scholars, for example,
consider the Jewish ritual of the Passover a
mythic ceremony. Its combination of story,
confession, and symbolic action evoke the
founding event of Jewish religion.5 Buber's
discussion of this ritual, called the Seder,
illustrates his understanding of myth as
communication. In his chronicle of hasidic
history, For The Sake of Heaven, Buber
includes a section devoted to "A Seder That
Went Wrong."6 Buber's description of this
Seder marks its mythic characteristics. Its
purpose is "by the might of one's yearning
to throw a bridge between that deed which
God performed in the liberation from Egypt
to that awaited deed of his which as yet has
no name."7 The myth of the Exodus recalls
an event that humanity shared with God. As
Jews recall that event, they prepare for
another event parallel to it in their own

lives. The story Buber tells, however, focuses on myth misunderstood. The Seer of Lublin, according to the story, instructed his disciples in a detailed set of Passover observances. They agreed to follow his instructions to the letter. Despite their good intentions, however, each disciple invariably failed in the attempt. Although Buber notes that "everywhere disturbances had taken place," the narrative records only three of them. Each of the three stands for a particular kind of mythic misunderstanding.

In the first and, according to Buber, most crucial misunderstanding, family quarrels disrupted the ceremony. A rivalry between mother and daughter-in-law delayed the beginning of the ritual. Although the ceremonial proceeded according to plan, still "the lost time could not be retrieved."8 The problem here stems from a misunderstanding of the meaning of the ritual. When seen at as a set of actions, as behavioral directives, the Seder had been performed accurately. As an evocation of liberation, however, the Seder demands an atmosphere of freedom. Strict observance of detailed laws alone cannot fulfill the obligation of the ritual. The lack of fellowship, the air of hostility, and the familial tension in the household all impaired the experience of freedom essential to the religious goal of the ceremonial. The Seder went wrong because of a false definition of the ceremony and its purpose. While accomplishing the superficial purpose of the ritual, those performing it failed to achieve its real purpose.

The second disturbance Buber reports apparently seems trivial. The entire Seder went well until its final moment. When the time came to eat the special wafer eaten at the conclusion of the ceremony, "no one could find it."9 Here myth proves its authenticity only when its performance reaches its fulfillment. The myth may be recounted accurately yet still fail. Despite an accurate definition of myth, an assessment of its achievements depends upon studying its consequences. Buber's own concern for the modern meaning of myth represents his effort to avoid losing the special wafer by ignoring the consequences that make the myth a living reality rather than a relic.

Buber calls the final disturbance "the strangest report of all." In that Seder everything followed the prescribed pattern. Only one alteration occurred: the leader recited the ritual not in Hebrew but in his native Hungarian. He justified this change by declaring "an account must be communicated in such a manner that all who hear it understand it."10 Buber certainly should approve such a recitation of a mythic ritual. Yet the assumption made in the defense for this ceremonial innovation suggests something with which Buber would not agree. The leader assumes that by translating the ceremony from an ancient language to a vernacular he has accomplished his task of transmitting its meaning.

Buber's own experience taught him the fallaciousness of that assumption. While he had begun his task of communicating hasidic lore by transforming its antiquated style into modern language, he discovered that the closer he remained to the original tale, the more accurately he transmitted its meaning. Too vernacular a translation may lead to miscommunication of myth. Buber's contribution as theorist of myth depends on his new definition of myth, his insight into the purpose of mythology in human cultures, and his ability to communicate ancient myth to moderns. The next sections evaluate the importance and the limitations of Buber as theorist of myth in these three areas.

BUBER'S DEFINITION OF MYTH

Buber defines myth as a story preserving the memory of an I-You relationship between the divinity and either a human individual or a group of people. This definition contributes to the theory of myth by attacking an uncritical identification of myth and polytheism, by opposing the existentialist ploy of demythologizing mythic tales, and by proposing an explanation for the evolution and change of mythic traditions. The distinctive aspects of myth accordingly lie in its narrative, in its origin in a factual event experienced as a meeting with the divine, and in its function as a transmission of the memory of that meeting. This definition expands the

possibilities for discovering myth in Jewish
tradition. Were myth defined by its content
alone, it would exclude much of biblical and
post-biblical writings. Those defining
mythology as stories about the various gods
inevitably define the Bible as non-
mythological. Buber's definition of myth
identifies biblical stories as myth wherever
they point backward to an actual event in
which the divine and the human meet in
genuine relationship. Without further
refinement scholars might find it difficult
to distinguish between biblical and
nonbiblical myths. Rudolf Bultmann responds
to this problem by distinguishing biblical
myth on the basis of its philosophical
ideas. Buber opposes that approach as
destroying the distinctiveness of myth.
Buber's definition takes its narrative form
as essential. Reducing a myth to its ideas,
to a vehicle for conveying existential
truths, misunderstands the importance of its
structure as a story. Buber not only
expands the scope of what may count as myth
but also refuses to dilute the specific
characteristics of the mythic form.

Buber recognizes a problem in defining
myth as the recollection of a single event.
Biblical and post-biblical stories often
appear in duplicate or triplicate. The same
motif may be transformed as it is retold
again and again. The story of Enoch, for
example, evolved and changed in the course
of centuries. Buber provides an explanation
for these changes even in the face of his
insistence that they all recall a single
event. The event of an I-You meeting occurs

outside of experience but must be
communicated in experiential language.
Myths often change their form to communicate
their truths more adequately. Sometimes,
however, a society or its leaders consider
I-You meeting too spontaneous or
unpredictable to maintain a stable
community. They therefore seek to
discourage it. Myths change in response to
these fears, and Buber traces this kind of
mythic evolution as well as the more
positive changes occurring in a tradition.
In this way he contributes a method for
analyzing the transformation of mythic
motifs.

While Buber's definition offers a
positive program for expanding the scope of
myth, for taking its form seriously, and for
tracing mythic transformations, it does lack
specificity and precision. This problem
springs from a difficulty inherent in
Buber's presentation of his I-Thou thinking
from the beginning. When Buber first
presented his "I-Thou" insight, Franz
Rosenzweig questioned this aspect of his
theory.11 Buber's description of "I-It"
relationship seemed too constricted, while
the "I-Thou" appeared too broad and
inclusive. Since, as Rosenzweig put it,
Buber portrayed the "It" as a "cripple," he
needed to expand the I-You to fit anything
alive in human experience. The "grab-bag"
approach to "I-Thou" extended its dimensions
so widely that it lost shape and definition.
The same criticism applies to Buber's view
of myth. Buber defines myth so broadly that
reflection on any event experienced as true

meeting falls under that definition. While
distinguishing between myth faithful to its
original experience and myth already
subordinated to religion, Buber never
distinguishes between genuine myth and other
records of authentic relationships.

Going beyond Buber himself, one can note
that the cases he studies display a common
theme of divine intervention in human life.
Abraham Joshua Heschel devotes considerable
attention to the question of God's "pathos,"
by which he means God's passionate feeling
for human beings.12 The drama of biblical
stories represents the changing pathos, the
changing responses of God, to human events.
Buber took exception to Heschel's views and
focuses more on "the blood and soul of the
theomorphous man," that is, on the way
people try to identify themselves with God
rather than on the way the divine identifies
itself with human concerns.13 That focus,
however, blurs the distinctiveness of mythic
narrative. What distinguishes myth from
other stories and legends is its concern
with the divine involvement in human
affairs.

THE PURPOSE OF JEWISH MYTH

Buber continually judges myths by their
effects: do they stimulate new opportunities
for I-You meeting, or do they succumb to the
temptation of religion and fossilize the
memory of a past event? Buber's

understanding of myth goes beyond that of psychologists and existentialists. Psychologists reduce myths to truths about the human mind. They identify the patterns of thinking and response developed in the human past and recapitulated by each individual. Since psychology discovers these patterns independently of myth, the ancient testimony merely confirms a scientific discovery. Outside of that confirmation myths no longer serve useful functions. Like the Passover Seder that proceeded perfectly until it misplaced the Afikomen, psychology uncovers truths about myth, only to learn that myth itself is dispensable. Existentialist interpretations of myth tend to fall into the same trap. They explain the meaning of myth in terms of truths previously discovered. Reducing myth to propositions about human life makes it a poor substitute for existential philosophy. Existentialist interpretations of myth, like psychological ones, make myth superfluous.

For Buber, only myth can stimulate both response and imitation. Buber recognizes that myth in Genesis 1:1–3:24 differs from myth in Exodus or in the Psalms. He explains these differences as consequences of the different events each myth celebrates. Because Buber rejects the view that all myths convey the same message and that myths project an eternal return, his interpretation of diverse myths explored their distinctiveness. The social experiences underlying the stories of Moses complement the personal reality expressed in

the stories of good and evil. Buber's
approach allows him to describe the
historically conditioned nature of hasidic
myths of cosmic disorder and human
reparation of it.

   Unlike Gershom Scholem and Yoav Elstein,
Buber traces the personal and social
realities that shaped different trends in
hasidic myth. Sometimes persons experience
their return to selfhood as a miracle
effected by divine power. Sometimes they
find their journey back to themselves an
ascent through stages of self-knowledge.
Sometimes they learn that they must change
the structures of society and conditions of
human life. Buber uses a different hasidic
tale to suggest these possibilities. His
approach encourages a flexible rather than
dogmatic understanding of different mythic
alternatives. Once again, however, Buber's
strength hides a weakness. Rosenzweig's
criticism of Buber included a concern that
he had reduced the number of "primal words"
to a false duality. People relate to the
world in more than the two ways Buber
suggests. They can acknowledge the divine
creator and say He-It, and they can speak
from their own awareness as creatures and
say "We-I."[14] Buber's characterization of
myth as a record of "I-You" meeting includes
too many different kinds of stories under a
single rubric and ignores the distinctive
purpose of myth. Not only myth but other
stories serve the same function of
stimulating I-You relationships. Not only
mythic memory but historical memory and
imaginative, didactic tales fulfill a

similar purpose. While Buber reminds
theorists of myth to look at the
consequences of myth, his own definition of
those consequences seems rather broad.

Looked at from a theoretical
perspective, the stories Buber includes as
myth serve a far more mundane purpose than
that of encouraging I-You living. They
serve to preserve and communicate norms of
human behavior. This normative function
seems more adequately explained by
Rosenzweig's category of "We-I." As a
society recalls its origins, the experiences
that shaped it as a coherent group, it
retells those events as narratives filled
with supernatural power. The forging of the
"We" in the I-We relationship appears as an
act of divine grace. Narrowing the function
of myth to this normative purpose focuses
attention on the characteristic elements of
myth. The Genesis stories imply norms of
gender-specific activities, of social
organization, of economic division of labor.
The stories in Exodus supply norms for
leadership, for ritual process, and for
social identification. The hasidic tales
offer their audience a new normative
tradition focused on the zaddik. This
tradition embraces norms of personal
behavior, of political allegiance, and of
morality. Buber's contribution to the study
of myth suggests the need to take seriously
the differences among myths; going beyond
Buber by defining the consequence of myth as
normative action helps specify those
differences even more concretely than Buber
himself does.

A DEEPER INSIGHT INTO MYTH

Buber's development as an exponent of Jewish myth reveals an extraordinary aspect of his theory of myth. As his general understanding of the I-You relationship deepened, his ability to transmit and communicate the meaning of myth increased. He insists that the true aim of hasidism was not to continue an ancient kabbalistic tradition, as Scholem suggests, or to point to enduring eternal patterns, as Yoav Elstein thinks, but to aim "toward the revolution of values, toward a new order of rank in which it is not the man who 'knows' the Torah but the man who lives in it, who realizes it in the simple unity of his life that stands in the highest place."15 Following this insight, Buber does not emphasize esoteric doctrines or impose complicated literary structures on the stories he retells. He tries to communicate the myth simply. Even those who doubt whether Buber communicates the full message of hasidic thought testify to his honesty. One critic considers Buber's For the Sake of Heaven a valid and genuine evocation of hasidic life in which his fidelity to his sources leads him farther "than his own personal leanings would have permitted."16 Buber's attention to the sources of hasidism and refusal to reduce the meaning of myth to simply an existentialist, esoteric, or psychological significance allows him to present it honestly.

Buber's approach to his sources reflects his view of how myth communicates its message. He denies that myths communicate an esoteric idea or theory. Instead, he suggests that myths transmit their message by evoking a life, by projecting the image of human beings in the midst of a lived relationship. He identifies the "stream of mythn-bearing power" within Judaism with stories about human heroes calls forth in response to a summons. He tells these tales to help evoke the reality of that call.17 That approach, however, illustrates what one critic considers a fixation on the phenomenon of presentness.18   Buber's restlessness with "religion" and his fear that institutionalized religious forms would sap the strength of myth leads him to over-emphasize the importance of the moment. Buber judges the value of the past by its conversion into a present opportunity. Often myth celebrates history or anticipates a future without immediately opening a door or window. While Buber refuses to reduce myth to some other reality, he limits its value to its immediate significance.

The most crucial failure attributable to Buber's bias for presentness, already intimated by Gershom Scholem and his disciples, lies in his avoidance of the esoteric philosophy included in mystical myths. Buber correctly realizes that the theoretical aspect of hasidic myths represents a legacy from an older kabbalah and conveys a secret message about a mysterious future. In neither case for Buber does the mystical theory advance the cause of I-You meeting in the present. That lack, however, may not in and of itself mean that the story has abandoned its mythic purpose. Certainly theorists of myth should applaud the honesty and nonreductionism that Buber's approach to myth inspires. They should, however, also question the appropriateness of such a simple and straightforward immediacy. Myth often contains hints and signs that draw attention not to the here and now but to an esoteric past or a hidden future. Elements within a myth act as stimuli pointing beyond the story itself to its significance. Buber's self-conscious selection of stories limits the applicability of his theory of myth. Israeli scholar Mendel Piekarz notes, that for Rabbi Nahman popular stories provide "an external expression of exalted spiritual realities." Nahman told stories to provide his listeners with hints of such realities, to indicate a truth beyond the literal tale being told.19 Buber seems oblivious to this dimension of the mythic tale.

Students of myth should learn from Buber to pay attention to the substance of the myth, to take its literal meaning and form as a point of departure. They should not ignore indications of esoteric meaning, of myth as a signal of transcendence, as something other than an invitation to I-You relationship. The message communicated takes the shape of myth because myth makers seek to hint at special meaning, at a hidden purpose. The structure and vocabulary of myth point its readers to an esoteric realm of reality that does not necessarily

coincide with Buber's sphere of I-You
meeting. The student of myth should move
beyond Buber to take seriously the elitist
elements in mythological traditions.

CONCLUSION

Buber's definition of myth, his
explication of its purpose, and his
understanding of it as a form of
communication contribute to the work of
theorists of myth. That legacy remains an
important one despite limitations in his
definition of myth. His sense that the
purpose of myth is to stimulate I-You
meeting needs to be more conservatively
identified as an attempt at normative
direction. His interpretation of the
hasidic message should be tempered by a
greater awareness of its esoteric appeal.
Buber's greatest contribution remains that
of a teacher instructing students how to
learn. He shows by example the meaning of
"humanity the student." Maurice Friedman
explores the master-disciple relationship
that Buber developed with Hermann Gerson as
a paradigm of how Buber understood his own
role as teacher. Buber was the "helper" who
would encourage "the handing down of values,
the institutional linking of the generations
through teaching." The problem with the
Jewish Youth Movement, Buber argued, lay in
leaders who were "not persons who hand down
existence and teaching." When Gerson turned
to Buber for help, he received the teaching

that "There is no reliable yardstick for ethical decisions ... but there is the <u>one</u> direction to the living truth."20 Buber refused to let his students substitute his thinking for their own creative being. He remained a "You" and enabled his students to maintain their individuality before him.

Buber's relation to other theorists of myth exemplifies the same response. Buber's challenge reminds fellow theorists of the importance of their definitions of myth, of their understanding of its purpose, and of their transmission of its message. His theories help identify the problems facing interpreters of myth. Buber's theory arises from his openness as "humanity the student." That spirit of studenthood pervades his work on myth and remains an important contribution for all who study myth.

NOTES

1. See Mircea Eliade, <u>Myths, Dreams and Mysteries: The Encounter Between Contemporary Faiths and Archaic Realities</u>, trans. Philip Mairet (New York: Harper, 1967), pp. 244-45.

2. The story calls him "Reb Eisik ben Reb Yekel" using a shortened Hebrew form of Rabbi and the Hebrew word "ben" for son of.

3. Martin Buber, <u>Hasidism and Modern Man</u>, ed. and trans. Maurice Friedman (New York: Horizon Press, 1958), pp. 170-71.

4. J. W. Rogerson, <u>Myth in Old Testament Interpretation</u> (Berlin: Walter de Gruyter, 1974), p. 96.

5. Will Herberg explores the existential and ritual implications of the story of the Exodus as the central myth in Judaism. See his discussions of the Exodus in his <u>Judaism and Modern Man: An Interpretation of Jewish Religion</u> (New York: Harper, 1951), pp. 261-72, and <u>Faith Enacted as History: Essays in Biblical Theology</u>, ed. and intro. Bernard W. Anderson (Philadelphia: Westminster Press, 1978), pp. 32-42.

6. Martin Buber, <u>For The Sake of Heaven: A Chronicle</u>, trans. Ludwig Lewisohn (Philadelphia: Jewish Publication Society of America, 1945), pp. 270-76.

7. <u>Ibid.</u>, p. 271.

8. <u>Ibid</u>., pp. 274-75.

9. <u>Ibid</u>., p. 275.

10. <u>Ibid</u>., p. 276.

11. See Bernhard Casper, "Franz Rosenzweig's Criticism of Buber's <u>I and Thou</u>," in Haim Gordon and Jochanan Bloch, eds., <u>Martin Buber : A Centenary Volume</u> (New York: KTAV, 1984), pp. 139-59.

12. See Abraham Joshua Heschel, <u>The Prophets</u> (Philadelphia: Jewish Publication Society of America, 1962), pp. 221-31.

13. Martin Buber, <u>The Prophetic Faith</u>, trans. Carlyle Witton-Davies (New York: Macmillan, 1949), p. 112.

14. See the remarks in the appendix to Caspar, "Franz Rosenzweig's Criticism," pp. 158-59.

15. Martin Buber, <u>The Origin and Meaning of Hasidism</u>, ed. and trans. Maurice Friedman (New York: Horizon Press, 1960), p. 60.

16. Schatz-Uffenheimer, "Man's Relation to God and World in Buber's Rendering of the Hasidic Teaching," p. 431. Contrast, however, Buber's rendition to the sources presented in Joseph Dan, ed. <u>The Hasidic Novella</u> [Hebrew] (Jerusalem: Bialik Institute, 1966), pp. 73-82.

17. See Martin Buber, <u>The Legend of the Baal Shem</u>, trans. Maurice Friedman (New York: Schocken, 1955), pp. 10-13.

18. Caspar, "Franz Rosenzweig's Criticism," p. 153.

19. Mendel Piekarz, <u>Studies in Braslav Hasidism</u> [Hebrew] (Jerusalem: n.p., 1972), pp. 83-84, 108-9, 114-15.

20. Maurice Friedman, <u>Martin Buber's Life and Work: The Middle Years, 1923-1945</u> (New York: Dutton, 1981), pp. 143-45.

BIBLIOGRAPHY

(1)   BIBLIOGRAPHICAL

Cohn, Margot, and Rafeel Buber. <u>Martin Buber: A Bibliography of His Writings, 1997-1978</u>. Jerusalem: Magnes Press; Munich: K. G. Saur, 1980.

Moonan, Willard. <u>Martin Buber and His Critics: An Annotated Bibliography of Writings in English through 1978</u>. New York: Garland, 1981.

(2) BY BUBER
        (a)   BOOKS: GENERAL

<u>Between Man and Man</u>. With an afterword by the author and an introduction by Maurice Friedman. Trans. Ronald Gregor Smith and Maurice Friedman. New York: Macmillan, 1965.

<u>Eclipse of God: Studies in the Relation Between Religion and Philosophy</u>. New York: Harper, 1952. Paperback: New York: Harper, 1957.

I and Thou. A new translation with a prologue and notes by Walter Kaufmann. New York: Scribner's, 1970. Original ed. ed. and trans. Ronald Gregor Smith. Edinburgh: T. and T. Clark, 1937.

Israel and the World: Essays in a Time of Crisis. First ed. New York: Schocken, 1948. Second ed. New York: Schocken, 1963.

On Zion: The History of an Idea. With a new foreword by Nahum N. Glatzer. Trans. Stanley Godman. New York: Schocken, 1975. Original ed. Israel and Palestine -- The History of an Idea. New York: Farrar, Straus and Young, 1952.

Pointing the Way: Collected Essays. Trans., ed., and with a new intro. Maurice S. Friedman. New York: Harper, 1963. Original ed. New York: Harper, 1957.

    (b) BOOKS: BIBLICAL

Darkho Shel Miqra [Hebrew]. Jerusalem: Bialik Institute, 1964.

Good and Evil: Two Interpretations--Right and Wrong, Images of Good and Evil. Trans. Ronald Gregor Smith and Michael Bullock. New York: Scribner's, 1953.

Kingship of God. Third ed. Trans. Richard Scheimann. New York: Harper, 1967. Paperback: New York: Harper, 1973.

Moses: The Revelation and the Covenant. [No trans. given]. Oxford: East and West

Library, 1946. Paperback: New York: Harper, 1958.

The Prophetic Faith. Trans. Carlyle Witton-Davies. New York: Macmillan, 1949. Paperback: New York: Harper, 1960.

Two Types of Faith: A Study of the Interpenetration of Judaism and Christianity. Trans. Norman P. Goldhawk. New York: Macmillan, 1951. Paperback: New York: Harper, 1961.

(c) BOOKS: HASIDIC

For the Sake of Heaven: A Chronicle. Trans. Ludwig Lewisohn. Philadelphia: Jewish Publication Society of America, 1945. Paperback: New foreword by author. New York: Harper, 1966.

Hasidism and Modern Man. Ed. and trans. Maurice Friedman. New York: Horizon Press, 1958. Paperback: New York: Harper, 1966.

Tales of the Hasidim: The Early Masters. Trans. Olga Marx. New York: Schocken, 1947.

Tales of the Hasidim: The Later Masters. Trans. Olga Marx. New York: Schocken, 1947.

The Legend of the Baal Shem. Trans. Maurice Friedman. New York: Schocken, 1955.

The Origin and Meaning of Hasidism. Ed. and trans. Maurice Friedman. New York: Horizon Press, 1960.

The Tales of Rabbi Nahman. Trans. Maurice
Friedman. New York: Horizon Press, 1956.

      (d)   BOOKS: ANTHOLOGIES

A Believing Humanism: Gleanings. Credo
Perspectives, ed. Ruth Nanda Anshen.
Trans., intro. and explanatory comments
Maurice Friedman. New York: Simon and
Schuster, 1969.

On Judaism. Ed. Nahum N. Glatzer. New
York: Schocken, 1967.

On the Bible: Eighteen Studies. Ed. Nahum
N. Glatzer. New York: Schocken, 1968.

The Way of Response: Martin Buber.
Selections from his writings. Ed. Nahum N.
Glatzer. New York: Schocken, 1966.

The Writings of Martin Buber. Selected, ed.
and intro. Will Herberg. Cleveland and New
York: Meridian Books, 1956.

(3)   ABOUT BUBER
          (a)   BOOKS:

Breslauer, S. Daniel. The Chrysalis of
Religion: A Guide to the Jewishness of
Buber's "I and Thou." Nashville: Abingdon,
1980.

Diamond, Malcolm L. Martin Buber: Jewish
Existentialist. New York: Oxford University
Press, 1960.

Friedman, Maurice. <u>Martin Buber and the Eternal</u>. New York: Human Sciences Press, 1986.

_____. <u>Martin Buber: The Life of Dialogue</u>. Chicago: University of Chicago Press, 1955. Paperback: New York: Harper, 1960.

_____. <u>Martin Buber's Life and Work: The Early Years, 1878-1923</u>. New York: Dutton, 1981.

_____. <u>Martin Buber's Life and Work: The Middle Years, 1923-1945</u>. New York: Dutton, 1981.

_____. <u>Martin Buber's Life and Work: The Later Years, 1945-1964</u>. New York: Dutton, 1981.

Gordon, Haim, and Jochanan Bloch, eds. <u>Martin Buber : A Centenary Volume</u>. Faculty of Humanities and Social Sciences, Ben-Gurion University of the Negev. New York: KTAV, 1984.

Hodes, Aubrey. <u>Martin Buber: An Intimate Portrait</u>. New York: Viking, 1971.

Horwitz, Rivka. <u>Buber's Way to "I and Thou": An Historical Analysis and the First Publication of Martin Buber's Lectures "Religion Als Gegenwart"</u>. Heidelberg: Lambert Schneider, 1978.

Kohanski, Alexander S. <u>An Analytical Interpretation of Martin Buber's I and Thou, with a Biographical Introduction and</u>

Glossary. Barron's Educational Series. Woodbury, NY: Barron's, 1975.

_____. Martin Buber's Philosophy of Interhuman Relation: A Response to the Human Problematic of Our Time. Sara F. Yoseloff Memorial Publications in Judaism and Jewish Affairs. Rutherford: Fairleigh Dickenson University Press; London: Associated University Presses, 1982.

Schilpp, Paul Arthur, and Maurice Friedman, eds. The Philosophy of Martin Buber. The Library of Living Philosophers, Vol. XII. La Salle, IL: Open Court, 1967.

Silberstein, Laurence J. Martin Buber's Social and Religious Thought: Alienation and the Quest For Meaning. New York: New York University Press, 1989.

Vermes, Pamela. Buber on God and the Perfect Man. Brown Judaic Studies, Vol. 13. Chico, CA: Scholars Press, 1980.

Wood, Robert E. Martin Buber's Ontology: An Analysis of I and Thou. Northwestern University Studies in Phenomenology and Existential Philosophy. Evanston, IL: Northwestern University Press, 1969.

(b) ARTICLES:

Bergman, Samuel Hugo. "Martin Buber: Life as Dialogue." In his Faith and Reason: Modern Jewish Thought. Trans. and ed. Alfred Jospe. Hillel Book. New York: Schocken, 1963. Pp. 81-97.

Berkovits, Eliezer. "Martin Buber's Religion of the Dialogue." In his <u>Major Themes in Modern Philosophies of Judaism</u>. New York: KTAV, 1974. Pp. 68-137.

Dreyfus, Theodore. "Understanding the Term 'Umkehr' in the Philosophy of Martin Buber." <u>Daat</u> 9 (1982): 71-74.

Glatzer, Nahum N. "Aspects of Martin Buber's Thought." <u>Modern Judaism</u> 1:1 (1981) 1-16.

_____. "Editor's Postscript." In Buber, <u>On the Bible</u>, pp. 233-40.

_____, ed. <u>On Jewish Learning</u>. New York: Schocken, 1965.

Gordon, Haim. "Method of Clarifying Buber's I-Thou Relationship." <u>Journal of Jewish Studies</u> 23 (1976): 71-83.

Kaufmann, Walter. "Prologue." In Buber, <u>I and Thou</u>. Pp. 9-48.

Levy, Zeev. "Demythologization and Remythologization" [Hebrew]. In <u>Bar Ilan Annual</u>. Vols. 22-23. Ramat Gan, Israel: Bar Ilan University Press, 1987. Pp. 205-27.

Mendes-Flohr, Paul. "Martin Buber's Reception among Jews." <u>Modern Judaism</u> 6:2 (1986): 111-26.

Scholem, Gershom G. "Martin Buber's Interpretation of Hasidism." In his <u>The</u>

<u>Messianic Idea In Judaism and Other Essays</u>
<u>on Jewish Spirituality</u>. Trans. Michael A.
Meyer. New York: Schocken, 1971. Pp. 203-
27.

_____. "Martin Buber's Judaism." In his <u>On</u>
<u>Jews and Judaism in Crisis</u>. Ed. Werner J.
Dannhauser. New York: Schocken, 1976. Pp.
126-71.

Swarcz, Moshe. "The Concept of Myth and the
Question of 'Demythologization' in Martin
Buber's System." In his <u>Language, Myth, and</u>
<u>Art</u> [Hebrew]. Tel Aviv: Schocken, 1966.
Pp. 216-49.

Talmon, Shemaryahu. "Martin Buber's Way of
Interpreting the Bible." <u>Journal of Jewish</u>
<u>Studies</u> 27 (1976): 195-209.

Weiss, Meir. "The Secret of Scriptural
Speech" [Hebrew]. Intro. to Buber, <u>Darkho</u>
<u>Shel Miqra</u>. Pp. 9-33.

(4)   ABOUT BIBLICAL MYTH

Cassutto, Umberto. <u>A Commentary on the Book</u>
<u>of Genesis: From Adam to Noah</u>. Jerusalem:
Magnes Press, 1961.

Frankfort, Henri. <u>Kingship and the Gods: A</u>
<u>Study of Ancient Near Eastern Religion as</u>
<u>the Integration of Society and Nature</u>
Chicago: University of Chicago Press, 1948.

_____, with H. A. Frankfort, John A.
Wilson, and Thorkild Jacobsen. <u>Before</u>
<u>Philosophy: The Intellectual Aventure of</u>

Ancient Man. Baltimore: Penguin Books, 1949.

Goldziher, Ignac. _Mythology Among the Hebrews and its Historical Development_. Trans. Russell Maretineau. Marandell Book. New York: Cooper Square, 1967.

Kaufmann, Yehezkel. _The Religion of Israel: From Its Beginnings to the Babylonian Exile_. Trans. and abridged Moshe Greenberg. Chicago: University of Chicago Press, 1960.

_____. _Toldot Haemunah HaYisraelit_. Vol. I Tel Aviv: Dvir, 1937.

Rogerson, J. W. _Myth in Old Testament Interpretation_. BZAW No. 134. Berlin: Walter de Gruyter, 1974.

Uffenheimer, Benjamin. "Myth and Reality in Ancient Israel." In S. N. Eisenstadt, ed., _The Origins and Diversity of Axial Civilization_. Albany, NY: SUNY Press, 1986. Pp. 136-67.

Zeitlin, Irving M. _Ancient Judaism: Biblical Criticism From Max Weber to the Present_. Oxford: Oxford University Press, 1984.

(5)   ABOUT HASIDIC MYTH

Agnon, Shmuel Yosef. _Sefer, Sofer, Vesippur_ [Hebrew]. Tel Aviv: Schocken, 1978.

Band, Arnold J. "The Function of the Enigmatic in Two Hasidic Tales." In Joseph Dan and Frank Talmage, eds., _Studies in_

Jewish Mysticism. Cambridge, MA:
Association for Jewish Studies, 1982. Pp.
185-209.

Ben-Amos, Dan, and Jerome R. Mintz, eds.
and trans. Shivhei HaBesht: In Praise of
the Baal Shem Tov. Bloomington: Indiana
University Press, 1970.

Biale, David. Gershom Scholem: Kabbalah and
Counter-History. Second ed. Cambridge, MA:
Harvard University Press, 1982.

Bloom, Harold, ed. Gershom Scholem. Modern
Critical Views. New York: Chelsea House,
1987.

Dan, Joseph. Gershom Scholem and the
Mystical Dimension of Jewish History.
Modern Jewish Masters Series. New York:
New York University Press, 1987.

_____, ed. The Hasidic Novella [Hebrew].
Jerusalem: Bialik Institute, 1966.

_____. The Hasidic Story--Its History and
Development [Hebrew]. Jerusalem: Keter,
1975.

Elstein, Yoav. In the Footsteps of a Lost
Princess: A Structural Analysis of the First
Tale by Rabbi Nachman of Braslav [Hebrew].
Ramat Gan, Israel: Bar Ilan University
Press, 1984.

_____. Maaseh Hoshev: Studies in Hasidic
Tales [Hebrew]. Jerusalem: n.p., 1983.

Green, Arthur. Tormented Master: A Life of
Rabbi Nahman of Bratzlav. New York:
Schocken, 1981.

Idel, Moshe. Kabbalah: New Perspectives.
New Haven, CT: Yale University Press, 1988.

Levin, Meyer. The Golden Mountain. New
York: Behrman House, 1932.

Nahman of Bratzlav. Rabbi Nahman: The
Tales. Ed. and trans. Arnold J. Band.
Classics of Western Spirituality. New York:
Paulist Press, 1978.

Scholem, Gershom G. Kabbalah. Jerusalem:
Keter, 1974.

_____. On the Kabbalah and Its Symbolism.
Trans. Ralph Manheim. New York: Schocken,
1969.

_____. Major Trends In Jewish Mysticism.
New York: Schocken, 1946. Third Ed., 1954.

(6) ABOUT MYTHOLOGY GENERALLY

Eliade, Mircea. Myths, Dreams and
Mysteries: The Encounter Between
Contemporary Faiths and Archaic Realities.
Trans. Philip Mairet. New York: Harper,
1960.

Segal, Robert A. "In Defense of Mythology:
The History of Modern Theories of Myth."
Annals of Scholarship I:1 (1980): 3-49.

INDEX